PRAGMARKETISM

Advance Praise for *Pragmarketism*

'*Pragmarketism* is an extremely useful and timely addition by Trupti and Arvind to the cause of better, more focused, less wasteful and more meaningful initiatives in the marketing world. Using Indian references, anthropology, best-in-class examples and analytic structures, the book takes a young marketeer, or a seasoned professional looking for a "refresher", on a systematic journey from concept to execution and results. I am sure *Pragmarketism* will become a guide to marketing propositions and products in the Indian context.'

Suresh Narayanan, Chairman & Managing Director, Nestlé India

'A timely and essential guide on how to build enduring brands in India. Backed by their decades of on-the-ground expertise, Trupti and Arvind meld classical marketing concepts with the unique Indian context to craft a powerful playbook with great practical insights. You will want to read this more than once!'

Vivek Gambhir, MD & CEO, Godrej Consumer Products Ltd

'*Pragmarketism* by Trupti and Arvind Bhandari is the kind of book that marketing needs today. It is a thoughtful and comprehensive exploration of concepts and issues that businesses deal with in today's rapidly evolving world. Written in a conversational and accessible style, this book will engage lay readers and practitioners alike.'

Santosh Desai, Author, MD & CEO, Futurebrands Consulting

'A fantastic combination of practical marketing with a strong conceptual framework of what and how to make brands win.

Strongly recommend as a must-read-and-keep for practicing and aspiring marketeers.'

Navneet Saluja, Managing Director,
GSK Consumer Healthcare

'A step-by-step prescriptive and introspective guide to winning the Indian consumer's heart and pocket. Truly interesting blend of practice and theory making it an actionable must-read for anyone aspiring to do business in the Indian market.'

Nandu Nandkishore, Professor, Indian School of Business;
Former EVP & Head of Asia, Africa,
Oceania, Nestlé S.A

'I wish a book like *Pragmarketism* was available thirty-odd years ago as I was joining the FMCG industry. Trupti and Arvind have done a great job of bringing to life the Indian consumer in the context of society and tradition and then gone on to share thoughts on how great brands interact with these consumers. I really liked the way they have demystified marketing terminology and shared the best practices followed by brands we interact with on a day-to-day basis. The sections on digital and cause marketing got me thinking about what could be next for some of the great brands I have had an opportunity to work on. *Pragmarketism* truly brought out the meeting points of theoretical marketing and the realities of the Indian market place and is an interesting and easy read.'

Manu Anand, Former President, AMEA, Mondelez
International; Former Chairman and CEO PepsiCo, India

'I adored the story-like flow of a classic textbook on marketing in the varying realities of India. The complexities of consumer behaviour and the marketing thinking to shape it in the demographically criss-crossed subcontinent could not have been handled better.

Pragmarketism is a mandatory read for anyone who wants to sell anything to the Indian consumer. And a delightful read for anyone who cares to understand the psyche of India better.'

Prabir Jha, Ex-President & Global Chief People Officer, Cipla; Founder & CEO, Prabir Jha People Advisory

'*Pragmarketism* is a unique read. Hands-on experience meets common sense meets deep consumer and cultural insights to create a truly pragmatic view of marketing. Making this your daily go-to handbook to help find simple answers to complex marketing problems.'

Rohit Ohri, Group Chairman & CEO, FCB India

'*Pragmarketism* is very useful for managing and overcoming the challenges of marketing in the complex market of India. Full of insights drawn from the rich experience of the authors, the book presents numerous highly practical templates and models that can be taken and applied to any marketing challenge. A highly relevant book that should be a must-read for all marketers.'

Ambi Parameswaran, Author, Independent Brand Coach and Founder, Brand-Building.com

'Arvind and Trupti have written a marketing book that balances contextualized theory and practice, and is written in a simple, conversational tone. I enjoyed reading it. I think many marketers will feel the same way.'

Ranjan Banerjee, Dean and Professor, Marketing, SPJIMR

'We have always valued the ear-to-the-ground, first-hand knowledge of any domain and a practical, rather pragmatic, understanding of why something happens and how to engineer it. Trupti and Arvind are two marketing/business practitioners who have blended their own first-hand experiences of building brands and businesses with pragmatic analysis of trends, ideas, society, marketing successes and especially the uniqueness of India and the peculiar nature of Indian consumers. They have blended practical theory, their own experiences and learnings from their observations and market successes and come up with a framework for creating brands and businesses by of understanding the Indian consumer. *Pragmarketism* is seminal, real and, dare I say, a must-read for all marketers, practitioners, start-up founders and students to refresh and stay pragmatic.'

Dr Anurag Batra, Chairman & Editor-In-Chief,
***BW Businessworld* & Exchange4Media Group**

'Trupti and Arvind Bhandari not just report live from the frontlines of the marketing world but dive deep. Their perspective refreshingly picks up the unique Indian nuance. A rewarding read.'

Prasoon Joshi, Chairman McCann Worldgroup, Asia Pacific; CEO & CCO, McCann Worldgroup, India

'What makes *Pragmarketism* effective is the frequency of examples of the brands that touch our lives every day, making things easily relatable. The book challenges the classic frameworks used by marketers and looks to suggest new innovative ones that can be more relevant to achieve corporate goals in today's times, especially in India. Written in lucid language, it is not just for professionals but for anyone looking to take a deep dive into the dynamics and excitement that prevail in the Indian consumer markets.'

Harsh Goenka, Chairman, RPG Enterprises

'This is Kotler 2.0. A practical marketing toolkit for trainees to CMOs and digital marketers to start-up entrepreneurs. Descriptive, rich in detail, with new-age marketing frameworks with lots of real-life examples make it a very sticky read.'

Prashant Sinha, Co-Founder, Momspresso.com

'This book lives up to its name. It explains marketing concepts simply and clearly and illustrates their application, capturing the wealth of practical experience the authors have. It is a great reference book for start-ups, students and practising managers across all disciplines.'

Rama Bijapurkar, Management Consultant;
Author of *A Never Before World: Tracking the Evolution of Consumer India*

'An informative read based on real marketing experiences. It demystifies some of the complex marketing situations, provides a structured mechanism for building an effective 360-degree marketing strategy and gives away the secret for customizing solutions for the diverse Indian consumer. Who said marketing products or solutions to 1.3 billion people, who communicate in twenty-two different languages, was easy? Although there is no set standard for cracking the winning marketing strategy, a strategy that is tossed with market research, consumer insights, manages to connect and engage with the audience through the right platforms and, most importantly, catches the pulse of the Indian audience – can inch closer to becoming a hit.'

Deep Kalra, Founder & Group Executive Chairman,
MakeMyTrip Ltd

PRAGMARKETISM

PRAGMATIC MARKETING INSIGHTS FOR WINNING INDIAN CONSUMERS

TRUPTI BHANDARI

ARVIND BHANDARI

HARPER
BUSINESS

An Imprint of HarperCollins *Publishers*

First published in India in 2020 by Harper Business
An imprint of HarperCollins *Publishers*
A-75, Sector 57, Noida, Uttar Pradesh 201301, India
www.harpercollins.co.in

2 4 6 8 10 9 7 5 3 1

P-ISBN: 978-93-5357-733-9
E-ISBN: 978-93-5357-726-1

Typeset in 11/14.2 Aldine401 BT at
Manipal Technology Ltd, Manipal

Printed and bound at
Thomson Press (India) Ltd

To our best new product launches ever,
our daughters Rishni and Nandini

Contents

Introduction

Despite having been in the profession for forty-five years between the two of us, we can't say if marketing is as objective as science or as subjective as art. The book in your hands has been triggered by the indeterminate allure of marketing, a subject that everyone in the world seems to have an opinion on but none a mastery of. Consumer need, the beginning and end of this perilous subject, defies prediction and standardization as a tool to approach it as much as spontaneity and reactive thinking. Such are the frustrations and challenges of marketing that it makes billions as easily as it sinks them. Take three examples to this point:

Nano, the revolutionary car manufactured by Tata with a dream price tag was conceived through an incredible collaboration between engineering and cost management. It was positioned clearly to upgrade the solus two-wheeler owners to the collective dream of family excursions on four wheels. A great product and a clear marketing strategy that should have taken the market by storm, right? Wrong. It's been recently laid to rest. Forever.

Parle-G, the brand that sells nearly a lakh tonnes of biscuits every month at a price that sometimes appears cheaper than the cost of raw wheat, has been thriving despite being in marketing oblivion for years. The packaging looks archival; it's communication or brand equity is hardly worth a recall, except for the ominous finger-raising child splashed across acres of walls throughout India. Is it even a brand? Ask the billions who live and die by it and you will be ashamed you even posed the question.

Lehar Kurkure, the twisty snack by Frito Lay that made messy hand-held namkeens a finger-food rage overnight. Spreading across age segments and socio-economic types ahead of all other snacks, it defied the normal growth cycle of a new product. This hybrid Western snack with traditional masalas converted a staid category into a rollicking business across shops dotting the nation's highways creating a new consumption opportunity. The product became a brand even before it could be advertised or promoted in any serious way.

Product, place, price and promotion (the classical four Ps), the trio of segmentation-targeting-positioning, big idea, innovation grids, digital marketing – however deftly you juxtapose these time-tested models, disappointment is never far. But ignoring them will doom you. That's marketing in essence – hard to cast into theory, equally impossible to build on with just common sense.

Hence, we propose Pragmarketism: the tinkering of theory with practice, or elevating practice with some theoretical abstraction, or infusing Western models with adequate Indian sensibilities. Whatever the blend, the result is a solution that works in happy combinations for ... well, India. For a country that displays a remarkable diversity on the surface – languages, dialects, cultures and customs – it is eerily glued together with a very Indian way of looking at things. This is where the highest statistical number of mobile owners and internet users sit easy with the quaint reality of joint families and arranged marriages.

But the enigma is that for these uniquely paradoxical billions in the tricolour nation, we have only one Kotlerian model of marketing. Something seems amiss, doesn't it?

Pragmarketism has brought marketing closer to home, to Indian soil. The Indian consumer is represented as sending off religious morning greetings on WhatsApp and wearing lightly embroidered formal business shirts. The dichotomy of India's consumers is mirrored in the nifty brand-building formula and framework we have developed, which adequately reflect their reality and are not an adaptation of the reality for their Western cousins. Therefore, success from marketing endeavours becomes more certain and replicable.

That's not all! We noticed how scores of managers walk out of management campuses into haloed corporate offices and instantly experience academic amnesia with their first brush with real life. Equally, we observed how the successful 'reality-weary' professionals depend on their experiential learnings to run marketing on 'gut feel'.

In this book, we have tried to close the chasm between academia and industry, stereotypes and originality, potentiality and realization so the Indian market can get its due from the best of practitioners' experiences as well as the best of scholastic learning, whether it's from the East or West, from marketing or any other adjacent field. The approach of Pragmarketism is as indifferent to geographical borders as it is to subject divisions; we have taken liberally from Indian sociology and religious aspects of the country to evaluate consumer need, the society, the segmentation and so on in order to retrieve gems of consumer insight that will not only satisfy their needs, but also enthral consumers from deep within their psyche.

Why us?

Because between this duo sits forty-five years of successes, failures, thrills and mundanities of running thirty-odd brands across most of India's blue-chip companies, supported by our countless business associates. This is a situation that places us at the advantageous intersection between marketing problems and opportunities to reflect its madness, truly and fruitfully. Like an experienced chef who not only knows his ingredients but also his consumer's favourite cuisines, we look at marketing trends to plate a fare that reflects external trends as much as an insider's consumer knowledge. What we deliver at the end is not just a well-considered menu but also a well-practised one.

Living and writing from within this marketing milieu has ensured that the dynamism of marketing is well captured, as shown in the chapters on digital marketing, innovation and communication. This makes Pragmarketism an evolving and dynamic idea. This book attempts to infuse the freshness of our contemporary perspective, mounted on the solidity of past learnings.

Who will this book benefit?

Well, a range of business-inclined folks, such as:

- The theoreticians, who need real application and validation of their ivory-tower views.
- The practitioners, who need some theories and relevant Indian frameworks as well as cross-industry examples to sharpen their saws, blunted by the monotony of their approach.
- The MBA students, who want to cut through reams of academia to progress quickly and comprehensively to grasp what really matters when it comes to real business battles.
- The mid-ranking managers, who want to rekindle the balance between theory (that doesn't appear to guide) and practice (that has been repetitively unproductive).
- The business leaders, who want a holistic business perspective so they can navigate their ships with the knowledge of all the issues they will face at sea, especially issues they haven't had adequate exposure to.
- The entrepreneurs of various hues, new or old, who want to appreciate the operations of large corporations run by specialist employees so they can bring order to their home-grown organizations.
- The foreigners, who want to understand what it is that motivates or paralyzes the 'irrational Indians'.

- The Indians, who want to see themselves as consumers from a holistic marketing lens.
- The professionals from any field – doctors, lawyers, artists – who want a commercial make-over of their endeavours that comes with an understanding about consumers and their needs.

Pragmarketism abounds in cross-category comparisons to benefit people who have only worked in their fields and lacked the perspective of other industries. This sort of cross-pollination always brings fresh ideas in even the most straitjacketed businesses. Durables companies can learn from FMCG (fast-moving consumer goods), pharmaceuticals can be inspired by retailers and even the disruptive e-commerce sector can learn from the staid brick-and-mortar companies. This cross-sectoral knowledge is the spine of our 'Pragmarketing' approach.

Finally, the book presents a whole ensemble of marketing opportunities so readers can play a perfect business symphony without missing any notes. It's comprehensive without being unwieldy, aiding more than brow-beating with academic jargon. The usual topics are enriched with new insights, and fresh mantras are shared to accelerate success with the rapidly evolving consumers. As a result, the reader will find new inspirations: they will learn how to structure and stitch together wild digital marketing with the traditional marketing, how to segment in a Desi way, how to innovate using roadblocks as stepping stones and how to lead start-ups to inspire awe in the diverse Indian consumer base.

In sum, *Pragmarketism* will reward its readers with a perspective that is holistic, dynamic and truly Indian. Marketing professionals will imbibe the two values that help them succeed the most – walking in the consumer's shoes and being effective solution-providers for their needs.

In other words, this book will enable them to become pragmatic marketers to win in the world's most complex consumer landscape.

1

The Indian Society

If it works elsewhere across the globe, it should work in the tri-colour nation, shouldn't it? After all, it's made up of the same human species with universal needs and wants, right?

Not really.

In the West, you can sell a product to a woman and she gets it. But in India, you have to sell to a mother, a wife or a daughter and through her child, her husband or father, respectively. And you still may not get it right – not if the last frame of the advertisement (directed at them) does not include a happy and approving family.

Again, in the West, you can sell a fairness cream with a display of a contented, beautiful smile framed in a mirror. In this country of a billion gazers and approvers, fairness often is an easy ticket to a top corporate job, a 'fair' marriage or quantum social mobility. Exaggeration? Not at all. This is the exact brief of Fair & Lovely's TV commercials, which led to the creation of the iconic brand.

Moreover, in the West, products and advertisements show an adult satisfied when his individual grooming needs are met, saying this is the 'best a man can get' (Gillette). Not enough for India. Here, you will do better if you make the promise to 'become hero number one'.

Welcome to the Indian society. A vibrant patch of earth which looks like anywhere else on the planet but hides craters of complexity in its consumers' psyche. In our experience, the sharpest or the most astute professionals can't predict which path their ideas take in the Indian marketplace where the rubber meets the road. Given below are some likely outcomes to any business initiative in this befuddling country:

- **Replication**: India responds exactly like other markets in the West, where consumers have shared similar experiences and companies just tweak some elements of a product and scale up, sending a firm's cash registers ringing. The iPhones, the Mercedes or the Paracetamols can be transplanted from one market to another and consumer experience remains the same.
- **Fusion**: External models undergo a change, thereby creating an entity where the original version makes room for an adaptation, making it look like a hybrid. Air conditioners with an inverter and Nokia's mobile phones with a torch are examples of such local twists that enhance the user experience of universal product categories.
- **Indifference**: Western inspiration fails to turn the consumer towards energy bars, dental hygiene products, vitamin supplements and so on, as consumers have found little relevance for these products in their traditional lives.
- **Creation**: Local ideas or usages not intended by the brand spring up – Eno antacid for cooking, submersible pumps as engines for low-cost trucks, washing machines for churning buttermilk, etc.

Why does India defy, modify or deify Western ideas? Is there a way to predict the future of business efforts? To answer them, we need to understand the Indian society.

The Indian Society: Ethnocentricity

What does it take to WOW the bustling billions of this paradoxical nation?

Do Indians, like the rest of the folk around the world, exhibit universal needs to demand universal marketing solutions? Or are they a tad different? Or could it be that this diversity merely hides the universal consumer truths deep inside? An MBA education provides a paltry perspective on Indian society, so it's worth pausing here to look at ourselves as a community – historically and culturally – before we plunge into our current context.

Ethnocentrism is a common malaise in all societies. It means emphasizing your *own* culture and having a perspective that sees it as different, even superior. The Chinese thought their country was a 'middle kingdom', with all insignificant countries strewn around, before the British invaded and the opium wars exposed otherwise. The 'white man's burden' is another such example, where the arrogance of 'pale' Westerners resulted in them regarding it their onerous task to 'civilize' other 'barbaric cultures'. Could we also have a similar bias about ourselves when we say India is 'diverse, religious, crowded and a miasma of insane contradictions', claiming that it is 'like none other'? Or are we just like everyone else, with superficial variations? Let us dive into the Indian society.

Caste, Not Class

Inequality is an inevitable reality of collective human life. We are not born equal, and in a society, members are arranged into a pecking order due to differential access to wealth, power and prestige. Simply put, this is the layering of society by rank, depending on one's access to material resources. In the West, this takes form in a 'class system'; a Marxist description which aggregates people on different levels depending on their relationship to ownership of factors of production, namely land, capital and labour. Human history is the history of class struggle between those who own the factors of production and those who are controlled by them.

Earlier, in slave societies, slaves were ruled by royalty. In feudal societies, the landlords had their land tilled by the peasants, and in the current industrial societies, the capitalists have their factories run by the working class. The class struggle results in revolutions once in a while to restore equitable distribution of wealth. But everyday strife is about upward social mobility and climbing the social ladder towards the rung above one's existing class. The blue-collared wants to be white-collared and the white-collared wants to be an owner. Ownership of resources and wealth is a legitimized form of rising up in society. In other words, if you have the cash, you have the position and respect too.

But that is not true in India, which is what makes the Indian consumer different and more complicated. It's not enough to climb to the next economic class – lower to middle to upper – as you acquire more wealth. You have to also climb in terms of caste. Otherwise, you remain in cultural limbo, because you may have all the ostentatious symbols of wealth but, ironically enough, you will be ranked below a higher caste. To circumvent this positional anomaly, people from lower castes often upgrade to the upper castes (Brahamans, Kshatriyas, Vaishyas, etc.) by renaming themselves with new titles and symbols (a process called 'Sanskritisation' by the eminent sociologist, M.N. Srinivas) or by embracing new religions, like Neo-Buddhism, to break free from the tyranny of the caste system. This cultural posturing isn't just rampant in Hinduism but has also impacted more egalitarian religions, like Islam and Christianity, which have coexisted in close proximity. They too have shown tendencies of segmentation into caste-equivalent layers, such as Bohra Muslims. Caste inequalities in India are rampant, that too with religious approval.

However, upward caste mobility isn't always possible. Caste membership is strictly by birth and although in crowded and modern urban environments one's identity can be concealed, in smaller towns it just isn't feasible. So, most Indians are left smouldering in the cauldron of unmet aspirations because education and economic success may take them upwards but the caste system refuses corresponding social stature. It, in fact, subverts it. In this respect, the caste system differs fundamentally from the class system, where economic success is a sufficient precondition for upward mobility.

How do Indians cope with this paradox?

They become schizophrenic. Publicly, they put up a great show: gaudy clothes, big cars, elaborate living spaces and ostentatious choices to assert their economic class. Privately, they resemble their older, humbler selves, reflecting on times before the economic climb. With regard to business, that means that goods which spell out economic prosperity are accepted unquestioningly, but for products that are not visible in their public lives, the same consumer bargains till the last rupee. Our schizophrenic consumer could bag a golden watch from Titan for a lakh while simultaneously haggling over five rupees for a better soap during the same shopping trip.

Acquiring mobility away from this suffocating caste system is given paramount importance, and consumers are willing to pay the price for it. Investing in one's offspring's health, education and even marriage into a better caste seems priceless, and consumers will spend on expensive baby food, tuition fees and grand marriage ceremonies to jump a rung in the social hierarchy. The luxury market in these segments appeals to consumers even from lower socio-economic segments, much to the surprise of those who segment strictly on the basis of economic wealth without considering the cultural realities underneath.

Caste, however, operates at all levels but is too embarrassing to accept as the determining vector in a society. After all, our society takes pride in the idea of being 'convent-educated', as most matrimonial adverts boost. Knowing the consumer's psyche, however, helps unravel their contradictory behaviour to customize plans that covertly appeal to caste aspirations without broaching such an inflammatory topic explicitly. Politicians in India do it all the time, whereas businesses perhaps do so less unabashedly. But times are changing and with increasing permissiveness, it's not hard to imagine brands aligning their marketing calendars with caste calendars: around festivals and rituals surrounding birth, marriage and sundry family functions *a la* the 'Kayastha Sabha' Holi Milan, brought to you by 'Tedhe Medhe Kurkure'.

Religious, Not Secular

The Indian worldview is deeply religious. This is not only true of Hinduism, but also of heterodox religions that have spun around it such as Jainism, Buddhism and Sikhism. Spatially, it means that temples, mosques, churches and gurudwaras intersect our roads, homes, public and private places all the time. It doesn't take a great memory to recall the myriad gods showering blessing, from calendars in people's bedrooms to Audis and BMWs lined up outside Ganesh temples for coconut and '*tikka-aarti*' rituals before they embrace the vicissitudes of Indian roads to idols of gods in science and technology offices to nerdy executives showing up at work with ash smeared on their foreheads – religion impacts every secular activity in India.

Does religious experience have a lesser impact on life outside of India?

Whatever the truth may be privately, it certainly isn't as ubiquitous as in the subcontinent. In the West, gods and goddesses reside mostly in places of worship and their memorabilia or avatars don't usually spill into calendars, badges, statues, clothes and curtains. In the West, religion requires the consideration of god and the good life and then steps back, letting individuals make their life's choices in consonance. In India, practitioners initiate the morning with an invocation to a devi/devta and through various appearances in posters, placards, WhatsApp messages, screen savers, desktop idols, *prasad* or god-laced greetings ('Jai Shri Krishna', 'Ram Ram', etc.) popping into every social and economic interaction.

Then you have prophets – Sai Baba, gurus, yogis, the Brahma Kumaris, ISKCON, the Isha Foundation, the Art of Living – to guide you through life's trammels. Fasts, abstinences, donations, rituals, stones, horoscopes, tarot cards, previous life visitations and innumerable kinds of clairvoyances are invoked to usher in positive results and fulfil our multitudinous wishes.

This is less conspicuous in metros and among the younger crowds, but as one goes towards the towns with lower populations and lower incomes, religion doesn't just become larger than life – it becomes life itself. Electricity, water and good air may run out but pious wishes never do. Religion is not a guiding beacon of light in the distance, but a walking stick with which one struts through life. Religion is not merely a voice and a conscience that tells us what is right and what isn't; instead, here, it comes intruding – through honks, loudspeakers and billboards.

Before we understand its implications for business, we need to understand why religion is so rampantly invoked everywhere. Indian life, like the Indian monsoon, is erratic. First, in spite of years of independence, we haven't managed to shake off the uncertainties of health, housing, sanitation and education. Millions fighting over diminishing resources makes everyday life a mini-war, and when you are pitched against this elbowing and shoving, the natural internal cry is, '*Hey bhagwan, kuch karo!*' (Good Lord, do something!). This frequent refrain indicates where the help is expected to come from. There are numerous 'gurus' (or conmen) who may answer the question, but they only further reinforce the yearning for god's mercy.

Second, we are bipolar as a nation and only religion is its cure – even though it is the cause of it too. A tug between wanting to indulge and being restrained by the cultural-religious ethos that exhorts abstinence is our reality. Capitalism throws irresistible goodies our way each day: fairness creams, men's grooming services, body sculpting and bliss-showering spas to sleazy vacations in Thailand. There is so much we can do with our money that we don't know where to start. But just then, religious guilt surfaces, crooning, 'Why waste so much? It's sinful. Save up instead, donate to a charity or hide it so others don't see it and get envious.' Essentially, don't consume it.

Why does Hinduism forbid consumption? In fact, other religions forbid indulgences too. After all, religion is concerned with non-material things. But perhaps no religious practice censures as severely as Hinduism. Why is the Indian experience unique?

The Bhagavad Gita, the conscious or unconscious basis of this particular Indian belief system, exhorts that humans look beyond the destructible body and towards the 'aatma' or the soul, which is one's lasting reality. The rest is mere delusion. Following this belief, indulging one's senses makes no sense because it takes one away from that which is real and towards that which isn't. However, the world of commerce pertains to providing goods for the body. Now, these two worlds stand in stark contrast with one another, creating uneasiness. You can't ignore religious moorings because propitiating gods is fundamental to need-satisfaction, yet gods themselves tell you to not run after these things.

Thus, you reconcile by sinning and then instantly cleansing, which allows you to indulge without alienating the gods. It is as if negative karma can be offset with positive karma, restoring the balance. This takes the form of integrating rituals of worship into your mornings to get the day started before you dirty your hands in pursuit of material goodies. You attend religious congregations, hold night-long loudspeaker chants of 'mata', make pilgrimages to holy places, shave your hair in Tirupati (which creates another market for hair, incidentally) and donate to orphanages. And then you are free to indulge in your desire for a Gucci bag with the conscience of a saint.

The other reconciliatory way is to infuse the religious calendar with festivity, fun and frolic. Dandiya, Durga Puja, Bihu or Onam become not only the time to worship but also the time to unleash the urge to consume. Why else would the sale of automobiles, paints and durables rise during the time for prayer? Fun is sanctioned through religious permissibility: pilgrimages come with five-starred comfort and helicopter rides for the devout;

luxuriant clothing is allowed during marriages because it's a sacred union between the bride and bridegroom; gamifying and watching content with slick graphics is permissible but only after marinating technology with mythology. Religion, once prohibitive, makes a U-turn and becomes a legitimized sanction for this boisterous fun through this very Indian logic.

The extent of this reconciliation may vary across many categories within towns, regions or age segments, but it never goes away. Businesses that understand this dichotomy resolve it through correct offerings and crafty communications and have consumers queue up; those who can't get the balance right don't understand how to sell an Audi to a dhoti-clad, temple-visiting geriatric in Cochin.

Religion can't be ignored in India. It flows uninterruptedly under the carpet of mass consciousness, and understanding how it motivates consumers provides priceless clues towards building businesses.

Collective, Not Individual

An Indian is always a part of a family and is never alone. Individuals have meaning only in reference to the collective unit they are a part of. This goes back to the strong feudal agrarian world, which is where India still lives; this is unlike the West, which has had a long industrial period. The patriarch of an agrarian family transfers his knowledge of sowing and the seasons along with a legacy of religious practices. In return, the kids till the land and look after the physically infirm members of the family. The family unit is thus consolidated as a whole, with mutually inter-fitting roles and responsibilities. India is still predominantly agrarian and its family structure is more traditional than that of the West.

Another reason why family and community prevail over the individual is because the young and the old live together perpetually in their natal homes in India. It's not unusual to find a boy going off to work but still coming home to his parents, unlike his compatriot in the West, who leaves home to fend for himself during college. Married couples continue to live in their parental homes and their children are looked after by the grandparents when they leave for work. Extended family tends to work to our advantage in India. With such economic and emotional gain, it's interesting that joint families statistically outnumber nuclear ones in India, even though sociologists are quick to point out that there are fractures within, highlighting how there exist different kitchens under the same roof.

Generically labelled relationships of uncles and aunts multiply into unique entities – *mama*, *tau*, *chacha*, *chachi*, *bhua* – as they evoke different expectations and justify these unique titles. With many relatives and frequent interactions with them (not limited to Thanksgiving alone), an individual maintains different identities. A woman is a wife, daughter-in-law, mother, *nanand* or a *devrani* or a *sali*. Frequently, a man occupies a placatory position between two roles: being a son and a husband. In such a situation, individual indulgences have little room because one constantly juggles these different roles. And when the desires do exist, it's only because other layers are not visible. For instance, products that indulge a woman's creativity rarely succeed in resonating with the consumer until they are supplemented with the idea of a doting husband or pampered kids. Individual storytelling comes alive when others are included.

Another complication is that the marketeer has to be conscious of the consumer not as a person, but with respect to the role he or she occupies. A mere toothbrush is endorsed by the kids watching the advertisement on the TV, approved by the mother if it fits her budget and only then bought duly by the shopping father. Research conducted with painstaking effort with respect to Mumbai's slum-dwelling women was foiled when the researchers discovered that the husbands were the ones buying, not the wives. Marketing campaigns have to understand this multiplicity to effectively convert consumers or they will be wasting money in utter consumer ignorance.

The subdued individuality of India, especially when compared to the more independent version in the West, is visible in people's life choices. Career choices often reflect the social mobility aspirations of one's family. Over generations, a mason's son can become a doctor with education and resources. Marriages are still by arrangement and digitization has merely expanded the choice of brides and grooms (but not the filtering by caste or region). Vacations are often with extended families, secured in rooms with extra beds. Big cars sell well because social outings require the whole family platoon to be packed in till the very last seat.

This kind of collective entity leads to business ideas based on economy, joint needs, comfort and variety. In fact, in the travel sector, groups from different regions and religions can travel together viably as operators offer Jain food or Malayali curries. Politics reinforces the value of the community further as groups with various affinities make coalitions to bargain for resources for themselves. And since democracy favours the voices of many over the whispers of a few, this tendency only grows. Finally, in a country where discounts accrue with bulk purchases, group booking during travelling facilitates the creation of all sorts of expedient groups too. Business conducted within such an Indian society must reflect the link between the individual and the group and the emotional and financial payoffs of such an investment, in addition to individual aspirations – a contradiction which need not be reconciled in the West.

In the final analysis, the individuals of India dream much like the individuals in the West, but their means of realizing it and even celebrating it are almost always within the full circumference of their near and dear ones.

Tradition, Not Rationality

Western political institutions are the offshoots of a long, rational and humanist movement that swept Europe from the middle of the fifteenth century to the Renaissance. Whether it was living in the prosperous mercantile world of the Bourbons and the Hapsburg families who made Europe culturally resplendent or following the host of Reformation movements that challenged the supremacy of the Church or the inquiry of science that interest in humanism engendered, medieval European citizens were inundated by cultural, intellectual and religious changes that brought rationality to the fore and created the industrial empires, and with it, bureaucracy. Max Weber highlights how, as a result of all these changes, the basis of authority shifted from tradition and charisma (based on an antiquated notion of rulers who were destined to command) to merit and rationality, as epitomized in modern-day bureaucracy. Power was not inherited but earned through hard work, recognized by all as legitimate in a meritocracy.

The Indian society, in contrast, moved from a feudal system to formal bureaucracy without the intervening industrial cultural revolution. The result was the creation of a '*mai-baap* sarkar', which looked like the bureaucracy in the West in its form and structure, but worked through the old patronage system of a princely kingdom. The Western-dressed babu was the '*janeyu*-wearing' (an investiture thread worn by brahmins signifying their twice-born status) pundit from within.

Today, we live in a world where material differences have been wiped out from the surface but old values are moulded internally into modern requirements, creating inconsistencies and fissures.

Marriages are not completely arranged any more because of the predominance of love marriages; but a system of what sociologists call 'survey marriages' prevail, where once the horoscope and caste have been matched, the prospective bride and groom spend some time together to decide if they will tie the knot or not. Offices have Western organizational structures, with KPIs (Key Performance Indicators) and other measurement systems, but deference towards authority or respect for seniority never fails to be rewarded – performance notwithstanding. The widespread practice of referring to one's boss as 'sir' and 'saheb' is in contrast to the West, where being called by one's first or last name does not amount to disrespect. Sensitization of a pre-existing gender bias is not even considered, even as the whole metric of evaluation is subconsciously structured on male values of aggression and independence. In corporate offices, when women take on positions of power, informal channels quickly spring up to disparage her and derail her climb. Strangely enough, products that are consumed by women are often marketed by men who have no real sense of what they are selling. But it doesn't seem odd.

At home, wives suffer from low self-esteem because husbands mirror the same old values inherited from their fathers, even though, unlike the past, they both work and earn equally. Politically, we vote and elect our leaders as in other Western democratic countries, but the driving consideration is caste and the choice of leaders is dynasty-based and not legitimized by merit. Cronyism and parochialism are rampant across the legislative, judiciary and executive bodies – communities of a kin canoodle with each other to maximize exploitation of public resources. In effect, rationality, which is the core of the Weberian bureaucratic edifice, is undermined, compromised and mingled with the Indian tradition that maintains a superficial semblance with the West, but blithely sabotages its spirit underneath to pander to feudal urges.

To set up a business in India requires being cognizant of this reality and often interacting with informal channels, enveloping our formal structures like ivy, to find one's way around.

Petite, Not Grand

The one thing that strikes any foreigner landing in India is the sheer size of our population. No matter where you go, there are swarms of people. Driving around, you discover that no land is untilled, no public facility is underused, no window is without a queue and no public place is without a jostling crowd. When the world's most populous country is huffing and puffing away on scarce land, dissymmetry is inevitable. Consequently, business, following the consumer, takes a shape that looks very dissimilar to the West.

As a result, the landscape of our country is petite, not grand. Landholdings are fragmented, leading to a familiar view of a countryside dotted with small farms around a cluster of basic dwellings, unlike the sweeping expanse of arable land in the West. Large industrial sheds in the West take the shape of cottage industries here, huddled up in a grimy corner. Unlike the sprawling squares of plush offices in the service sector in developed countries, here we have to settle for cramped quarters in urban squalor with poor amenities; across the streets, you find millions of traders, carpenters, job-workers, unskilled labour, white-collar employees, blue-collar employees and the unemployed going about their tasks feverishly, like diligent ants. They, however, build many molehills of daily perseverance and not impressive mountains of industrial enterprise or sprawling and glinting service sectors.

The Indian market, therefore, assumes peculiarities that Western products have only partially addressed so far. The first rally of growth happened and the size of western offers were miniaturized. Shampoo sachets, lower-grade tyres, lower quality food items – the list of pared-down versions of the original has brought endless business. Initially, for a country that was deprived of base-level quality and uniformity, the inherent standardization in western products had consumers gratefully lining up. Add low prices and the wonders of packaging and innovation to that and consumers and companies have become a happy couple.

But as the consuming market expands and local companies catch up, mostly through replication but also through innovation, the standardized low-cost model isn't working. Consumers are getting stuff that is especially made for them and the infusion of modern technology has helped local players improve the look of their offers too. And as the scale increases, mass media advertising becomes affordable and accessible to teeming consumers; the gap between global players and local wannabes narrows; and growth, which was the preserve of a few, is now like the fragmented landholding, shared by many.

What does a country with a petite consuming class have to offer as the next opportunity?

Not standardized, scaled-down versions of products but perhaps customized and regional delights – capturing the fine distinction between an Andhra sambhar and a Tamilian sambhar, catering to many cardiovascular patients with an easier and cost-effective electro-cardio GE (General Electric) machine, entertaining sports enthusiasts with the thrill of a rugby cast in the garb of kabaddi and even vernacular films with relatable locales and neighbourly characters with the technical finesse of a Hollywood production. As and when that happens, the many petites will turn out to be monstrous consumers – by the weight of sheer numbers. The Indian market, therefore, takes a tortuous growth trajectory when compared to the West, but the good news is that it delivers as well.

Modernized Tradition

Is India following the West and modernizing every day, brick-by-brick, to eventually resemble them in body and spirit? If so, the rest of the story of development is merely one of catching up, with some bumps, but a near-certain destination. Or is it going back to its roots, stealthily but systematically, consuming the edifices of the West with the nibbling soul of the East?

Neither. The model is fusion, best described as the 'modernization of Indian tradition' by eminent sociologist Yogendra Singh. This is best epitomized by the idea of a Bhojpuri song being heard on a powerful Dolby speaker in a five-dimensional theatre of the future – one that throws Holi colours on you as you jive to the local *jhatkas*. Sociologists typify this mingling of cultures by a churning of the wheel, where a 'little tradition' meets the 'great tradition'. A lower caste festival, like

Holi, grows to be embraced by the higher castes, the upholders of the greater tradition. Or a festival celebrated by Vaishyas, like Diwali, is assimilated into the mainstream. In this churning of the traditional wheel, not only are caste differences blurred, but even strands of modernity, which cling to contemporary life, are picked up and processed into a new unified hybrid. And so Diwali is celebrated with Chinese lights.

This unique Indian blend is not a new reality but a mere throwback. We have always blended. The original land of Dravidians was invaded by Aryans, Turks, Mughals, the British, the Dutch, the French and the Portuguese, yet it doesn't remotely display any of the remnants from the marauders' era. It only looks like itself, with imprints of all of the above ingrained into its cultural mosaic. It is often said that Hinduism isn't a religion but a way of life, but what isn't realized is that this syncretism or fusion is the essence of the religion and the country, not an accident of history.

Elsewhere, cultural invasion leads to the new being replaced by the old; it is borne out by the fate of the Incas after the Spanish invasion or numerous countries that came under the sway of Islam after the Crusades. But India has charted a novel path. It let the new sit atop the old for a while, before eventually subsuming it, rendering itself richer than before. This is how we have come to have the McDonald's Happy Meals that serve a McAloo Tikki burger. The tradition isn't strengthened nor is modernity reinforced, but both are humbled. On an iPhone X, a consumer watches a popular soap opera, *Icchadaari Naagin,* and nothing seems amiss.

Products and businesses that work in India must learn to live with this polarity and balance modernity and tradition with ease. They must also navigate the opportunity to celebrate the hybrids that this creates. With this balance, Haldiram's has opened a quick service restaurant and given McDonald's hot competition down the street.

So, where does that leave the Indian society? Is there an easy formula or a characterization that would help businessmen looking to understand it? Can they use it to come to grips with our colourful nation?

Yogendra Singh, in his seminal work, *Modernization of Indian Tradition*,* has highlighted a paradigm. The paradigm is 'hierarchy-holism-continuity-transcendence'. This is the value system used to comprehend India.

The Indian model

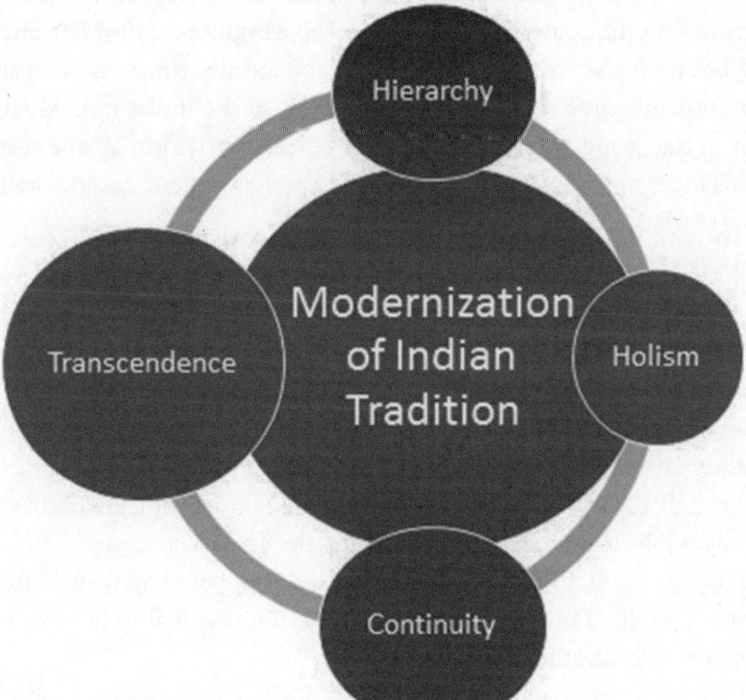

Source: Authors

Hierarchy: The compulsive Indian tendency to put things into a pecking order. Our gods (Shiv, Vishnu and Brahma at the top, followed by aerial gods like Surya and Indra and then the terrestrial

* Singh Yogendra, *Modernization of Indian Tradition*, (Rawat: Delhi, 1996).

gods), our social system (placing the Brahmins castes above Dalits and other marginalized communities), our family system (husband above wife, older sibling over youngsters), our icons (Bollywood's ranking of stars, painstakingly establishing a hero and heroine number one), our fruits (mango, the king of fruits) and our animals (lion, a the king of the forest) – the tendency to put everything into hierarchies goes on and on. It's so pervasive that without it we can make no sense of how our world is structured. Hierarchy creates a unique need amongst us to be, simply put, number one. Whether it's at work, in relationships or social settings, we feel an inescapable urge to rank and see if we are at the top as individuals or in the group we belong to. Other cultures may or may not have this intangible tug, but for Indians it's almost a genetic compulsion.

Holism: Where an individual is to be seen with respect to his roles. His responsibility acquires meaning only in the context of the collective entities around him: family, caste, community, religion and nation. Self-pursuit is alright, but cloak it with the spirit of family betterment and you become a hero! What you do isn't anybody's concern, unless it doesn't include their concerns. And strangely enough, before you know it, even you are seeing yourself through the eyes of others. You are the son chasing his father's dream job and the daughter marrying the groom cherry-picked by her parents. It so happens that others know your interests better than you do. This creates the need for an individual to be seen in the context of others.

Continuity: Life is eternal (*shaasvata*), and through our karma we live perpetually – from one life to the other, our souls carry the never-ending spiral of our desires. This perspective imbues life in India with a circular dimension. Nothing terminates definitely but merely transmutes from one stage to another. Our explanations on all aspects of life are circuitous, not linear. Conversations aren't concluded easily as we argumentatively approach a problem. And no perspective is complete without an infinite regress of circular reasoning. In a sense, it joins the hierarchy and the holism together.

Once we have ordered our universe in a ranking system (hierarchy) and found a way to situate the individual within the context of the community (holism), we must arrive at a cause-and-effect relationship between various elements of our ecosystem.

Thus, our mutual conversations or our public narratives make endless connections, drawing elaborate and causal relationships: what should be our goals in life, what constitutes a good life, what makes an ideal son, daughter and mother-in-law, what models define success – there is no dearth of readymade blueprints to live a virtuous life. And when we deviate, our reasons are no less elaborate. Either way, this makes our culture replete with vivid stories (as seen in our elaborate commercials packed into a mere thirty seconds), where reason seamlessly gives way to emotion and our universe appears chiming in happy unison.

Westerners find such ambiguity paralyzing, while Indians find it hugely energizing. In fact, this fulfils our need to have meaning behind every action.

Transcendence: Traditional values, which are reflected in our caste and religious systems, are kept outside the domain of rationality. Faith is a viable alternative to logic; to understanding the world and living a life without frequent recourse to rationality. When you live beyond logic, it may become difficult to arrive at a mutual understanding, but in India, no functionality is lost. We are perfectly at ease living beyond logic, steeped in non-verifiable (and often, non-utilitarian) values that are rooted in obscure dharma. But we exude the same confidence as those with rationality. In fact, for us, faith can supersede rationality when there is a clash between the two frameworks. That explains how, in spite of irrationality, we continue to live on amicably. The unjustified faith in various religious leaders (although many have been exposed as criminals or conmen), the caste-based voting behaviour in a modern democratic and apparently meritocratic government, lavish expenditure on weddings that result in debt and so on show how comfortable we are living dangerously on the edge.

So, what sort of a consumer does our social system generate?

One who is argumentative, emotional, rank-conscious, ridden with contradictions (between the emotional and the rational, between individual glory and social validation) and thriving in ambiguity (for a complicated world with coalescing winds of modernity and tradition). In short, we are nuanced.

Marketing begins and ends with consumers. We believe that our knowledge of Indian consumers and the unique background of their socio-cultural experiences, is absolutely necessary if we are seeking to create endearing brands with enduring values. In the chapters to follow, Pragmarketism imbues Western models with Indian colours, and also creates new paradigms to better service the sons and daughters of this diverse soil.

2

Business and Vision

Every morning, when we drive past mirrored monstrosities – our modern offices looming over dhabas and shacks – we can't cease to be amazed at the dichotomy of the new India. Humble dhabas coexist next to the upmarket DLF Cyberhub. The food inside is probably one-tenth the price of Cyberhub, and perhaps it feeds ten times more customers too. However small, these guys also do business. We look a little closer and notice the dangling board of Mahesh Dhaba that reads, 'Delishus chole bhature every day, since 1925'.

To compare, we recall the gilded letters behind the glitzy reception at the McDonald's office: 'To be the world's best quick service restaurant experience'. This is the office of one of the world's biggest QSR (quick service restaurant) that has satisfied many weary 'n' hungry travellers. Their business runs like clockwork, but only because it is highly sophisticated organizationally. Where and how does the difference between Mahesh Dhaba and McDonald's start?

It's in their **vision** – the foresight on ways of fulfilling consumer need that determines if a store selling a mere burger grows into a global enterprise or stagnates as a single ramshackle outlet.

What lands on a highway consumer's table? A McAloo Tikki burger or *chola bhatura* may be marginally different in taste. But how long does the experience of the consumer last? Does it echo time after time and how many such consumers consistently feel the same has to do with the founding thought of the enterprise – its vision. It looks distant and unconnected? Let's look deeper.

McDonald's burgers have the same bite and flavour every time you have them; the delivery time is nearly always the same and the parlour experience is almost blameless insofar it is inspired by core values of cleanliness, value, convenience and quality, which have been adhered to with an obsession. Also, behind the simple burger sits the best of American business concepts: standardized operations, quality control, continuous consumer feedback on new products, rigid consumer forecasting models, tight cost control, streamlined logistics, motivated employees and years of America's successful capitalism, exported to developing countries.

Against this, the backend of our delicious *chola bhatura* is somewhat shallow. It includes a favourable deal with the potato vendor, who narrowly escaped a blight last year, and the chef with the magical touch, who has been persuaded to stay longer in spite of his failing health. Also, the owner is not sure what will happen to his business after his passing; he has never thought that far ahead.

What differentiates Mahesh Dhaba from McDonald's, therefore, is in the comprehensiveness of their outlook regarding the future of their businesses – the vision. It not only justifies the everyday trammels of running a business, but also sets a direction. It indicates *why* a firm is in business or in the value-creation game, *what* good will it bring to consumers and *how* it intends to secure its objective and keep its employees motivated. By all this, it provides a destination and paves the way for choices that need to be considered to reach that destination.

Without a vision, Mahesh cannot be sure if his business will survive after two years, but with it, he can even think of opening a branch in Manhattan. Vision clarifies one's objective and enables steps to be taken to meet it. It's that fundamental. Indian companies must start here to delight their consumers if they want to play big.

Below are a few distinctive and inspiring examples of powerful visions that have powered multinationals:

- **IKEA**: *'To create a better everyday life for the many people'*. 'Many' and 'everyday' are terms that cue their mass ambition with the umpteen product range and 'better' the visionary contribution to improving life.
- **Amazon**: *'Our vision is to be the Earth's most customer-centric company; to build a place where people can come to find and discover anything they might want to buy online.'* This clearly spells out their leadership ambition with regard to both customer-centricity and online availability.
- **Universal Health Services**: *'To provide superior quality healthcare services that patients recommend to friends and family, physicians prefer for their patients, purchasers select for their clients, employees are proud of, and investors seek for long-term returns.'* Amazing perspective from the outside, but this doesn't reflect how they will make it happen.
- **Apple**: *'Committed to bringing the best personal computing experience to students, educators, creative professionals and consumers around the world through its innovative hardware, software and internet offerings.'* A comprehensive run-through of customers and offers, but it hasn't captured the crispness and memorability of Steve Jobs' vision: *'To make a contribution to the world by making tools for the mind that advance humankind.'*
- **Disney**: *'To make people happy'*. You can't beat this one. It's simple to the point of sounding generic. This shows tremendous potential, which only Disney can bring to fruition without sounding ridiculously pompous.

A few others for a quick run-through:

- **Google**: *'To provide access to the world's information in one click.'*

- **Instagram**: *'Capture and share the world's moments.'*
- **LinkedIn**: *'To connect the world's professionals and make them more productive and successful.'*
- **Microsoft**: *'A computer on every desktop and in every home (using Microsoft software)'*
- **Nike**: *'To bring inspiration and innovation to every athlete in the world.'* Inspired by the founder, Bill Bowerman, who said, 'If you have a body, you are an athlete.'
- **Quora**: *'Quora connects you to everything you want to know about.'*
- **Walmart**: *'To help people save money so they can live better.'*
- **Wikipedia**: *'Imagine a world in which every single person on the planet is given free access to the sum of all human knowledge.'*
- **Ben and Jerry's**: *'To make the best possible ice-cream, in the nicest possible way.'*

It would be instructive to also know how NGOs state their visions, especially as companies get conscious about the communities they impact directly or indirectly.

- **ASPCA**: *'That the United States is a humane community in which all animals are treated with respect and kindness.'*
- **WWF**: *'We seek to save a planet, a world of life. Reconciling the needs of human beings and the needs of others that share the Earth.'*

Looking at all the above examples, one cannot help but notice that they contextualize their product with regard to a specific human need. And then they go on to state it while being strictly economical with their words. This not only makes it relatable, but also memorable.

Against that, how do top Indian companies fare? Some are inspiring, but some are downright blasé. Here are a few examples:

- **ONGC**: *'To be the global leader in integrated energy business through sustainable growth, knowledge, excellence and exemplary governance practices.'* This spells out the ambition but follows it up with general adjectives; these values could be relevant in other industries as well.
- **ITC**: *'Sustain ITC's position as one of India's most valuable corporations through world-class performance, growing value for the Indian economy and the company's stakeholders.'* Like the one above, this also suffers from generalization and is somewhat inward-looking, perhaps forced by the diversified nature of their operations. Do they inspire or provide direction?

Let's look at a few more:

- **Asian Paints**: *'We want to be an innovative, agile, and responsive world-class research and technology organization that's aligned to future consumer needs and catalyses the growth of the company across existing and future businesses.'* Not very different from the ones above.
- **Titan**: *'We create elevating experiences for the people we touch and significantly impact the world we work in.'* Interesting – a breeze of a humane touch, but the vagueness regarding its plan fails to impress.

Now, a quick run-through of a few others:

- **J K Tyre**: *'To be amongst the most admired companies in India, committed to excellence.'*

- **HCL**: *'To be the technology partner of choice for forward-looking customers by collaboratively transforming technology into business advantage.'*
- **Infosys**: *'To be a globally respected corporation that provides the best-of-breed business solutions, leveraging technology, delivered by best-in-class people.'* They also aim '*to achieve our objects in an environment of honesty, fairness, courtesy towards our clients, employees, vendors and society at large*'. This is very verbose and inward-looking.
- **Airtel**: *'To enrich the lives of our customers. Our obsession to win customers for life through an exceptional experience.'* However, their mission reads, '*Hunger to win over customers for life*' – this is crisper than their vision.
- **Dabur**: *'Dedicated to the health and well-being of every household.'* This could be better, especially if the Ayurvedic aspect of their business could have been covered.
- **Aditya Birla**: *'To be a premium global conglomerate, with a clear focus on each of the businesses.'*
- **Tata**: (the text appears in the mission of the Tata Group) *'To improve the quality of life of the communities we serve globally through long-term stakeholder value creation based on Leadership and Trust.'*
- **Reliance Industries**: *'To be our client's first call and preferred collaboration partner within our business areas. To consistently exceed our client's expectations for our professionals and value-adding advice.'*

Compared to their Western counterparts, Indian companies seem to lack inspiration and a sharpness in their intent. You could swap a vision of one company with another in quite a few cases and this would create no dissonance. The words are trite and the visions are somewhat blurred. They seem to have a universal desire to be 'number one, best in their class' and contain more such woolly exhortations that provide no specific direction for their employees to pursue.

The second aspect is the lack of consumer centricity. One has the sense they are written with a censoring government or disapproving public in mind. This may reflect the 'Licence Raj' that these companies evolved within or serve as an indication of socialistic mooring that frowned upon wealth accumulation unless it was intended for public welfare.

Another piquant aspect of the vision of Indian companies is that they don't spell out the industry they are operating in or the products they are offering. And understandably so. Indian companies with their diversified portfolios couldn't have covered all their motley businesses under one umbrella, and specificity would not allow their foray into emerging business opportunities in the future. While this may be a difficult situation to circumvent, it certainly limits the potential of the vision to provide direction and drive choices in a volatile world. More importantly, as Simon Sinek argues in his book, *Start with Why*,* a specific vision enables companies to attract the right kind of people – much like great companies such as Google and Microsoft inevitably do. A good vision answers the existential question, 'Why are they in the business in the first place?'

So, how do Indian companies reconcile their diverse portfolios under a common vision and yet not lose the sharpness required to provide direction?

Looking at the example of iconic companies, the primary task would be to identify the basic human need the business is fulfilling. Apple fulfils the need for tools that advance humankind, Disney

---

* Sinek, Simon, *Start with why: How great leaders inspire everyone to take action*, New York, Portfolio, 2009.

makes people happy (so does Coke, but more through an advertising tagline), Google fulfils the need to be informed, Walmart helps people live better by saving money and Wikipedia fulfils the need to have access to all knowledge. There is no ambiguity regarding what needs they satisfy. It puts the consumer first and gives them a real face for all thc company's employees and shareholders to connect with. In a world where situations change often and lead to confounding possibilities, knowing the consumer and his need builds sails to harvest the uprooting winds of uncertainty.

In their vision, the Tatas, Reliance and Birlas talked about touching the common Indian with an ideal to become more human, but the risk is that they start to look like each other. A simple way to expand their vision would be to write it in three parts, encompassing it as follows:

1. **Why**, or their reason to exist in the business world. They can justify their reason to exist as giving consumers the opportunity to meet their needs of connecting (telecom), grooming (apparel), bridging distances (infrastructure), enabling electricity and so on. This would bring a much-needed consumer face for the purpose of these industrial behemoths.
2. **How** they would bring the resources to bear towards the objective above: using the 'latest technology' in a 'world-class fashion', with 'enduring roads, bridges, airports' and 'reliable supply'.
3. **What** the result or benefit of the above two points would be: phrases such as 'making people happy', 'driving self-confidence', 'coming together', 'dispelling darkness or ignorance', etc.

For companies that do not have multiple segments, a vision that enables them to stay focused on the broadest platform of their initial set of products or services would impart a sharpness and enhance their core competence. For instance, Dabur needs to capture Ayurveda (or Indian traditional medicine as their unique focus if they want to do unani or homeopathy in the long run), Titan could choose lifestyle (leveraging the benefit of watches and accessories) or Paytm could choose 'pocket banks' over the current image of a payment portal. Does being specific limit the options available to these companies in the future? Not really, if words are chosen to include both the medium- and the long-term priorities of the firm. On the contrary, writing the vision may help companies articulate what they currently do and even include other adjacent innovation possibilities that they may not have considered.

Can vision statements be changed if the company decides to change its direction? Hopefully, they need not be, but modifications can certainly be made if a core philosophy is retained and only its application altered. This would not only infuse a certain discipline and keep the company anchored in its core competence, but it would also enable flirting out of it when the situation warrants. The advantage is that even if you depart from your core, you will know. Otherwise, companies drift any way unconsciously, lured by momentary expediency over sustainable strategy.

Mission, another popular word, usually refers to the tools required to shape the vision. Here, a whole lot of common words float on the charter of Indian companies: 'company of choice', 'performance-driven', 'innovative', 'caring', 'environment-friendly', 'integrity', 'teamwork', etc. These terms are exalted to the level of unique company philosophies, when in reality, they are rather generic. Without a sharp vision, the mission reflects the same ambiguity. Without specifically knowing where to go, you cannot choose the best route – it's a bit like that.

In the final analysis, the vision or the question of 'why' needs to be addressed before the 'how', 'what' or 'when' of business. When we look at the visions of some companies today, their windscreens appear hazy and require wipers so a clearer view emerges regarding what their consumer/customer needs are and what they are around to address.

Clearing the dust off their visions, or writing them afresh, Indian companies can set their GPS coordinates so they can go far and fast without being driven off course by unknown routes. The sharper and more energizing the vision, the greater the chance of a firm to create value for its consumers.

3

Consumer Need

Until my (Arvind's) mother-in-law started to use it, I didn't realize how rampant the usage of YouTube is for recipes. She is a fine cook, but even she finds inspiration on the net to add to her already-rich repertoire of dishes. Needs can exist, even when consumers seem overtly saturated with experience.

Our daughter, Nandini, loves to go to restaurants, giving boring home-cooked food a miss. But when we are not around during her dinner time, early in the evening, with a phone and some cash at hand, this issue is solved. Everyone gets to test their hunger against images of delectable food on Zomato and Swiggy, to know and get what they want and not depend on the kitchen. Technology has not only satisfied a vague need but also empowered people, creating a base for new needs. Nandini now extends her new-found power to buy cakes and bouquets online for unimagined reasons.

We want to have many friends and impact those around us. Dale Carnegie's book, *How to Win Friends and Influence People,* succinctly captures this need and continues to top the list of bestsellers. This is a case of a universally relevant need.

And as we strut through our need 'n' satisfaction matrix every day, new vistas open up. Quick, reliable services for home repairs through Urban Company, furniture deliveries with an assembling option through Pepperfry, help for aged parents with trained nurses and escorts, home catering for a small family party, personal grooming at home during those in-between times, toilets that provide Western comfort with Indian familiarity – it appears that the Indian consumer's specific needs are finally being heard and provided for with solutions that have been developed with only him or her in mind. Need is where ideas take root and against which consumer satisfaction is registered.

Therefore, our recommendation is a motto: *When in doubt, think of the consumer need.*

This is the most important advice we can provide from our collective experience. The complexities of business can drag us into paralyzing debates and prevent us from looking at the final beneficiary of all our efforts – the consumer. It is not what the company can offer, what it can manufacture efficiently, what satisfies the manager's objectives, what makes great financial sense or what the boss's wife needs ... *but what the consumer needs*.

Sometimes, the need is explicit and sometimes it has to be mined for, uncovering the consumer's complex motivations, while sometimes it's ambiguous and needs to be clarified and sometimes it's just not there and manufacturers create a need. A need has many avatars. And while success can take diverse shapes at the end, a need is a necessary and enabling condition for it. Consumer need clarifies the business's purpose, defogging the glasses of confusion. But it can be easily forgotten.

In a different context, Gandhiji said, 'When in doubt think of the poorest Indian ... and ask yourself if it will benefit him.'

We could restate the same. Embracing Mahatma's spirit and also keeping business as the focal point, we would like to restate as follows: 'I will give you a talisman. Whenever you are in doubt, apply the following test. Recall the face of the consumer whom you may have seen, and ask yourself, if the step you contemplate is going to be of any use to him/her. Will he/she gain anything by it? Will it restore him/her to a control over his/her own life and destiny? In other words, will it lead to 'swaraj' [freedom] from want? Then you will find your doubts and your "strategic dilemma" melt away.'

Consumer centricity, with need and want as the fulcrum, ought to be an obsession for all marketers. We cannot overemphasize this any more than we already have. We have already quoted the father of the nation. Indeed, this is the way out of many strategic dilemmas that all corporates routinely confront.

From Need to Want

Consumers are the measure of all commercial activities. They are the ones who use goods or services, not the producers who make them. The Hindi word for consumer is '*upbhokta*' – one who indulges in '*bhog*' or consumption. Another word for it is '*grahak*' – one who accepts (*grahan*) what is provided. Both the words imply a passive beneficiary of goods from suppliers who are supposed to be conscientious sellers. Hard-selling of goods is alien to India and consumption is taken for granted if quality goods are made in consonance with the need, following a spirit of mutual benefit. This is as enshrined in the '*jajmani*' or barter system, which has laid the foundation for Indian commercial activity.

The consumer consumes what he needs. What is a need? The word is derived from the Germanic or Old English word, '*neodian*', which implies, 'be necessary, be required, be under obligation of'. Need is, therefore, a response to something more elemental than a want.

'Want' is derived from the Old Norse word, '*vanta*', which implies, 'be lacking in'. Since a want is based on the deprivation of something, it is more urgent. For instance, there may be a genuine need for mobility, but advertisers can turn that into a want for a BMW. This is one way among many to meet that need. But advertisers may convert diffused yearning into a pressing want.

How do you convert a need into a pressing want? One way is to list its benefits. Another is to give an emotional benefit so compelling that the mind sees no alternative. It is a bit like choosing your friend or relationship over anything else; the heart, and not the mind, must and will steal the show.

Needs are, therefore, inextricably linked to our emotions. The word 'emotion' originates from the Latin word '*movere*', combining the word 'move' and the French word '*emouvoir*', meaning 'move out' or excite. If a want tells us what is lacking, an emotion tells us what has 'moved' into our being as a result of it. An emotion is the catalyst that converts a dormant need into a throbbing want.

Marketers try their best to find veritable emotional needs, and rightfully so, because if no movement is achieved, the potential captured in the need is not met. So, a Hush Puppies shoe is not just valued for its lightness and comfort but also because it helps me work harder so I can be more successful, which positively impacts my self-image and eventually determines if my life has been worth living at all. The moral of the story – do well and put your best foot forward while wearing Hush Puppies. Seems implausible? Well, big brands do just that – they partner with the consumers, converting dreams into reality. And the brands are with them wherever it matters so their consumers are foremost for them. Consumers then reward them by making that brand the first choice when a need in that category arises.

Types of Need: Want, Access and Quality of Experience

Need has a direct correlation to accessibility. After all, what good is a need that cannot be met? What sets a fantasy apart from a desire is accessibility. If we plot a graph of want versus access, the needs are recast in different ways, offering differentiated ways in which to capitalize them.

Need-want model

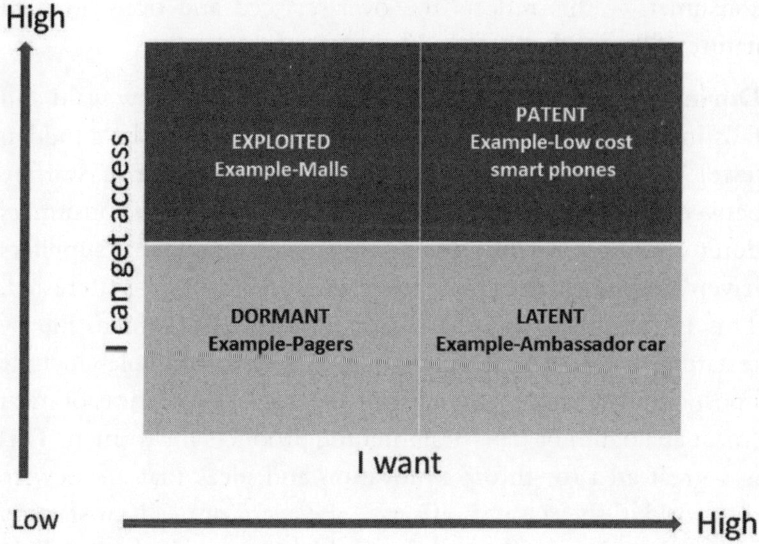

Source: Authors

Patent needs: In the top-right quadrant are needs which are visible to all and highly serviceable, leading to over-segmentation and over-investment. Everyone wants these, and while participation here is lucrative, it clearly comes at a cost and is competitively intense.

Latent needs: The needs in the bottom-right quadrant are cloaked, either by the level of development that has occurred in the industry or through inhibitive regulation. It, however, represents a high degree of want but poor consumer access to the opportunity. Until cars were deregulated, the Fiat and Ambassador were the fate of Indians, even though the desire for decent mobility was much higher. Maruti Suzuki JV tapped into this, leading to their meteoric rise.

Exploited needs: These occur when the options to satisfy a need outweigh the need itself. The plethora of malls for shopping compete for footfall and real estate players aim for housing-hungry consumers – this reflects the over-serviced and over-saturated nature of the market.

Dormant or dud need: This has low access and low want and falls in the bottom corner quadrant. It could either be a hidden jewel or a dud. Tucked away from the competitive warfare between segments and lying over it, it may be what consumers don't want because they don't know about it and what suppliers haven't yet created because they are clueless or disinterested. This is the space where dormant needs are brought to life by restating the need and reinventing solutions. Examples include liposuction, WhatsApp, hair weaving, vegetarian replicas of meat (meat analogue) or hair-straightening products for women. This is a great area for future innovation and ideas that are new to the world. Otherwise, it reflects a graveyard of need-satisfactory ideas: the ideas of yesteryears, which have failed to delight consumers – the Walkman or innumerable tablets for common cold with dubious side effects.

Alternatively, these needs may be a junkyard of stale innovation or incongruous ideas, like pagers or bromide films. Whether the junkyard of today can be turned into the goldmine of tomorrow will depend on the re-articulation of the firm's vision in accordance with the changed times. Nirula's, a popular fast food chain in north India, fell prey to slicker outlets like McDonald's or other Indian parlours like Haldiram's. If the company's vision and relevance had been re-articulated, they may have led with a portfolio of nostalgia (their trademark pizzas or their '21 Love' ice-cream) and ventured into new fusion foods and salads (which it pioneered successfully with its potpourri range of salad bars).

We could draw a third axis, that of the **quality of experience**, on a 2 × 2 grid between access and want above. In the patent need segment, consumers can be *delighted* because their disposition to accept new innovations is high and suppliers have the capacity to provide them. An iPhone with a slowfie or a slow-motion selfie feature or a hotel stay with free spa services could provide new ways to delight within a saturated segment. In the latent need segment, consumers can be *surprised* positively because the suppliers under-service this segment, due to which consumers have low expectations even if the demand is high. In the exploited segment, suppliers have to *value up* the demand as consumers are spoilt for choice. Suppliers have to, therefore, constantly redefine their offers to be differentiated in a commoditizing space. Small freebies, like free parking tickets to service guarantees, are ways to increase the value of their service in their consumer's eyes. And in the lowest quadrant, consumers either return with indifference or a thumping endorsement, depending on whether the suppliers are abandoning or recasting this segment in a new way.

Therefore, in a world of needs, there is no stagnancy. The interplay between suppliers and consumers can change a dormant segment to an exploited segment overnight, or a patent to a latent. Successful entrepreneurs are those who spot an opportunity in the interaction among the axes of want, access and quality of experience. Indian companies, with their inherent ability to innovate in unconventional ways (as epitomized in the word 'jugaad'), can get ahead by utilizing the new vector of quality of experience on the want/access grid.

Need Spectrum

Maslow's hierarchy is a comprehensive overview of consumer needs for any MBA student worth his salt – starting from physiological needs, like hunger, sex, shelter and security, to social needs, like belongingness and love, to needs of self-esteem, like when you want your worth in society to be recognized because it gives you self-confidence, to the higher-order needs of self-actualization, where, paradoxically, one looks beyond oneself, taking on higher responsibilities (more vivid in art forms and in business, when people act out of motivations beyond profitability and growth) to experience higher self-realization.

Maslow hierarchy model

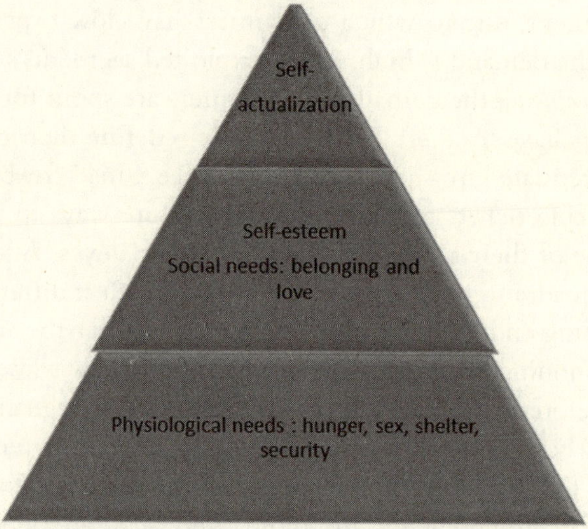

Source: Maslow, 1943

However, some limitations of this need-hierarchy are:

1. It assumes a sequential occurrence of needs from the lower to the higher states. However, exceptions often exist. People are known to fulfil basic needs, like sex, even after achieving great material success and people down and out often think of the interests of the larger community and do not focus on their basic wants, as is the case with social activists. Consumers may appear and disappear between the layers of Maslow's needs randomly and not in an upward vertical trajectory, as predicted.
2. It doesn't predict the turning point – that is, when a consumer moves from one layer of need to another. At what point does a hungry man, satisfied by food, reach out for social security? Empirically, we know that people rarely feel

satisfied completely and that they are rarely also completely unsatisfied, often reconciling themselves with their existing lot. At what level of satisfaction are they propelled to move to the next level?

3. The arrow of cause to effect doesn't run linearly in the human mind. It's a lot more complicated than that. Insufficiently met libido may fire off creative urges, as 'sublimated' art often proves. Deprivation of food may spur a desire to be powerful in an unrelated direction. Real life isn't always in a straight line.
4. Consumers may not be aware of their own needs. How would other people be able to ascertain this on their behalf?

Hence, Maslow provides general guidance that proves inadequate for predicting and modelling human behaviour based only on sequential need-satisfaction.

Fear-avoidance

Maslow's hierarchy can be supplemented with a more detailed understanding of human emotions. Robert Plutchik, a renowned psychologist, provides a 'wheel of emotions', which has simplified the primal human responses to correspond to eight basic emotions:

- Fear
- Anger: tending towards rage
- Sadness: momentary grief to depression
- Disgust: at something nasty or unjust
- Surprise
- Anticipation
- Trust: acceptance to admiration
- Joy: plain happiness to ecstasy

One thing clearly stands out from Plutchik's list above: negative emotions are as important as positive ones. But Maslow's hierarchy leads us to think of need-satisfaction, not *fear-avoidance*. Can marketers better meet needs by knowing not just the wants of the consumers but also their fears?

To delve deeper into the Indian psyche, let's evaluate the views of Indian philosophers on human needs.

Indian Philosophy on Understanding Consumer 'Justifications'

Desire – where need finds expression – has been disregarded by Indian religious philosophers. Also, since religion consciously and unconsciously influences consumer psyche, could it dampen the enthusiasm of Indian consumers to splurge? Buddha, who identified desire as the root cause of suffering, highlighted three seminal needs:

- *Kama-taṇhā*: craving sensual pleasures – wealth, prestige and power – and attachment to one's ideas and beliefs.
- *Bhava-taṇhā*: craving for existence – an urge to unite one's entity (or ego) with some expression.
- *Vibhava-taṇhā*: craving for non-existence by way of suicide, when the craving or '*tanha*' ends as the person gains insight into the impermanence of nature and the reality of his non-self.

It appears that Buddha had foretold Maslow's hierarchy, and even gone beyond it, 2,500 years ago. Other theologies point in the same direction.

The Bhagavad Gita talks about the futile chase of *naam*, *rupa* and *yasha* (name, beauty and fame); Jainism celebrates those who conquer their senses (*arihant*); the Upanishads urge humans to look beyond cravings in search of the pervasive and eternal (*Parabrahma*) to recognize the non-existence those one who crave; Shankaracharya stressed the fundamental unity between those who wish and what they wish in '*advait*' (non-dualism), therefore, making needs redundant; and Islam has vows and regular 'namaz' to direct the indulgent towards sacrifice. The history of the Indian subcontinent is the saga of abstinence.

Does it mean that Indians are averse to need-fulfilment? Not really. Indians disguise their carnal needs within a religious garb. We spend unabashedly during religious festivals and even resort to gambling during Diwali. We spend on tourism because half of the picturesque places are 'tirthas' or pilgrimage sites, which need no justification. Calendars of all religious communities provide enough occasions to splurge in myriad ways, where people can bring out their material wealth in religious shades.

This means that Indians can splurge within a restrictive framework if 'justifications', like the ones below (which are couched within the framework of hierarchy-holism-continuity-transcendence), are available to consumers. Justifications can be founded in the consumer's mind on the basis of fear-avoidance or need-satisfaction, as noted above.

- *Fear of obscurity*: Blame it on our crowded living spaces or the hierarchical mindsets, but Indians are pulled towards recognition and fame. Whether it's about having a superior opinion ('I told you so'), better grades, being bigger or having a better home or vacation, there is no joy without being relatively ahead of others. Therefore, brands which make us stand out or impart significance to our lives emerge as winners. Onida's slogan, 'neighbour's envy, owner's pride', or Asian Paints' '*har ghar kuch kehta hai*' campaign touch this chord.
- *Fear of being outsmarted*: Linked to the above is our fear of being beaten by someone. This may have to do with our

hypercompetitive society. Endless commercials replay concepts such as being smarter than your neighbour, spouse, friends, peers, bosses and even your mother-in-law. In a resource-scarce country, there is a premium for getting to a coveted thing before others. From catching the crowded school bus to cutting queues and jostling with others to scoring better grades with coaching to wooing that girl to grabbing a deal better than your neighbours – this list has no end.

- *Need to be elitist:* Following the logic of Sanskritization (upward mobility by imitating upper-caste symbols of consumption), Indians spare no opportunity to be elitist – appearing like Westerners is the safest way to stand out. Brands that hint at an imported flavour, look and feel, find easy acceptance, beating the price-conscious consumer. This explains the relatively elitist backdrop of Indian advertisements that consumers voyeuristically delight in or the heavy growth of Indian-made foreign liquor (IMFL) in the subcontinent.
- *Need for spiritual endorsement*: Our self-actualization is a bizarre hybrid. Draped in designer clothes, we step out of a BMW 5 series to attend lectures on renunciation. Spirituality gives our conmen and their followers an unquestionable licence to be consumption-ogres. Brands that have a pious and other-worldly feel have a great market in the premium segment where these consumers orbit.
- *Fear of being left out*: This is linked to the aspect of holism, where an individual acquires meaning in the context of the group. We feel an inherent tug to be part of a group: whether it is caste, religion, region, alumni, kitty parties, clubs, age-based or vacation-centred, the lure of groupism extends far. WhatsApp is creating new social affinities so we can fulfil Maslow's social need in newer ways. Groups also, by design, create newer groups. A society like India, which

has ostracized others for violating the caste order, loves to exclude others. This creates a great fear of being left out. Very often, in chat groups and kitty parties, you can't tell if the cohesiveness comes from intimacy with each other or hostility towards the excluded.

Being aware of these peculiar needs allows marketers to thrill consumers, either furtively or ostensibly, as we will explore in later chapters.

Fusing Maslow's need-satisfaction with the fear-avoidance framework and justifications based on typical Indian needs and fear, we are now ready with a more useful framework to meet the needs of a billion consumers.

Negative-positive need model

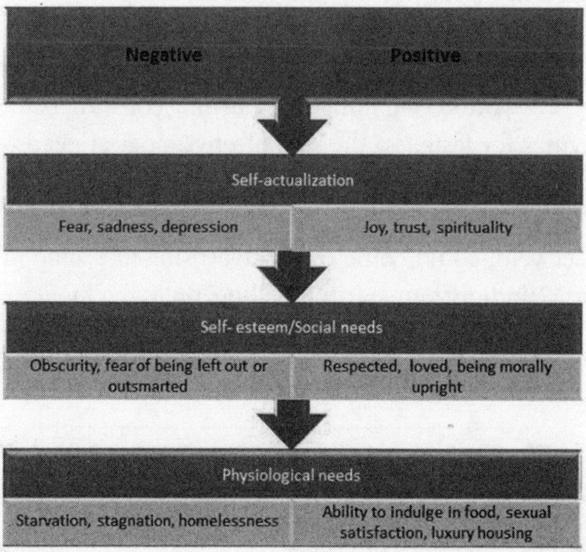

Source: Authors

From the above grid, one can see emotions of various hues being created at different need-levels. Negative emotions can be used to remind consumers of the risk of ignoring a brand benefit and positive emotions that entice them towards availing higher potentialities of need-fulfilment. Therefore, consumers can be reminded of what they want and what they don't want. What they want is often already understood, but what they don't want can be used more effectively because fear also haunts them into action.

The cross tabulation between positive emotions or needs and negative emotions or haunts gives us a useful 'want-haunt' pathway to move consumers towards brands' offering.

'Want-haunt' Pathway

Situate a fun food brand, like Lay's potato chips, between Maslow's grid and the grid of positive and negative emotions and you get an interesting and somewhat piquant 'want-haunt' pathway of options (the options are italicized below to indicate a negative emotion or haunt). You can get an option like 'start gaining control of your life' and meet it by countering hunger or pushing consumers to indulge their cravings for taste, on the side of physiological needs. On the social side, you could be left out of your community or alternatively become the most desired. And self-actualization for a chip category, in a lighter vein, could come from advertising like 'chipping away to nirvana', 'finding your spiritual calling' or 'living life, lost forever without knowing one' – a great creative multiplier for advertising.

Want-haunt model

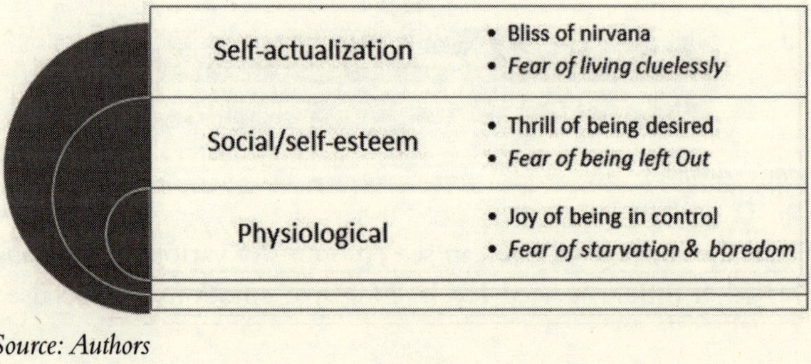

Source: Authors

A similar want-haunt pathway can be made for other categories, like durables – for example, a washing machine.

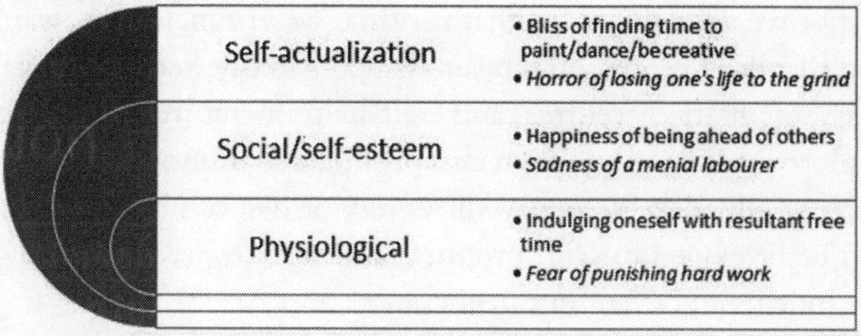

Source: Authors

The want-haunt pathway of an e-wallet company could look as follows:

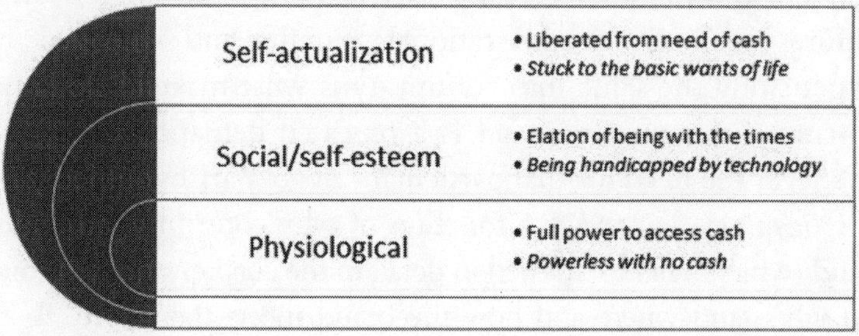

Source: Authors

A want-haunt pathway can yield some interesting options. Not all categories at all times will yield possibilities that can be leveraged (some may be outrightly bizarre, as in the case of Lay's – even though it could be used for communication), but exploring the pathway will generate newer, more effective ways to satisfy the consumer. Understanding the negative haunts and the positive wants will enable business owners to play the best chord to delight consumers. Finally, soaking these with the peculiarities of Indian need-requirements, such as spirituality, probity or fear of being left out or outsmarted, would endear consumers.

Lastly, a passing mention should be made of '*Vibhav-taṇhā*' or the desire to be beyond desire. It's a unique reflection of the topmost ladder of self-actualization in Maslow's grid. Whether or not we actually go for that nirvana, we are inclined towards it and that itself represents a business opportunity. Scores of spiritual spas, meditation centres and self-help literature have already explored this need and then also proliferated it into products quite successfully. Kerala's Ayurvedic equity or that of Himalayan states can be leveraged to offer products and services, creating a market for Indians and even for outsiders.

More examples of untapped needs that various industries could leverage are detailed in the need types framework on page 46-47.

Demand Plasticity

Converting a want, which can either be done once or a few times, requires spelling out the rational benefits and emotions but perpetuating the same into continuity is what makes a consumer demand. Consumer demand is a repeated demand for a brand, whenever the need for that particular category arises.

Consumer demand is a function of why consumers want your brand (which will be explored in detail in the chapter on positioning) and when and where and how the brand meets their need. As the brand becomes equated with all or most of the expectations of a need-fulfilment, it becomes more entrenched with consumers. For instance, if a brand fulfils a basic need, such as quenching thirst, it must then outscore all its rivals in the totality of that experience. Consumers should feel satisfied and the feeling should soothe their throats (the beverage has to be pure and refreshing), their minds (it must stand up to the critical assessment of quality and safety) and their hearts (quenching thirst goes a long way towards establishing the internal poise of consumers). A lot of the work on product development, innovation and communication centres on these conditions.

Need types framework

Industry	Tapped Needs	Untapped/Semi-tapped Needs	
	Core Expression	Basic Needs – Physiological, Social	Extended Needs
Food	Taste, health, growth	Food for satisfying hunger or Nostalgia/comfort food	Longevity and independence Daily health, traditional ayurveda Well-being – yogic food
Cosmetics	Looks	Hassle free hair-dyes/dental implants Home visits by barbers, beauticians Annual maintenance plans Grooming counselling and checks	Local fame opportunities Public speaking/appearance tips Self-confidence classes
Durables	Functionalities (TV, AC, toasters, machines)	Electricity costs covered/reduced Annual maintenance of toasters Discount on clothes and dish dryers as follow-up purchase	Holiday packages/hobby classes made possible due to free time

Industry	Tapped Needs	Untapped/Semi-tapped Needs	
	Core Expression	Basic Needs – Physiological, Social	Extended Needs
Mobile	Pictures, calling	Wi-Fi packages to enhance connectivity in public places	Photography contest Video content-curation opportunities
Medicine	Ailment cure	Instant relief, discount on doctor visits on loyalty card	Wellness packages, gym packages Health food offers
Infrastructure	Travel	Bump-free, toll-free driving experience	Better passage to new destinations Services on roads, restaurants

But once that happens, it's equally important to complete the whole gamut of need-fulfillment, as follows:

- **Where** and **when** is the brand when the need presents itself before the consumer – at home, out of home, in restaurants, on highways – during different parts of the day?

- **How** is the channel and product strategy configured: are there right stock keeping units (SKUs), secondary packaging and supporting infrastructure (for e.g. chilling equipment), enabling the where and when of the brand demand?

A lot of time is spent in decoding the **why** behind the brand, which pertains to product innovation or communication; only somewhat residual energy is deployed towards the corresponding **where, when** and **how**.

How well is the consumer demand being tapped into by a company? This can be tracked by measuring the demand plasticity of a brand. In other words, of all the occasions where a brand could be consumed, how plastic is the brand to stretch itself to cover all those occasions? The table below illustrates how demand plasticity can be measured.

Consumption Occasions per Month	**At Office**	**At Home**	**At Play**	**Shopping**	**Other Occasions**	**Total**
	21	10	7	8	4	2 billion occasions. (50 total occasions* size of target audience of 40m)
Brand's share of occasions						2 million (total unit sales of a product)
Demand Plasticity						10%

This may seem tedious to start with, but multiplying the target audience (the brand's chosen consumption universe) with occasions of where and when the brand is required will give a good idea of the real market potential – more robust and challenging than the classic way of garnering market share from the competitor's pie. This may also spur innovative ideas, since one product or selling unit may not be able to cover all the occasions.

As the demand plasticity of the brand improves, consumers will see the brand more often, which in turn will impact consumption positively. For diverse Indians on the move, brands will not really satisfy the consumer's needs unless varying demand moments are captured by demand plasticity and all occasions are fully met.

Pragmarketism's approach has taken the fulcrum of marketing, namely consumer need, and expanded its scope to reflect human emotions as the eventual pay off, when a consumer is satisfied. Brands that are able to capture a wider and deeper set of emotions, including Indian expression, will better explain their proposition and be able to build equity.

Plutchik Robert, 'The Nature of Emotions', *American Scientist*, Vol. 89, No. 4, (July–Aug 2004).

4

Consumer Insight

Back in the day, when I, Arvind, was area sales manager at ITC Agrotech Ltd and posted in West Bengal, we launched a premium oil called 'Natura Mustard Oil' with a lot of marketing hoopla. However, the results were downright embarrassing: unsold inventory, high trade spends, wasted advertising money and managers scuttling for cover. It was so bad that it caused the then-CEO to pose the imminent question: 'What was the consumer insight?'

'There is a market for premium cooking oil, if we look at the local products in the retail shelves …' Somebody attempted an unconvincing answer.

'What was the CONSUMER insight?'

'That consumers are looking for first pressed *kachi ghani* mustard oil.' Another futile explanation followed.

'Really, and what will they do with it? How much extra will they pay for it? What is the cost of a cooking dish with this oil versus normal oil …' A volley of questions were fired, ending with, 'Did someone check with the consumer?' This was followed by a resounding silence.

Consumer insight can be the road to glory or perdition. Developing capabilities to build consumer insight, however tedious, is an absolute must for all marketers. It links the need to the benefit. In doing so, it delivers two things: it clarifies the need-gap to consumers and facilitates the correct situating of the product; and it sets up the right expectation so that benefits are in consonance with the delivery of the product.

The inevitable result is consumer delight.

Then, 'What was the consumer insight?' needn't be a post-mortem question but a pre-birth inquiry.

What does the consumer really want? If this question could be answered in its entirety, business would be an effortless win. Without it, business is a relentless misery. But stepping into the consumer's shoes to understand her latent, patent, exploited or abandonable demand takes the mickey out of the most seasoned professionals. But before the fishing net is tossed to catch the fish, one has to know what to ask and how to elicit the answer. It doesn't help matters that the gamut of research methodologies is so wide and sometimes so ambiguous that even with good intentions, marketers could make errors in solving the riddle of what the consumer really wants.

We pulled back to simplify what the research is triggered by so that marketers can ask the right question and seek the right answer, while avoiding expensive mistakes. Here is what it boils down to:

- What is the consumer doing?
- Why is she doing that – what is her motivation?
- What is her attitude towards a category/brand/issue?
- What will be her reaction to my products and concepts that she sees in the future?

Let's understand the gamut of research methodologies to know what to ask and how, but after considering all the options. Often, research decisions are made not knowing the options available, leading to expensive mistakes down the line.

What Is the Consumer Doing?

Before a brand issue is explored, before even a category is sought to be deconstructed in the consumer's life, sometimes it might be very revealing to just see what he is up to? The consumer is not always us, not our boss's wife, nor what we read of him in secondary data, nor even our impression of him. He is what he is in his environment, and it takes a lot of objectivity to see him just as he is.

ADILO: Marketers and researchers could make a huge leap if they just became flies on the walls of their consumers' homes, watching them go about their lives on a typical day. ADILO, or 'a day in the life of' a consumer, is a non-participative, non-intrusive observation to just note all the things a consumer is doing religiously, without sparing any detail, however banal. This is the way anthropologists study tribes to understand the hidden or apparent motivations behind usual behaviour. Their lack of knowledge about the subject forces them to watch their subject with utmost curiosity and openness. Marketers must show a similar approach, with as blank a slate as possible. They must assume that they know nothing to prevent their bias from getting in the way of an objective study.

This simple device of sincere observation may not only prevent huge mistakes based on assumptions of a non-existent consumer, but also provide critical clues for innovation, communication, media, distribution strategy and a host of business applications later.

Marketers can even take help from ethnographers to decode deeper socio-cultural meaning through the technique of ethnography. Companies like Unilever are known to mandate a minimum number of direct consumer observation hours for their brand custodians. Institutionalizing this may be highly advantageous for other corporates as well.

In-depth discussion: One-on-one discussions with consumers are tremendously useful to determine the hypothesis of a research and to further validate a finding or to just determine consumer motivation through elaborate probing. Deep-seated cultural inhibitions can be uncovered through such a technique, like in exploring the reservations against birth control or indifference towards a category due to the relevance issue (like tea drinking amongst coffee consumers). However, adequate care should be taken in the language used and mannerisms deployed while probing the consumer. Once, while probing an aspect of an advertisement copy, it was realized that the accent of the moderator had caste implications, which dampened the consumer response.

Focus groups: Pulling homogenous clusters of consumers based on demographics and socio-economic groups into a controlled environment, professionally moderated with the client watching non-intrusively over a TV monitor, works well to fathom consumers' collective views. However, very often a dominant consumer may sway the group into submission, denying the researcher access to individual reflections. If moderators are not trained to screen out the dominant strands of conversation, the researcher can be misled to believe an individual opinion as a collective truth. Since qualitative studies are often critical in supporting a manager's instinct on a subject, it's best to have a couple of pilot sessions before the full-scale research gets underway – this helps evolve consensus on the scope of consumer study and its methodology. Too often, after money has been wasted, clients discover that the actionable part of the research has been weakly probed, requires more research or, they still resort to applying their gut feeling (a frequent impulse of clients), citing the inadequacy of research. Over time, research gives way to whimsical business calls, causing huge losses. Painstaking attention to detail in research is what even the smallest test is to flying a Boeing. Detailed diagnostics never fail to impact businesses positively. Indian companies don't do this enough, whereas multinationals can overdo it. Clarity in research brief can help strike the right balance.

Projective techniques: Consumers don't always articulate themselves very easily. This could be because they don't care, or because they don't say or don't understand, or because they say something and mean something else, or because they say it very subtly, causing researchers to miss the fine cues that could be very critical. Therefore, researchers deploy projective techniques to tease out responses that aren't easily elicited. Some examples of projective techniques that are frequently deployed are as follows:

- *Picture collages*: Consumers are asked to depict their thoughts by looking at pictures cut from random magazines and newspapers and stick them on a piece of paper to form a collage. At first, it seems silly to describe your desired brand of shampoo through images of food, clothes or things even more unrelated, but the clarity it brings to describing a brand vis-à-vis others is simply amazing. Besides, it gives a rich set of cues within which to clothe your brand. For instance, a beverage drinker may describe the texture of his beverage as velvety, biscuit-like, fragrant like a lotus, placid like a lake, sharp like a samurai warrior … the imagination that your consumers display can be a great way to know what is and isn't acceptable to them. The intensity of their beliefs tells a manager which idea will secure him consumer consonance.
- *Storytelling/role playing*: Consumers hesitant to express their own feelings or fearing embarrassment or disapproval can be asked to speak as a third person. Unexpected but authentic reactions tumble out as they under the guise of speaking for their friends, expose deep-seated internal complexes. For instance, consumers may show no hesitation in buying a BMW car or an expensive penthouse but are very cagey about paying recurring, high maintenance costs. When probed on why their friends – not they – behave like this, they might expose that these brands are adopted for display value and

not for their inherent functional value. Thus, the researcher uncovers the real reason behind consumer behaviour.

- *Clustering:* When categories interact with each other and brand owners struggle to find a meaningful basis for differentiation, it helps significantly to ask consumers about their views. For instance, marketers can lay down chips, burgers, Indian snacks and their brands and ask consumers to cluster them on a continuum of healthy to junk food. This technique could be hugely illuminating to determine a brand's relative position vis-à-vis other foods on desired attributes, like health and junk. The clues thus gained can help direct the brand to the desired cluster.
- *Personification:* Consumers can be asked to imagine their brands, sometimes even categories, as people or animals. When asked, consumers can associate Cheetos to a cheetah or a cat, Lay's to a teenage girl, Haldiram's to a trusted uncle, Bingo to a fun-loving vagabond and so on. Seeing brands as animated characters helps understand brand persona that in turn provides clues towards building a consistent and desirable brand image. Consumers love consistency in a brand's approach, much like they value it in relationships. Personification is a great way to gain insight into the brand's make-up. Quite often, home-bred brands in India lack consistency or richness while narrating the brand story, which creates a diffused brand image. Think of Balaji Wafers and Lay's chips – the images the two brands conjure clarify this point.

Mining Consumer Insight: What Is He Doing? Why Is He Doing That?

There are many definitions of insight, but, in essence, consumer insight highlights the obscure reason behind a need so that it can be resolved to introduce the solution. It's not so obvious that anyone can uncover it; at the same time, it's not so remote that it doesn't appear to be a consumer's reality.

Insights can start from an attitude towards a category ('I wish there was a healthier alternative to carbonated drinks because I get burpy and fat') or gendered reality ('My health is going down, but I don't have time to think of myself,' said by mothers/other women) or from behaviour ('I would rather sleep longer than have a sit-down breakfast') or from a human truth ('Fairness increases the chances of success at the workplace and in relationships' to sell women fairness creams) or from a national reality ('Vandalism in a country where guests are like gods is unacceptable').

Insights eventually help satisfy a consumer need. There are many emotional yearnings that consumers seek to bridge (derivatives of extended Maslow's need). A few of these that could be considered for writing an insight are given below:

- Saving: to hoard, to collect for a better tomorrow
- Order: to reduce ambiguity and rule with predictability
- Vengeance: to square-up an old wrong
- Curiosity: the desire to explore, grow, learn
- Family: the desire to raise and look after people
- Romance: the desire to be loved or indulge in physical pleasure
- Independence: to stand out, to carve one's destiny
- Honour: to conform with order and values
- Acceptance: to belong to a community
- Peace: to live without stress
- Hunger: to crave for physical satiation

- Social standing: to seek stature, to matter more than others
- Power: the desire to influence others beyond their own will

But how does one convert a lumpy set of information, feelings and hunches into a crisp expression of consumer need? It turns out that insight generation is distillable if approached with discipline and honesty. Here is how the process could run.

The insight generation process starts with adequate **information** about the consumer's current attitude towards a problem or issue. Too little of it can leave out crucial factoids and too much unnecessary data can drown out the essence – information should be gleaned with care to take what is relevant (it should answer the central question or reference of research), material (it should not be too trivial to not make an impact) and authentic (the source, quality and quantity of data should be objective, as far as possible, and not a whimsical observation of one or two consumers or researchers).

Information leads to **observation**, which allows disparate pieces of data to be summed up into single statements of consumer realities that in turn highlight an attribute of relevance. Observation turns mere data into meaningful truths.

From observation, one comes to **interpretation**. This requires delving into the data to understand why it is the way it is. This is done by bunching together positively corelated observation points to fathom the motivation or the barrier that underpins consumer disposition or behaviour.

After distilling through the various intervening stages, we come to the end by adding or deleting some relevant points and reach the summit of consumer truth, which is called **insight**. It is the single expression of consumer want that contains the need and the key to unlock it. Below is an example of the insight mining process, based on current attitudes towards a bar of soap, which indicates future opportunities of innovation or communication:

Insight generation framework

Information	Observation	Interpretation	Insight
Soap bar sticks to the soap case			
Looks dirty	Soaps are dirty, unhygienic		
Is used by all			
		Soap bars are inconvenient, wasteful	
At the end has unused pieces	Inconvenient, wasteful towards the end	and unhygienic	
Leaves an impression behind			"I wish there was something that scrubbed easily and
			was hygienic without being messy."
Dissolves quickly	Unpleasant experience		
Smells awful after a while			
Takes lot of scrubbing to get soap suds	Usage is suboptimal	Dissolves quickly, Not Easy to use and messy	
Sticks to the surface of basin, remains on skin and rings			

The insight emerging from the above table can be seen as a solution amenable to individual dispensation, which is not wasteful, not unhygienic, produces good lather and is mess-free. The insight is a starting point for liquid soap or gel, or even a more customizable soap bar that can be used for longer with none of the after-effects. Insight mining not only inspires innovation but also provides communication clues to appeal to consumers.

When do companies collect the first level of information? Usually, the need for innovation is felt when the growth of an existing category has slowed down, but by then it is often late and reactionary. What if companies conducted **satisfaction and dissatisfaction studies** to evaluate the degree of the consumer's contentment with the brand through a mix of open- and close-ended questionnaires? Attributes, which are relevant for a particular category's performance, can be calculated directly on a rating scale and then the relevance of each attribute can be checked so that marketers know they are using the right yardstick. New, emerging attributes can be generated by asking consumers what actually matters to them, rather than going forward with internalized assumptions. Tracking consumer satisfaction in an ongoing process will not only establish the health of a brand's relationship, signalling drops and increases, but also provide rich data for generating **insight**.

Finally, what makes a powerful **insight**? A powerful insight *echoes* with the consumer because he identifies with it as it is *authentic* (not imaginary and based on intensive knowledge of his behaviour) and, when it is put to use, it will generate a positive *reaction* from the consumers as it promises improvement. If an insight doesn't qualify on all these counts, deeper mining is required – with due adherence to the process as outlined above. But it's well worth conducting; without it, the pain increases down the stream.

What Is His/Her Attitude Towards My Brand and Category?

While the above helps explore new options for his/her business, it's equally important to understand how a brand is being currently consumed. A knowledge of the current landscape is necessary before new horizons are sought.

U and A: To understand the consumer's attitude towards a brand, a usage (U) and attitude (A) study is set in motion once in three to four years (depending on the product life cycle and the speed of innovation in the category). Below is a run-through of how U and A can become more useful.

- **Who is my consumer?** Their age, where they fall in a socio-economic segment, are they urban/semi-urban rural residents and so on. A paramount task is understanding how a brand's consumption stacks up. Often, this data is sought at the incidence of consumption, which yields the answer in terms of a number of users, but not the quantity of the product/service they are using. By including a question on the depth of consumption, one can arrive at the total consumption. This yields a better appreciation of the loyal base of consumers and infrequent ones – a critical variable, which can drive marketing strategy.
- **What is he consuming other than my brand?** This could include other brands in the category, in lieu of my brand, around my brand and with my brand? This would help to understand where the business is coming from, what I could potentially lose out to (if substitutes are close and frequently available) and, more positively, what other benefits or features can be added or removed to focus on what delights the consumers.
- **When is he consuming?** This pertains to which part of the day, season, mood, need-state, social occasion and festival the product/service is being consumed during. An intensive follow-through on these questions can help determine heavy and light consumption patterns, which in turn can be leveraged to drive up consumption, increasing

brand remembrance at high points of consumption and driving new relevance at low incidences of consumption. With digital analytics and possibilities of sharp targeting, this data also drives content and the distribution strategy of creatives.

- **Barriers and motivations** of consumption need to be more direct and actionable. Loosely worded questions that don't add up create reams of data with little guidance to go on.
- **How and where is he consuming**? The consumer's state at the point of consumption: whether he is watching TV, travelling by himself, travelling in the company of friends, attending prestigious social events, etc. Along with this, the brand should consider what else can be economized – can he use it in a cup, plate, straight from the pack … the whole gamut of brand usage can throw ideas of promotions, partnerships and communication. However, often this data is either inconclusive or not connected adequately to the product/service to be useful.

Limitations of a U and A survey that needs to be kept in mind:

- It is conducted at a certain point of time and, therefore, it should be regularly updated to avoid carrying anachronistic assumptions into the decision-making process.
- Premeditated objectives (like justification to drive new projects) often exist and should be steered clear of to avoid a bias regarding the purity of consumer observation.
- Often, the recruitment questionnaire (RQ) is not done to fairly represent one's brand in the same percentage as the actual market share or the sampling is an imperfect representation of the users.
- It does not speak for the non-users. Possibilities for the penetration of the market can be actualized through non-

users, and unless they are studied separately or through additional research (by way of a booster quota of questions), the brand may miss out on understanding growth opportunities amongst the new non-users.

Because of its high cost, U and A studies are often not conducted. This could be a fatal mistake, tantamount to driving without knowing the road behind or ahead of the vehicle. U and A not only helps in knowing where the brand stands but also provides ample insight into growth opportunities.

Brand Track Study

Most brands look like the figure on the left (below), but marketers want them to look like the figure on the right. This means that there are as many consumers at the top who are aware of the brand – sum total of top of mind (TOM), spontaneous and aided awareness – as there are at the bottom levels of adoption – who have interacted with the brand – and those who have most often used a brand (MOUB).

Brand health funnel

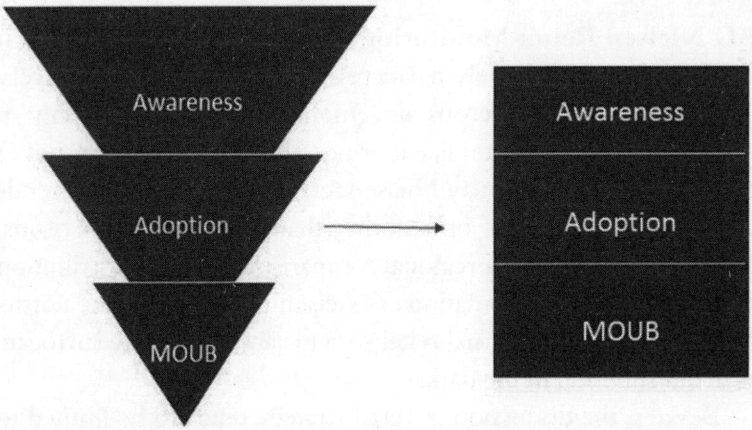

Source: Authors

However, for this to happen, it's important that marketers focus on driving the brand's positive association and experience with respect to attributes that actually matter. Attribute generation can be learnt through a satisfaction and dissatisfaction survey, or through a U and A. Once we know what consumers want, all marketing efforts must be driven to let consumers know what you stand for and give them an experience that draws them towards you.

A brand track study, which is a periodic stock-taking of the brand's health with respect to chosen attributes (like whether it is a 'brand for me', a 'brand that is good value for money', is 'trustworthy', 'helps me meet my need' or 'is my friend' may be answered through a battery of image-related questions on a agree/disagree or like/dislike scale). This provides marketers with an insight into how consumers regard their brand and also options to take corrective measures to move upwards, towards higher awareness and MOUB scores.

Brand tracks tend to be expensive but are indispensable. If the budget is an issue, a brand dipstick study can be deployed at a smaller scale and at a biannual frequency to track brand health. Digital technology can be used these days by small cash-starved brands to build their brand data repository.

AC Nielsen Retail Monitoring: Market share wars are fought on retail shelves and Nielsen data rewards or reprimands you every quarter. There is vociferous agreement regarding the veracity of the data, but whether you like it or not, this is the only snapshot of retail wars. Be that as it may, Nielsen retail should be used for trends over a longer period of time, rather than for short comparisons, and for inter-channel or regional comparisons to drive distribution strategy. Where representation of Nielsen is weak, as in the north-east, instituting an internal retail panel is an appropriate surrogate to avoid shooting in the dark.

Besides, the discussion in retail strategy tends to be limited to a numerical distribution since, in a country of almost ten million traditional outlets (mom and pop stores), reaching as far and wide as possible becomes a primary concern. However, a parallel discussion around weighted distribution (percentage contribution of your sales where category sales come from), out-of-stock dealers, per dealer offtake (PDO) and share amongst handlers of the category would go a long way in identifying the retail universe to focus on, especially by applying a Pareto principle (80 per cent of sales from a 20 per cent retail outlet base). Scanned data for organized trade (Big Bazaar and the likes) is beginning to become available, but the quality is not as reliable as it is outside India.

Household panel data: An ongoing study of consumer homes to facilitate a view of their in-home behaviour is priceless when subtle or big changes in purchase are tracked over a long period of time. Based on extensive consumer questioning on standardized templates and corroborated by used packs of the acclaimed brands, researchers are able to point out the level of penetration of a category, pantry stockings of new ones, lapsing and entry of new trialists, the source of new business for new categories and so on. Cross tabulation between U and A, panel data and brand tracks, if done on a periodic basis, provides a clear picture of a consumer with respect to their brand and the category. However, because of the sheer quantum of data and its non-comparable base, brand managers are not able to join the dots to complete such a picture. With sophisticated data analytics emerging in the field, this is a great opportunity for companies to invest and get a cohesive and comprehensive view of their consumers.

What will be his reaction to my products and concepts that he sees in the future?

A concept enables a marketer to check if the totality of his proposition – the concept – clicks with his consumer. It is the bridge between consumer need and potential consumer satisfaction. A good concept is rewarded with consumer action; hence, it becomes a perfect brew of brevity and essence. Concepts are used for product development and even for advertisement development. Elements of a good concept are:

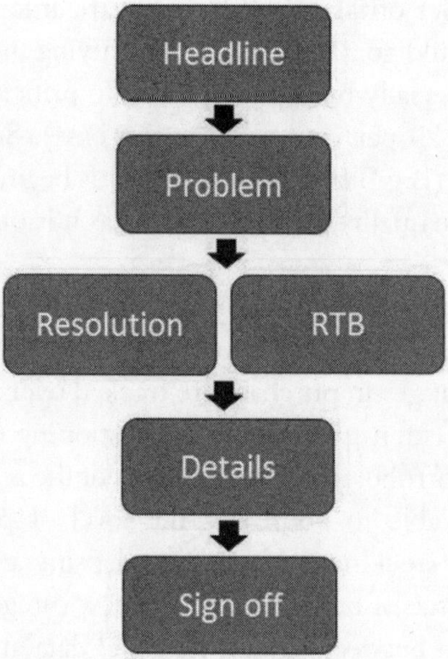

Source: Authors

- Headline: A brief but holistic idea of what is being proposed. It should be written after the other elements of the concept, as it sums up the essence.
- Problem: What unresolved and real issue is being addressed?
- Proposition: The product or a communication benefit to address the problem. A benefit should be a compelling and singular idea. If there are too many benefits, deeper probing is required till benefits converge into a single dominant one.
  - Functional benefit appeals to a physical need – it should be palpable.
  - Emotional benefit (refer to the earlier chapter on needs) speaks of the eventual emotional benefit.

An example of how the two benefits are layered:

- 'I like juice because it's a healthy hunger satisfier and it satisfies my taste cravings, making me feel good and in control.'

The brand should be embedded in the benefit so inextricably that the story cannot stand without it.

- A reason to believe (RTB) is a tangible reason that can support the claim. An RTB is based on hard facts, such as numbers ('90 per cent of germs are killed'), or expertise ('chefs use this recipe') or provenance ('strawberries hand-picked from Mahabaleshwar') or totality ('benefit of thirty vitamins and minerals'). However, these hard facts should be balanced and rounded off wherever possible to appeal to consumers. For instance, instead of referring to a thousand checks when talking about quality, you could draw equivalence with the elaborate checks conducted on aircraft to exemplify the point.
- Details: Product, pack, price, communication and even a sharper definition of target audience (demographic, typically).
- Sign-off: The happy ending that again connects the brand with the resolved world, which they can look forward to. Ideally, the headline and sign-off should chime together like a good title that draws you in alongside the closing line of the last chapter that closes the loop.
- Headline: Can be referred to again at the end, balancing the summary of all the relevant aspects with a singular benefit. For instance, for an inverter concept card, instead of saying, 'full power back for high-end products', you could write, 'now say goodbye to shutting off air conditioners'. This resonates with the consumer as the benefit is stated in the context of a familiar need.

- Visuals: Should elaborate the idea as well as the proposition (often mimicking the creative on print or televised advertisement), but not overpromise or understate while attempting to be as relatable.

Good concepts are painstakingly slow to create but are worth the effort as this can save many commercial disasters further down the line. Examples of concepts have been tackled in the chapter on brands.

Concept and Product: Various concepts can be exposed as stimuli, if the need-statement and the commensurate benefit explanation need to be fine-tuned. Once an idea of the concept is established, products should be introduced to capture the actual experience of consumption as far as possible. These are usually conducted in focus groups so it's a good idea to take responses one at a time from participating members at some point in the research to avoid influencing and being influenced by others. Three possibilities arise when the concept and product are evaluated:

1. Concept > Product: In this case, the concept should be toned down or the product uplifted to avoid disappointment due to asymmetry.
2. Product > Concept: This situation calls for improving the concept so it syncs with consumer experience of the product.
3. Concept = Product: This implies that the two are evenly matched and are helping each other. If purchase intention (PI) is high then it is a clear signal to go ahead. To avoid first-placed-bias (what is exposed first gets a natural preference from consumers), half the group get the concept first and the other half gets the product first.

The research on product and concept tends to be tedious and sometimes detailed quantitative diagnostics are required for product improvement, especially in case 1) above. This causes a delay in the launch, but it's better to stumble at the testing level than during the actual market conditions.

STM: Simulated test marketing is an elaborate tool that simulates real-life market conditions with marketing inputs to forecast actual sales. This is a result of complex modelling that works well if clients provide true and accurate data of the spends planned behind a new launch over three years and provide completely finished product samples to help researchers use regression analysis to forecast demand. BASES is a common model, but due to the elaborate nature of the exercise and the multivariables involved in a simulated setting, the results of the finding can be dubious. Accordingly, it may be wiser to take a test market which is spread over a small geography in a relatively media-isolated area before swinging into a full-blown national salvo.

Pricing studies: If you plot the price versus purchase intention, you hit a sweet spot where the price is just right (not too high or low) and the purchase intention is maximum. This will guide you towards the right pricing that makes money and sustains sales. Theoretically, this seems very attractive, but it actually has little practical utility for the following reasons: a) pricing decisions are usually made based on cost plus approach; b) consumers usually ask for the lowest price with the maximum benefits in research but may behave very differently in real life when a product's features are better known and positive or negative word-of-mouth communication sways their perception of the brand; c) category and cost realities within a company usually define the profit & loss of the brand, allowing little room for negotiation; d) pricing decisions can depend on the intention to penetrate the market (lower price) or skim the top end (higher price). For these reasons, pricing studies are usually not very popular. A qualitative call based on your product's uniqueness and the prevailing prices of comparable products seems to work fine in most cases.

Advertising or copy evaluation: Millward Brown's monopoly over LINK testing makes this a very single-minded space. Advertising copies in the form of animatics (and sometimes the final film) are tested with consumers, using a dial to capture their reaction to an advertising film based on likeability, memorability, persuasiveness and recall and compounded to arrive at an overall 'AI score' (awareness index). It also gives short term sales lifts (STSL: AI multiplied by persuasion) based on a trend of performance of other advertisements in the market. Since advertising budgets tend to be monstrous, even this high-cost research seems acceptable to avoid future disasters. However, given the qualitative nature of the advertising copy, LINK is no guarantee to advertising success and sometimes, its tepid results create indecision and embarrassment when huge production monies have already sunk. As a result, the most expensive input of marketing, namely advertising, goes live with the least testing.

Brand semiotics: This pertains to the study of signs, or words, gestures, images, sounds and objects, and their meaning for the brand. While traditional qualitative research looks at the way consumers think and feel, semiotics looks one layer deeper into the culture that shapes consumers' views. Examining the language (tone, metaphors, slangs), cultural symbols (archetypes, stories, ideas) and visual cues (fashion trends, designs) of the dominant or emerging culture, it attempts to understand our society. Then, by understanding how cultural symbols have evolved, communicated and interpreted, marketers can design new techniques to influence consumers at both the conscious and the unconscious level. Semiotic is a subtle science with a few qualifications.

- Context of signs: 'Thumbup' can either stand for a like if it's on Facebook or for somebody seeking a ride if the person is on the highway or a signal to go ahead if it's an armed force personnel standing at the tarmac.

- Consumer's interpretation: The word 'cheese' can be a cue to smile or for healthy, yummy, chewy, salty, creamy or sinful fat, depending on the consumer's state of mind. As can be seen from this example, the interpretation can vary from what a word denotes (what it means in the literal sense) or connotes (what it means in the extended sense).

Semiotics is, therefore, very useful for the visual rendition of the brand, but it is not limited to packaging alone. Colours, for instance, cue a lot about the brand.

- Red stands for passionate, active, exciting, bold, youthful, powerful and ambitious; the logos of Kellogg's and Coca-Cola embed that inherent advantage.
- Pink cues love, warmth, femininity, carefulness, intuitiveness and sensitivity, as seen in the logos of Barbie, Victoria's Secret and Disney.
- Blue cues control, content, spirit, openness and reliability, and it is the colour of many dairy brands (Amul, Mother Dairy), Skype and Intel.
- Orange cues warmth, freedom and extroversion. It is often the colour of food, beverage or children's brands.
- Purple cues depth, creativity, compassion, fantasy or being distinguished and goes with premium or indulgence brands.

Semiotic studies can help a brand choose those cues of colours, signs, symbols and textures which it wants to replace the current imagery with. For instance, a snacking brand found that on creating a 'semiotic map' (done on two or more variables for the brands in the same category; on natural–artificial ingredients on one scale and on functional–emotional on the other scale), its packaging, imagery and website reflected an artificial and sterile product profile. Consumers, on the other hand, preferred natural and real food cues with a human – not manufactured – feel. Marketers then proceeded to look for symbols of naturalness, humaneness and earthly elements to enrich the brand. Softer, homely pastels with a mother's face and a sack of potatoes cueing farm freshness became prominent symbols on the packaging, communication and website of the recast brand. The resulting change in imagery upturned the brand scores with a positive spin-off on sales.

Packaging Research

Packaging is one of the most critical aspects of branding, but is perhaps the most underutilized asset. When the product has been prepared, the usual packaging options are brought out to clothe a great offering, with minimal provision for change.

One reason this happens is because the packaging brief starts only after the product has been developed. Instead, it could and should start when the product is conceptualized. Starting early would make packaging a part of the brand idea and not a mere wrap for convenient cartage. Paper Boat, a brand of traditional Indian beverages, smelling of the nostalgia of yesteryears, demonstrated how the idea can be visually represented with great impact. What makes packaging work hard?

> **Distinctive**: Seek distinction from the start; don't be content with the mediocrity of the usual – challenge the shape, graphics and sealing, wherever possible. Think like a rebel: challenge, challenge and challenge. The industry is soaked with complacence and needs to be shaken up.
>
> **Holistic**: Look at the packaging holistically, like a piece of TV advertisement. Ask who is the target audience for the packaging; what consumer problem is being addressed and what makes it easy to use, breaks formality, allows multiple uses, is re-sealable/recyclable/environmentally positive,

etc.; what makes the idea cool or different – forcing brand managers to get more ambitious and think of the consumer first; and finally, visualize the idea, however roughly – this helps the managers express themselves more clearly and enables creatives to judge how far they can venture. If the discussion is freewheeling, great ideas can be hatched at this stage itself.

Digitally adapted: With bubbling e-commerce, the packaging world should be open to posting on e-commerce portals and websites. Creating impact with complexity in design was never a favourite, and now with digital platforms, it's definitely out.

Shopper Research

Consumers consume – that's obvious. But who buys? Consumers, right? Wrong. The absence of this basic question has trumped many business initiatives. An influencer has an impact on what's consumed like kids have on the choice of toothpaste or TV or mobile phone their parents buy. A purchaser transacts financially to bring the product home. A shopper stands in the shopping aisle or *kirana* (mom and pop stores) store and decides what to purchase. With the emergence of e-commerce, that chasm has been closed with the 'buy now' button converting want into acquisition. However, in modern trade, where about 5 to 10 per cent of everyday consumer goods of large companies continue to be sold, understanding and influencing shoppers is as critical as knowing the consumer. The two are not the same, and in the Indian environment of *kirana* stores, where products are dispensed upon being asked for, the study of shoppers is relatively meaningless because the purchase decision is made at home. The same behaviour also made TV communication critical because consumers had to be enticed and conditioned almost reflexively to ask for the product when they showed up at the store. But now, as self-service stores appear (many *kirana* shops are switching to convenient aisles) and big retail gets organized, the Western ideas about influencing consumers in the retail environment become seminal.

Shopper research understands and converts the uncertain walk in the aisles to the happy brand pick-up in the last mile of purchase. Consumers come pre-decided to the store, owing to print communication or a broadsheet of attractive offers delivered to their home or at the entry point. They are 'seekers': people who have to be guided to the brand with the least hassle so there is no loss of sale. And some others walk leisurely, tossing up options of price, promotion, grammage, imagery and benefits to close the sale. These 'evaluators' need to be informed about the relevant details so that they make the right choice in favour of your brand.

How and where brand choices are influenced or made differs from category to category, but in the path of purchase of the category, the following interaction points emerge with corresponding requirements:

Shopper pathway

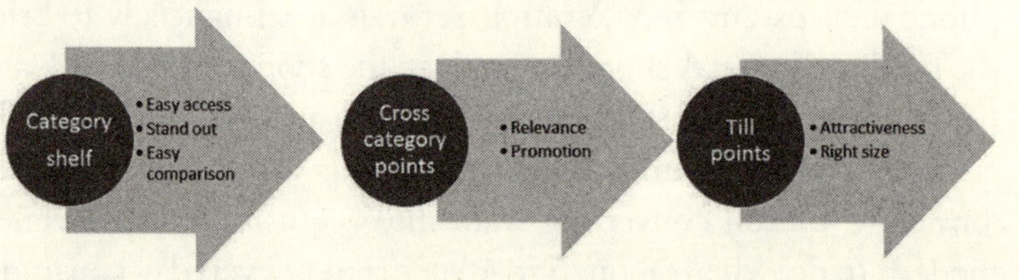

Source: Authors

At a category shelf, seekers look for their brand and move on. Hence, it's important to have a convenient location, preferably at eyesight, with convenience in packformat (which research can establish easily). For evaluators, information that highlights the relative benefits of one's brand needs to be placed prominently through point of sale (POS), leaflets in the shelf, better information on packaging or merchandising units (like LED lights) that attract the consumers (assuming these have been well-negotiated with the trade partner).

Cross-category placement, though costly, is a great way to communicate a new brand idea. For instance, soups can be displayed next to the fresh vegetables section, tea creamers next to the tea section, oils next to shampoos and so on to communicate a category proximity and hence a new usage which is not otherwise obvious to consumers. However, the relevance of the cross-category presence should be made clear through some POS that connects (soup that tastes like fresh vegetables) and a promotion that drives behaviour (a kilogram of papaya free with a week's supply of juices).

At the till point, consumers are captivated and waiting in the queue, but they are closed to buying any more. Hence, the packs at the till have to be attractive to induce a grab at a small price and size. This is a great place to plant 'trial packs' with miniature offers, but so far this space has been underleveraged, the focus having being on confectionery and toys only.

When consumers exit the shopping space, researchers interview them to understand their motivation and behaviour. Along with store observations, this forms the basis for designing and conducting research.

However, shopper research is relatively nascent in India, although it offers a huge opportunity as store owners look at insight to drive higher throughput per square inch of space and brands jostle for preference in cluttered aisles with lesser decision time. Moreover, there is hardly any research that guides how brands can be chosen in *kirana* stores. Joint business planning (JBP) offers advantages for both the supplier and the retailer if approached in the spirit of maximizing category offtake. However, the current level of negotiation is a far cry from this win-win situation, bearing a semblance to extortion, depending on the power equation.

Qualitative or Quantitative Research? Diagnostics or Statistics?

A very common disjointedness in a marketer's life is between what he wants to know and what he ends up getting at the end of a long research. A good understanding of qualitative and quantitative research is required to overcome this usual pitfall.

When do you go for qualitative and when do you go for quantitative research? When the researcher and the marketer are seeking the answer to a why or a substance of a consumer behaviour, qualitative with a specifically smaller sample size works. When the answer is where, when, what or how far, quantitative research is required to establish the spread of consumer behaviour with statistical data; here, the sampling size is big and random. Quantitative research can document existing behaviour with precision. Qualitative surveys uncover spoken and unspoken (subconscious) assumptions. The client should not expect precision in human motivation but be comfortable with the ambiguity a qualitative study produces. Likewise, a quantitative study can't conclude on the fuzzy aspects of consumer behaviour when the statistical dispersion of their attitude throws spider-like charts.

A practical way out of this quagmire is to do both. The diagram below illustrates how the choice pans out:

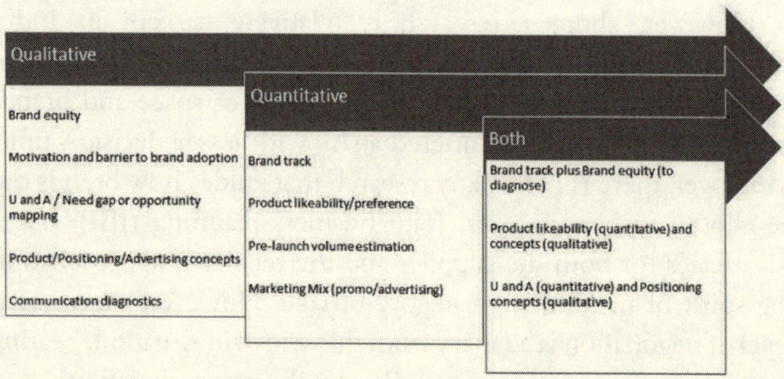

Source: Authors

Research Must Dos

In a fast-paced world, research is frequently viewed with doubt, and sometimes with outright dismissal. Action-oriented people argue against it by citing its inconclusiveness, the weakness in its sample size and methodology and its unpredictability. Researchers counter that without either a qualitative consumer validation or a quantified opportunity mapping; spending on consumers can be seriously flawed, wasting resources and time. The big question is when and why you must research. Or not.

Research should be actionable. In other words, one must be clear on what action will follow once the research result pops up on your screen. If it ends up as a 'good to know', then it might as well not have been done at all. From the actionability comes the research brief, and from the brief comes the methodology. This is a bit like if you know where you want to go to, you use a map and choose the shortest distance to the destination. That makes research conclusive and cost-efficient, thereby addressing the two problems with research, as illustrated below.

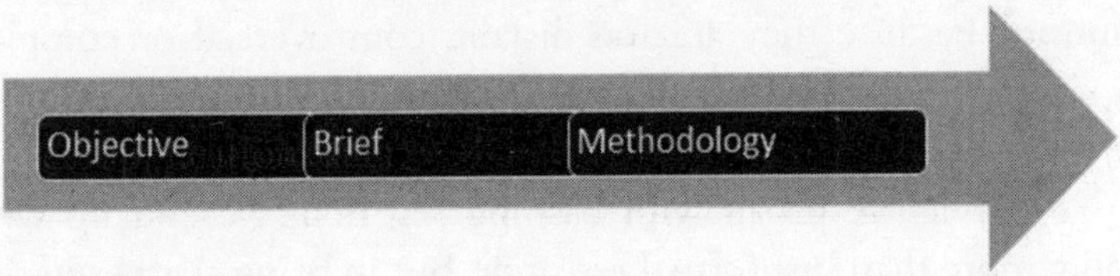

Source: Authors

Secondly, an awful lot of research can be avoided if managers can validate their hypothesis with **consumer conversation**. The dipstick studies elevate a gut feel to a resonating consumer reality. That may either provide much needed confidence to take a decision or point towards a more beneficial formal research. Either way, it's useful.

While the above pertains to research with an objective, there is also a need to do non-participative, agenda-less research: **consumer**

listening. It could be undertaken through listening to your consumers on social media or having an open-ended conversation with them on some issues of public or social relevance with least interference. Merely listening could give great insights for future innovation, delivery models or communication ideas. In fact, it may provide a great competitive advantage in these times when business actions are mostly reactive to consumer and competitor situations, denying one the leisure to explore breakthrough ideas. But this rarely happens.

Finally, this needs to be supplemented with the widest consumer understanding, that is, **environment gazing**: observations that pertain to macro-economic trends (demographics, migration, changing occupations and impact of digital technology) and socio-political awareness (evolving social structures, evolving family, Indian realities of caste and our idiosyncratic grain, as discussed before); would lead to very topical business ideas being brought to life. For example, what could the increase in white economy (after the recent demonetization), e-commerce, sale of smart phones and rising nationalism mean for my brand? Such issues are habitually shunned because they are too distant, controversial or complex to comprehend vis-à-vis my brand, which *seems* to operate in a microcosm.

So, while we began with bashing research, we end up with doing more than just formal research. But in being sharper in our prescription and wider in picking up emerging opportunities, we make research work harder for us. The consumer flywheel then expands from traditional research to include the research essentials, as illustrated below. Once these are in place, formal research can step in to sharpen situation diagnostics.

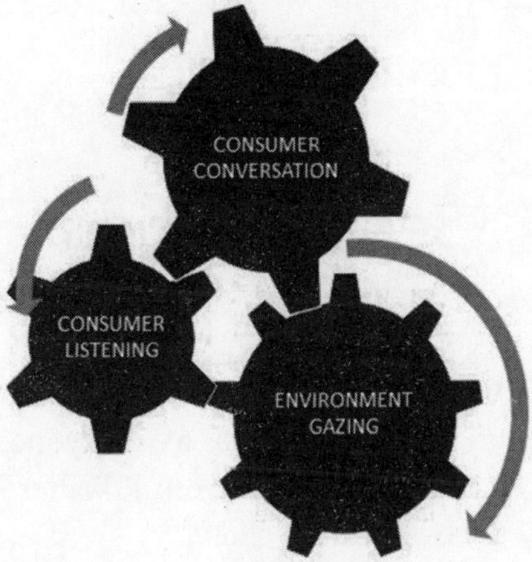

Source: Authors

What can the research not do? It can't give you action points with 100 per cent certainty. The managerial gut feeling is irreplaceable. Consumers also can't give you an idea about which creative works better, much like you can't get everyone to like the same painting. You can judge if a packaging or an advertisement delivers on stated objectives of relevance, likeability or persuasion with consumer feedback, but you can't ask them, 'So can I go ahead with it?' Finally, for very new ideas that consumers have very little exposure to and cannot even infer from given its prototype, research will very likely not tell you if they like it or not. You will just have to go and launch it and put your best foot forward. Research cannot eliminate unpredictability; it can anticipate its extent and verify possibilities to counter it, increasing the chances of success.

5

Segmentation

'Sell our new variant of Pepsi to everyone, Arvind.' The struggling account supervisor from J. Walter Thompson was commanded by the overbearing client.

'But we have segmented the market and believe the right audience ...' I protested meekly, as agencies usually start.

'That's marketing hogwash. Today, our brand is consumed by everyone, so our segment is the great Indian family.'

'We can't speak to everyone. We have to choose our audience and speak to them to be effective in our brand message. If we don't, the brand will lose relevance and we will lose differentiation, leading to loss of brand equity ...' I packed in all of my marketing wisdom rapidly before the imminent client bulldozing.

'But Pepsi is consumed by everyone – can you afford to ignore the elders in the family?'

'Pepsi is an irreverent youth brand. That is a choice we have made. We cannot let peripheral consumption impact the main brand consumption.' My voice trailed as I sensed that an honest point of view is not always welcome.

Segmentation is a tricky piece. There is no living with it, nor without it. It may help focus effort driving efficiency or it may limit one from building consumption in untargeted quarters. How can you be sure that your buck is going where it matters? And change swiftly to another segment when the current one dries out?

Segmentation

Segmentation refers to the slicing of the market in homogenous entities based on demographic, socio-economic, attitudinal, interest-based, geographical factors or any other commonalities to enable marketers to focus investments for generating higher returns by concentrating their efforts. Consumer satisfaction improves along with the return on investment when few are catered to with specific delights rather than resorting to several general benefits.

Segmentation was noticed in sixteenth-century Europe, where shopkeepers would sell their general wares for the masses from the windows, while reserving the inside space of their houses for detailed interactions with more elite clientele. During the course of Indian history, products were made for the royalty or the masses with a dual segmentation at best. The spawning of the middle class in India after the advent of the British rule opened up a new segment of anglophiles – Western-educated Indians who consumed products made by distant companies, who also incidentally became consumers of India's first brands: Polson butter and Bata shoes, Hercules cycle and Manchester cloth.

Today, the Indian market is super-segmented and unlike the West, which has big brands and private labels, we have a host of global brands jostling with locally developed small-scale or cottage industry brands, together with a sea of commodities, filling the needs of the teeming millions through stores.

Segmentation Menu

Demographic: Consumers can be categorized on the basis of age, gender, income, education, occupation, family size and other related raw data. This is basic and invaluable because it is quantifiable and verifiable. However, descriptors like YUPPY (young upwardly mobile professionals), DINKS (double income, no kids), SITKOM (single income, two kids, oppressive mortgage and pitiful discretionary income), GLAMS (greying, leisured and moneyed), good lifers and empty nesters (people over fifty whose kids have moved out of their home for education, leaving them with a second bachelorhood, albeit one that is more resourceful) gives character to sterile demographics.

Generational segment is a more qualitatively defined group of consumers who are brought together by comparable age or a stage in life during a particular period of time, like baby boomers (1945–65), generation X (1966–76), generation Y (millennials born in the '80s) and gen Z (from 2000 onwards).

Psychographics: The marketers' treasure trove of people-descriptors, which are based on lifestyle or societal and personality characteristics. Thus, a mother could be fun-loving, innovative, a conscientious homemaker, indulgent-creative and be given other such varied hues of human personality traits described in the context of their homes, society and social class. Categories may have their own psychographics, depending on their disposition towards the requirement of that category.

Behavioural: Consumers can be segmented on the basis of their purchases and usage behaviour. They could be non-aware, aware non-trier, users (frequent, infrequent/flirtatious), lapsers (forever to other categories/brands, seasonal), early adopters, laggards, followers, enthusiasts, hostile/fascist, brand evangelists, maven (full of knowledge about the brand/categories), indifferent, etc.

Online segmentation: It is based on the behaviour of netizens. They could be broadly classified as:

1. *Simpletons*: looking for the fastest route to get what they want so they can disconnect quickly – they hate distractions like pop-ups and other unsolicited messages, and are relatively slow and inept to navigate.

2. *Bargain hunters*: Those who make choices offline and then scout for the lowest price online.
3. *Usuals*: Navigate the net space generally and lap up the content and deals almost addictively. They avail products with elaborate details and cross-comparisons. They are early adopters and can become brand evangelists.
4. *Opinionators*: Use the net to vent their hitherto unexpressed feelings. Active on social media, blistering on Twitter and clicking merrily to share with all on Instagram; these people have found heaven with the advent of the net. They need to be cautiously cultivated because their base of followers, which is usually large, if not managed well, can turn against a brand.
5. *Mini-addicts*: Idolize the net for their passions – porn, sports, conspiracy theories and compulsive forwards of anything funny, lewd or iconoclastic. Are great for 'viraling' content but their love for pure content turns them against brands; content has to be designed deviously to be acceptable to their fun-prying eyes.

Indian (Desi) Segmentation for Sharper Marketing

Segmentation brings together homogenous groups for sharper marketing. Looking at the existing consumer base in India, the following segments could be created, providing insight into their needs and innovation opportunities, which will particularly resonate with Indian consumers. The segmentations suggested below are of great use in digital marketing, which allows us to break consumers into many sub-segments to target them specifically with relevant messaging (detailed in the digital marketing chapter later).

- *Generation-based segmentation* could help spot an Indian boy or girl who doesn't look or feel like his/her blonde cousin from the West.

- *Gargantuan kids:* The generation of infants, toddlers, '*babas*' and '*gudiyas*' who are fed even before they open their mouths because their parents will stop at nothing to indulge them – with diapers, baby products and so on. Prices can be at a premium as the demand is deep and market shelves are begging for more in a fast-growing country.
- *Growth metres*: The five- to ten-year-olds whose growth in height, weight, social skills and education are a barometer of their family's success – healthy food, drinks, brain tonics, education courses and hobby classes that are relevant for kids who have not grown up but represent miniature adults. Categories for this segment are ridden with hyperbole and ambitious consumers will expect nothing less.
- *Gawkeens*: The gawky tweens between the ages ten and fifteen, emerging from their first brush with puberty. Mothers are still their gatekeepers, but digital exposure has been stoking their independent demand also.
- *Rebellious:* The fifteen- to twenty-five-year-olds who find in their parents both the financier as well as the opponents of their dreams to change the world. Considering that over 35 per cent of country's population is younger than twenty five, this segment represents the fattest, most individually driven consumption band. The space is overcrowded, but it delights companies with the early adoption and frequent consumption of their products and services – if the value equation is right and comes with appropriate imagery.

  They are hyper-digital, glued to WhatsApp, Snapchat, Instagram and Pinterest way before they can spell right or qualify for exams. They order via voice, bypassing typing and traditional models of the earlier demand generation.
- *Saddled*: The generation between 25 and below 35, loaded with the cost of realizing their dreams – career, mortgage,

ageing parents and in-laws as added family members. They need a good lifestyle as much as counselling and education for their kids as well as support from their parents to run their extended households. They are the teeming consumers of food courts and shopping malls and content consumers of the internet generation. Deals and discounts work on these consumers. They are spending unabashedly and looking at the West for inspiration, glorifying India simultaneously.

- *Waist-fillers*: The health-wrecking, indulgent and sedentary years of thirty-five to forty-five, consumers who have resolved their career struggles, but not before fattening up at the waist. Sedentary customers who require general products for their nutrition needs before the prophylactics step in. They are mostly into insurance plans, house loans or just bundled up vacations-automobiles-spa trips from an e-wallet company.
- *Pre-retirees*: Retirement hasn't set in yet, but drained by cardiological or diabetic issues and fatigued from the urban drain of infrastructure, housing, health and finance, they value ease of living most of all. They express romance like Rajesh Khanna and knock at the antiquated walls of the Licence Raj like an angry Amitabh Bachchan. Having lived at the cusp of change, they require maximum cajoling with traditional and modern values to be won over.
- *Lost 60s*: Reconfiguring themselves after their retirement, this generation will scan every piece of information available, watch every program on TV with rising disdain, shop long hours at malls and consume syrups, tablets, intravenous drugs with both fear and hope. Yet, unlike China and Japan, where they are the apple of their marketer's eye, here they have to contend with leftovers of those above them. Customization, therefore, offers huge opportunity to capture these consumers. This generation, marked by

a mixed exposure to early state-controlled capitalism and lingering Gandhianism, lived a life of subdued and frugal consumption – choosing between an Ambassador and a Fiat to travel. Brands chasing them should explain the value of their products well because they are traditionalists and want a justification even to indulge (such as religion, family benefit, etc., as has already been explained before).

- *Time derelicts*: The fixture of grannies and grandads, celebrated as side casts in commercials but overlooked by most. Soaked in 'Gandhisms' and critical of the rampant consumerism of our times, sitting over piles of money, they could be willing customers for health products with frugal pricing, consonant with their mindset. If their purchasers and influencers could be appealed to, then a market of warm clothes, non-leaking water bottles, mobility options, large-print books, easy digital entertainment, valet/escort services, easy smart phones to operate or any service could be an innovation in this neglected market.

Geographic Segmentation

- *Metro-slickers*: Brash and hurried with a working command over the English language, with extraordinary patience regarding their commuting travails, hard-working and resilient – the quintessential metro-slickers. Convenience matters most to them and upward mobility is the chief dream. Wrinkle-free shirts and pants, hand-held fans for sweating brows and cheeks, 'time-pass' content on their mobile phones and easy stock market investment options to secure mortgages are the things that make their everyday strife endurable.
- *Millionaire club*: Those from towns with a population of over a million. They are the bastions of conservatism and the

harbingers of modernity. Family ties are stronger here, the houses are bigger and social functions are more elaborate, owing to shorter commuting distances. The population converges in a few parks and malls where they snack on dubious Chinese and Italian food, indulge in north Indian food in south India and south Indian food in north India. E-commerce has flattened the gap between metros and them and they have better space and infrastructure to indulge in metro-like luxuries.

- *Sleepy cousins:* The towns of Varanasi, Durgapur, Udaipur, Jalandhar, Coimbatore and Rourkela where bucolic charm thrives with patches of urban luxury mimicking their bigger towns. The opportunity for brands to raise consumer engagement, recruit future consumers and drive deeper consumption at lower trade and distribution costs is phenomenal. Deprived of goods supply, their inhabitants queue up at sales of Asian Sky Shop; but now, offline sales are as booming as organized trade expands its footprint here.
- *Rural fringes*: Years of mass media communication has spawned a lookalike market, similar to the big towns, in far-flung places. These are great to drive the penetration of durables, mobiles and personal care products with lower communication costs as regional channels multiply. Here, national matters but the **nat-regional** (a mix of national scale of brand with regional expression) explodes. A heaven for imitation brands, but still worth the headache because the multiplier for revenue is huge here with the sheer number of semi-urban towns in this category.
- *Rural-rural*: Difficult to tread with and expensive to cater to, but the usual battery of undergarments, cheap washing powder and spices of India is serviced by bullock cart wholesalers. Rural is not a down-priced version of the urban, but products and services need to be designed

specifically for the consumers' needs at the bottom end of the socio-economic structure.

Cultural segmentation is imminently useful in pluralistic India, where fashion, lifestyle, housing, cosmetic styles and so on vary from culture to culture. The *Puppy* (Punjabi yuppy) can be expanded and we will have the following: *Hurricane-vi* from Haryana, with loads of cash, rolling uncontrollably towards big labels, malls, male grooming centres and roadside wine stores; *Marwaris*, the quintessential money-spinners, who are also inveterate value seekers; *Bhaiyaas* from UP with intense self-righteousness, taking baby steps towards modernity with great traditional gusto; *Bohemian-Bongs,* hungry for intellectual and cultural indulgence; *Peripatetic Gujjus* looking for travel kits, savoury snacks and great hotel deals; *cool north-easterners,* with music, food and the leisure industry to celebrate their local richness; *Kool Kannadigas*, the cosmopolitan nerds who cavort on the traditional-modernity bridge with ease; *Brainy Tams,* who love voluptuous models, big cutouts of their leaders and are marked by an inherent austerity in their attitude, make a paradoxical market of people who love to experiment but only when their Indian-ness is safely entrenched; and *Efficient Mumbaikars who* have an affinity towards what can simplify life such as space-maximizing multi-utility items. The familiar stereotypes need to be detailed and built upon for marketers to pry deeper into their consumers' lives.

Segmentation on the Basis of Need-state and Consumer Typology

For instance, if you are into selling pants, you could segment the market on the basis of what you are inclined to wear, depending on the time of day or situation, as well as your general disposition towards the category. Cross-tabulating the two can yield twenty-five segments. The same consumer may inhabit different cells of the grid below at different times. Therefore, this approach looks intensely at the state of mind and consumption occasions to give a richer perspective for seeding one's brand. Since the size of the segment is visible here with actual numbers, brand managers can choose meaty segments to go after.

Pants

Need-state/ Consumer Typology -% Association	Fashionista	Scrupulous	Innovative	Easy-going	Rebellious/ Trend setter
Formal	11	10	20	19	40
Easy Wear	31	23	22	15	8
Outdoor	22	12	7	22	37
Evening Wear	10	23	16	33	15
Night	26	22	34	12	0

So, how does one grapple with so many segmentations to create a cohesive strategy? Let's take this forward with a hypothetical example.

Joy, the usual MBA, after a late night at work calls his equally frustrated friends at a nearby bar to rue their biggest mistake: joining corporate India. Three drinks down, he is looking at this freckled girl devouring yoghurt and wondering if that sinful yoghurt could give her smooth skin after a week of binge eating. Just then, his old college chum, Bobby, lands his burly, hairy hand on his shoulder and he wishes, What if there was a hair trimmer that could rid Bobby of all his body hair and that awful odour?

The next morning at his desk, when the boss is gone, he picks up a piece of paper to see if his night's imagination is worth a start-up. He maps his ideas – acne-freeing, skin-fairness yoghurt called Wonder Yoghurt and an all-hair trimmer – basis the segmentation on the criteria discussed above and he shades the relevant segments for his products as follows:

Wonder Yoghurt

Generation-based	Geographic	Cultural	Need-based	Typologies
Gargantuan kids	Metro-slickers	Hurricane-vi	No acne	Self-conscious
Growth meters	Millionaire club	Marwaris	Fairness	Grooming specialist
Gawkeens	Sleepy cousins	Bohemian Bongs	Great complexion	Look freak
Rebellious	Rural fringes	Peripatetic Gujjus	Seeking confidence	Modest effort
Saddled	Rural-rural	Brainy Tams	Seeking popularity	Mildly interested
Waist-fillers		Kool Kannadigas	High self-esteem	Indifferent
Pre-retirees		Efficient Mumbaikar	Achievement oriented	Anti-looks
Lost 60s		Puppies	Effortful	

All-hair trimmer

Generation-based	Geographic	Cultural	Need-based	Typologies
Gargantuan kids	Metro-slickers	Hurricane-vi	Looking good	Self-conscious
Growth metres	Millionaire club	Marwaris	Standing out	Grooming specialist

Gawkeens	Sleepy cousins	Bohemian Bongs	Self-confident	Look freak
Rebellious	Rural fringes	Peripatetic Gujjus	Attention seeking	Modest effort
Saddled	Rural-rural	Brainy Tams	Ease of grooming	Mildly interested
Waist-fillers		Kool Kannadigas	Low cost options	Indifferent
Pre-retirees		Efficient Mumbaikar	Less time utilization	Anti-looks
Lost 60s		Puppies		

From the above, he gets a sense of the consumer he is looking for, and since there are quite a few shadows, he is assured that the numbers would be significant. But to be able to compare them exactly, he would have to start quantifying. We will tackle that in the next chapter on targeting so we can help him make the right choice.

The segmentation options can boggle the mind, diluting focused marketing. However, with digital marketing (discussed later), the possibility of narrowing down on different consumer types with sharp messages is a real possibility, making multi-variate segmentation eminently useful. Further, this detailed segmentation can be of huge significance for a robust understanding of the Indian consumers. Marketers can then merge the segments strategically to design the product, packaging, pricing, communication and even distribution accordingly.

Segmentation: A New Perspective

Segmentation has been criticized for being unreal. It cuts holistic reality into imaginary segments. This limitation, however, offers the first opportunity to re-scope segmentation, by dissolving the divisions between segments to create newer segments.

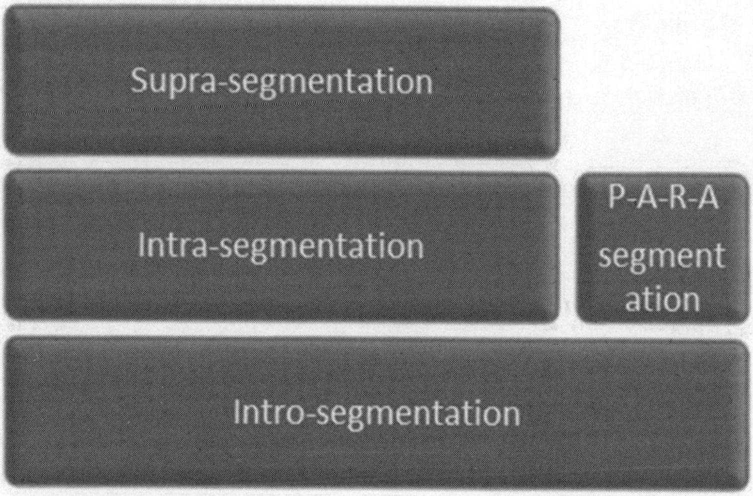

Source: Authors

Intra-segmentation

Combination products that combine the benefits of two segments arise when proximal categories coalesce: shampoo and conditioner, internet-enabled TV, chocolate with chilly, etc. Traditional segmentation would have only led these innovators deeper and deeper into the same category, blinding them to opportunities that arise between segments. Joining segments in this case not only creates an innovation but also draws in consumers from unforeseen segments. This is a perspective that expands categories and redefines usage.

Looking at the Desi segmentation opportunities above, one can be inspired to think of an innovation that serves the cause of the 'liberated new Gawkeens' who belong to the 'millionaire club' and who are 'Marwari' by origin – that could result in a technologically advanced product on the higher end, which comes with features that justify its high price. This can even provide cues regarding communication.

Supra-segmentation

The second criticism of segmentation is that it splits reality into divisions based on our own mental constructs. This offers a new opportunity, namely supra-segmentation.

In this, an opportunity over two or more segments is created. The output may not bear semblance to the original. Frozen yoghurt takes the product experience of ice cream but blends it with the fermentation and acidity of yoghurt culture, creating a 360-degree taste and health spin. Natural Ice Cream, originating in JVPD Mumbai, is expanding rapidly as it has fused natural fruits (also expanded traditional ice cream borders of strawberry and chocolate to the likes of 'chikoo' and figs) with home made ice cream, lower in fat and harking back to the old churned version in Indian homes. Or consider a tablet, which is neither a laptop nor a phone, but seems to find its unique uses in gaming and video streaming. Or an SUV, which is neither a saloon nor a multi-utility vehicle, but finds users well beyond its original customer base of golfers. Or the 'internet of things' (IOT) that converges a host of scattered needs but also creates new ones. Finally, going beyond non-banking financial services and credit cards, consider the creation of e-wallets like Paytm.

From the Desi segmentation above, one can create something for pre-retirees from rural fringes (a segment often ignored) who have the financial comfort of the insurance sector and can afford the health of nutritious food. Thus, you could have a meal plan with easy instalments, topped up with health plans for seniors in metros. Supra-segmentation has the potential to create unconventional (even if seemingly odd) ideas that sit above two or three segments, eluding the eyes of competition.

Supra-segmentation is a great disruptor and has the potential to redefine need, making trash of yesteryears' iconic brands as consumer usage gets altered.

Intro-segmentation

The third criticism of segmentation is that it is based on the concept of time and space. However, the tendency amongst managers is to go with historical descriptions of their category. This can be avoided if the existing segments are redefined by probing deeper, like an introspection every now and then that would recharge the context. This gives birth to our next opportunity: intro-segmentation.

If you look between segments in intra-segmentation and above in supra-segmentation, the prior takes you down below. This approach can evangelize what is already there to a new level, like Keventer's milk which has come back to celebrate the legacy of the dated bulbous bottle, turning it into a collector's item. Or it can look deeper for solutions that don't exist, until they are found. Like the hair fixing gels for the Sikh community or a backscratcher for the inaccessible part of the body or a tongue cleaner that is designed on the back of a toothbrush or a hair-reviving oil with an applicator that delivers the hair formulation to the roots (Indulekha hair oil) or a low-cost but high load-bearing '*jugaad*' in upcountry India, made from submersible pumps. Intro-segmentation drills deeply into small inconveniences or big gaps, and surfaces with unforeseen opportunities from deep within the segment.

Para-segmentation

A frequent criticism of segmentation is that the process of selection of segments is based on our existing knowledge of categories, so we end up recreating and justifying what we already know without actually exploring new options because they are just not in our sight. In other words, where we stand limits our view, and a novel perspective of segmentation is literally out of sight.

Para-segmentation is a technique that would allow you to look at a completely unrelated category and use that experience to refashion the category you wish to recast. For instance, the pioneers of Aravind Eye Hospital got inspired by the swift service at McDonald's to treat cataract patients in large numbers by standardizing and simplifying operations, and conducting simultaneous surgeries in make-shift camps, thereby multiplying their benefit to the community exponentially.

Para-segmentation is unusual and requires the following steps:

- Classify your category basis the known variables: low-income patients seeking eye operations, away from home, away from hospitals which they don't access, etc.
- Within your vision of treating the maximum number of patients for the least amount of cost in least time (hence, the importance of setting the vision as stated in the first chapter for making the right business choice), you segment the market on the patients' desired need-states of accuracy, speed, reliability and low cost (as also done above with the basis need segmentation of pants) – the critical thing here is to identify the core need-states.
- Once you have the core need-states, you leave your industry reference and start to go paranormal (beyond the obvious) to evaluate any other industry that is inspiring for those need-fulfilments.
- Then, ruthlessly apply the same by hybridizing objective one and two. Below is how the segmentation grid could work to spot an inspirational segment.

Basic Needs	*Categories/Brands That Index High on Need-states*						
Eye clinic							
Quick	Street shops	Formula race	Maruti manufacturing	Postal services	Railway counters	Mc Donald's	
Effective	Police station	Fire brigades		Postal services		Mc Donald's	Big Bazaar
Low cost	Dabba food distribution	Primary health centres	Co-operative stores	Public library		Mc Donald's	Big Bazaar
Large scale	Transport	Hospitals	Sweet shops	Public library	DPS school		
Customer ease	Banks					Mc Donald's	
Humane	Hospital	Public parks					

If core values are considered as above, then clearly McDonald's is the best carrier for most need-states. An analysis like this allows the best practices to be exported from one segment to another once the clarity of the core needs emerges. We could have also chosen post offices or fire brigades as inspiration, but for the consumer orientation of McDonald's. That makes McDonald's, a distant and unrelated example, relevant for Aravind hospitals, resulting in a truly disruptive idea.

Segmentation, accordingly, is a great tool if it is used to map the market extensively. But choices arising out of that should be made by looking around and above and not just within the segment. That way, not only can the potential of the existing segment be assessed correctly, but even a product's extension into unrelated areas can be tackled. In sum, being aware of segmentation's limitations is a great way to circumvent it for creating breakthrough ideas.

India is growing at a furious pace with dynamic segments every day. The techniques suggested above offer lucrative opportunities to delight the billion consumers in newer and better ways. Pragmarketism advocates making segmentation based on Desi realities unabashedly so that we can better understand and delight our local consumers.

6

Targeting

'What is the market share for our chips?'

'Seventy per cent,' I answered perkily.

'In what?'

'In potato chips in the north and west, where we are the market leaders amongst national players.'

'Oh, and what is the all-India market share with local players included?'

'It's around 40 per cent,' I stammered.

'And amongst salty snacks, including namkeens?' The next rejoinder was even more damaging.

'Less than 2 per cent.' The fall from glory was rapid.

Seniors in the room looked around, wondering whether we could break out of the room for some celebratory drinks or sheepishly head back to work. The question that hung heavily in the room was, 'What are we targeting – the narrow definition of the market based on our product format or the larger category of salty snack from where we drew our business?'

After understanding segments in the last chapter, we now come to the selection of segments that businesses will choose to go after in the classical marketing model of segmentation-targeting-positioning (S-T-P), namely targeting.

Potential > Available > Convertible: Sizing the Consumer

A fundamental qualification that is lost in rough pronouncements is that the whole country of 1.4 billion is not the consuming population when this huge consumer-base is decomposed to reveal the layers within.

Potential consumer refers to those who can buy into the category because they need and have the capability to purchase. *Available* consumer refers to those who not only have the potential but are also available because they can be accessed by suppliers. Suppliers have demand for their products but are blocked by regulation (big co-operatives like Arla and Fonterra cannot export dairy products to India), by treacherous terrain (like the states of north-east India) or by religious beliefs or cultural taboos (like the inability of restaurants to sell meat during Navratra).

From the *available* market emerges the whole gamut of consumers with different levels of predisposition to a category. The sum total of all these forms the *convertible* consumers, and they come in various hues. Eager to lap up the new offers, the kind that will queue up for hours outside an Apple store even before it's opened forms our *early adopters*. Following them are *followers*, who don't jump in first but scamper to fill up the empty front seats as news of a good film starts to pick up traction. They don't lead the pack but follow earnestly. *Contemplators* need to be nudged bit by bit – partly by outside information and partly from internal discussion. Finally, *laggards*, who spring up long after everyone is gone and just before the shop closes. They are non-risk takers; hence, their journey of buying into the idea takes longer or they are merely uninterested in acting out even if they believe the product is right for them. And a significant number may not be interested (falling into what is called DKCS – don't know, can't say), no matter what.

So, in effect, and while these estimates vary from category to category, only about 60 per cent of the available market is convertible into consumers for a business. Targeting can help overcome the error of generality and quantify the exact size of the consuming base. Probing deeper into various segments and sizing them up is an antidote to this mistake, as we will see in the example below.

Sizing Up Markets

Joy, working for Wonder Yoghurt, is trying to estimate the size of his market on a piece of tissue paper before his friend arrives. He then proceeds to highlight the relevant ones. It looks like this:

Wonder Yoghurt

Generation-based	Geographic	Cultural	Need-based	Typologies
Gargantuan kids	Metro-slickers	Hurricane-vi	No acne	Self-conscious
Growth metres	Millionaire club	Marwaris	Fairness	Grooming specialist
Gawkeens	Sleepy cousins	Bohemian Bongs	Great complexion	Look freak
Rebellious	Rural fringes	Peripatetic Gujjus	Seeking confidence	Modest effort
Saddled	Rural-rural	Brainy Tams	Seeking popularity	Mildly interested
Waist-fillers		Kool Kannadigas	High self-esteem	Indifferent
Pre-retirees		Efficient Mumbaikar	Achievement oriented	Anti-looks
Lost 60s		Puppies	Effortful	

To estimate the size of this target, he has to get some figures from census data, some from secondary research and some from surrogate information or through plain smart assumptions. Then, he has to use the chain ratio method of taking the biggest segment and multiplying it with various sub-segments to arrive at the potential market.

- On the basis of demographic-geo segmentation, we can arrive at a broad size for our target market for Wonder Yoghurt to arrive at available consumers. Thus, it's composed of the Gawkeens and Rebellious (10 per cent of 1 billion Indians or 100 million), living in metros, millionaire towns and in some sleepy cousins totalling to 25 per cent of the Indian population. That makes 100 million × 25 per cent or 25 million available consumers.
- However, to understand how many of these consumers are 'convertible' and are going to be early adopters and followers, we need to look at other segments too, aggregating them with as best an estimate as is available. From the other types of segmentation, we can size up the market:
    - Efficient Mumbaikar, Puppies and a few others seem like the right audience – it's a qualitative call that can be verified if the concept of Wonder Yoghurt is checked for acceptability in these towns in comparison to towns where it's not expected to be acceptable (marketing, being an imperfect science, rewards intuition verified by research, as discussed in the earlier chapter). So if you take data from these cities and slice for the demographic audience, you now have an idea about the geographies to launch in first but the market size here is down to 6 mio (by taking the population of these cities and skinning it based on age and socio-economic standing).

- From a parallel study of another category, like facial creams or chilled products, Joy estimates that those in the need-state of seeking 'great complexion' and 'confidence' and those who fall in the consumer typology of 'self-conscious', 'grooming specialist' and 'look freaks' (all of whom are conscious and take steps to improve their physical appearance) are about 18 per cent of the total population, as defined above.
- Now, if you multiply 6 million by 18 per cent, you arrive at a size of 1.1 million.

Thus, we are talking about an available market of 25 million (this is already a largely truncated version of the one billion market that outsiders expect India to be) with a convertible audience of barely 1.1 million generating positive word of mouth, before the followers come. Assuming he sells three packs to each consumer in the first three months since the launch, he is looking at an initial sale of ₹100 million (₹90 for three packs of yoghurt for a 1.1 million consuming audience consuming audience). In the calculations above, we have multiplied various segments that are assumed to be subsets of each other. However, for adjacent segments, we would add the numbers instead of multiplying, discounting by an overlap factor (but since estimating overlap is not easy, multiplying is usually the better option).

This is not bad to start with, but just then, Tarun, the torrid number-cruncher, comes along and says he has found an idea that is bigger than carbonated beverage because it tastes like healthy buttermilk while still being fizzy like a carbonated drink: Fizzy Buttermilk! He estimates his product sale at about ₹200 million. But Tarun says he has not estimated the market size based on the number of consumers available but on the size of other categories. He simply took the size of the beverage market and assumed a 10 per cent share, and then added to it a 5 per cent share of the buttermilk category. Then, he discounted the summation by 30 per cent on account of the overlap (the number of consumers common to both).

They look at the data from both approaches and agree that Tarun's Fizzy Buttermilk is a killer proposition. Joy is walking back home sullenly, wondering why he is always the runner-up in life.

Well, based on surface analysis, he is right. And if the size of the business is anything to go by, Tarun's idea seems better because it has large numbers, and he pulls out the concept and the product research to prove that consumers are excited about its uniqueness, thereby showing a high propensity to purchase.

Cost of conversion (COC)

Another factor that has a bearing on this case (but is habitually overlooked) is the cost of converting these consumers. In the final analysis, it's not how many consumers you win but how profitably and with what operational ease you win them with.

So, the next day, Joy feels enlightened and challenges Tarun to do a COC calculation between Wonder Yoghurt and Fizzy Buttermilk. This is how the two stack up:

Decision table

All figures in millions	Fizzy Buttermilk	Wonder Yoghurt	Comments
Size of available consumer	10	1.1	Basis demo-geo and category segmentation
Cost of awareness	50	5.6	Number of users times the cost of reaching one
Number of aware consumers	5	0.5	50 per cent of available consumers reached by media

All figures in millions	Fizzy Buttermilk	Wonder Yoghurt	Comments
Sampling cost	2.5	0.8	Product cost for 10 per cent of aware consumers × ₹5 and ₹15 respectively
Revenue from trial purchase	5	1.5	10 per cent of aware × ₹10 and ₹30 price per unit respectively
Revenue from repeat purchase	3.8	1.1	25 per cent of trialists × three times ₹Rs. 10 and ₹30 respectively
Total revenue	105	31.5	Sum of the above two × twelve for annual vols.
Total cost	52.5	6.4	Cost of awareness plus sampling cost
Cost of conversion	0.5	0.2	total cost/total revenue

Joy argues that his business is better because the cost of conversion is low, the per-unit revenue is better, the turnover is not bad for his personal ambition and the idea has uniqueness, which will allow it to carry on for longer. So, when he grows the business, its multiplier is high – which means that for every buck he puts in, he gets a return of five times that amount (revenue/cost). Tarun argues that the scale of the business in his case is huge, making it truly promising and, therefore, more attractive as he can continue to gain share in a large category, unlike Wonder Yoghurt, which is a new-fangled idea.

So, what started off as a sheer game of numbers has thrown up many issues that need to be considered, as often happens in business. These issues are as follows:

- What is your vision and what business does that lead you into – scale or impact (with higher profitability and better returns)?
- How much are you willing to invest and how far will you extend it?
- What is the risk being taken with the operational complexity?

Targeting, thus, helps make a quantitative comparison of the pros and cons, enabling one to make the choice, sometimes even clarifying what one wants (which is also often not clear). Also, due to the large number of qualitative issues that have to be considered to reach a decision, the tendency is to not size up the market and estimate COC. Sharp targeting estimation and the cost of entry into each segment would help firms reach a consensus on which segments to target for investment and for how long.

Targeting Techniques

Search engine targeting: Searching on Google provides insight into the keywords used by consumers to access the categories they want. Using data analytics, technology now allows marketers to strike exactly those consumers who are in need of their products instead of carpet-bombing all potential consumers. This increases the chances of conversion. With facilities like the 'buy now' button that links to an e-commerce site, the gap between awareness, interest, decision and action (the classical AIDA model) is scrunched, yielding action straight after intention.

Search engine optimization (SEO) allows marketers to seed their brands when consumers are searching for the relevant category, allowing them to be ahead of the competition. Lapsed consumers, who linger on the site but do not purchase, can be retargeted using specific messaging appropriate to them. Targeting by SEO is far more specific and relevant than the diffused targeting that mass media, like TV, offers.

Social media targeting: Analysing the consumer's habits on social media, relevant products and services can be offered ahead of it being asked for. Bearing an eerie semblance to stalking, this technique can and does help if marketers are genuinely helping consumers choose better deals. However, the frequency and intrusiveness of a brand's message should be tailored to prevent putting consumers off.

Contextual targeting: Another boon for the advertisers in the modern day is the ability to know when the consumer is around and, therefore, become more relevant. A consumer looking for housing is in the right frame of mind to take home loans. Or somebody shopping for vegetables can be presented a promotion on fruit juice. Or somebody buying a phone can be offered a screen cover through a bundled promotion. Contextual targeting leverages the consumer's inclination to a category or an adjacent category for closing sales.

Behavioural targeting: A related concept that goes one step back in the consumer's buying journey, it captures the opportunity of converting a consumer when his behaviour points towards an inclination. While looking for a gym bag, a consumer can be tempted to try a high protein drink. This way, new categories can be introduced if the communication being served at that moment educates the consumer to an unconsidered benefit.

Targeting has taken on a whole new meaning as brand owners have the opportunity to be in personalized conversations with willing consumers. More of this will be explored in the chapter on digital marketing.

Penetration Versus Frequency of Consumption

A very frequent dilemma in marketing is to go for more consumers or target more consumption from the same consumers. If we take more consumers as the x-axis and more consumption as the y-axis, the options before marketers can be summarized as follows:

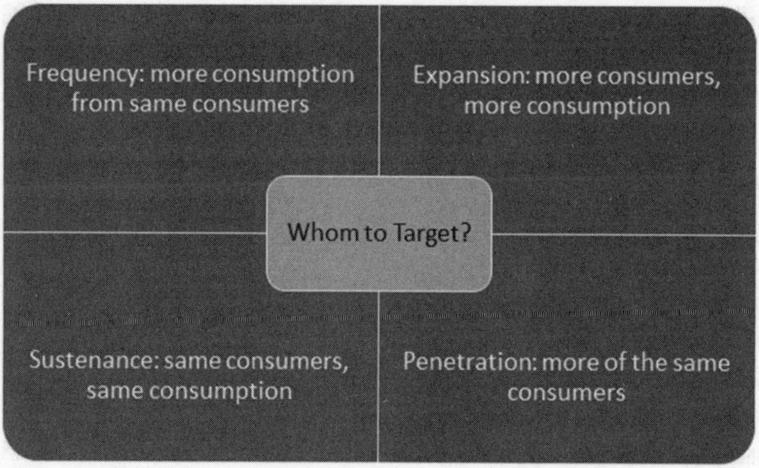

Source: Authors

Frequency of consumption: Targeting more consumption from the same consumers amounts to reminding consumers to consume more often or creating occasions or reasons to widen consumption. Impulse categories thrive on frequent brand recall to spur consumption from people who are disposed to consuming brands, but haven't considered or adopted the brand. Pepsi on a hot day or Lay's chips to satiate hunger pangs works when the brand name is heard or seen when the opportunity strikes. A pack of Lay's designed for a picnic – with dip – is an example of increasing consumption with the same consumers through a new association of the brand.

Choosing the frequency of consumption leads to pack adaptation or line extensions, making creatives and buying media that reminds consumers to consume at the right time and place. It is measured by increased sales amongst the same audience and has a positive impact on brand loyalty.

Penetration: Targeting a higher number of consumers to increase category usage belongs to the bottom right quadrant. Most market leaders of today have invested in aggressive penetration strategies in the past, creating relevance for their brands through low pricing, extensive distribution or mass communication drive. In developing markets like ours, unless it's a premium brand, penetration makes perfect sense. Today's leading FMCG, durable, pharma players, to name a few, have built their businesses on single-minded penetration drives.

Expansion: This relates to absolutely new usage creation. Dettol's usage from nursing wounds to being a component of the daily mop or on one's shaving brush as lather is an example of extending a brand to a new usage segment, which may or may not draw from its already penetrated user base. An even more radical expansion area is Uber Eats, where the former business of travelling is diversified to include the online delivery of food. Expansion can offer outrageous opportunities if a brand's essence and a firm's core competence is well understood and leveraged.

Sustenance: This is not a strategic output but can be a result of strategic omission. In a dynamic environment, if a firm keeps all business efforts static vis-à-vis other competing firms, it can either go down or rise up. Even if all players in the category decide to take the same approach, some other proximal category will cause the erosion of the category, impacting the sustenance-mode brand adversely. Hence, sustenance cannot be a strategy unless one is divesting or selling out.

Since sustenance is not an optimal option and expansion opportunities are seldom, a firm is left with either penetration or frequency as possible vectors of consumer acquisition. Again, here, the experience of business managers is that penetration is favoured over frequency in our bustling nation for the following reasons:

1. *Low-category penetration*: Most categories in India, barring basic commodities, still show low penetration as per the Indian Readership Survey (IRS). This means that whether

you are a leader or a follower, there is always a large and equally profitable segment to exploit either vertically (on the socio-economic ladder) or horizontally (geography or target audience). Given the relatively cost-effective media and low cost of entry in retail, most players have gained significantly from just acquiring new consumers even after decades of existence in the market. This, along with a growing population (twenty-seven million babies added every year), means that even the fatigue of the existing consuming audience is not a worry due to the new additions every year.

2. *Limited solus brand usage*: Most brands don't enjoy exclusive solus usage or die-hard loyalty. Most advertised brands build category relevance over others and eventually sell basis consumer convenience of availability or visibility. With limited tangible differentiation between brands, consumers can flit across options, showing loyalty more out of situational conditions (too lazy to look for more options, going with retailer recommendation, relying on a first-found bias or showing deep loyalty to category instead of brand, amongst other reasons) than a deliberate pre-planned choice. In such a condition, targeting a niche audience, communication or media can make a brand vulnerable among its light users who are quite content to try competing brands. A broad-based marketing effort often wins the day.
3. *Brand lapsage*: As study after study in household panels show, even the biggest brands show lapsage. These could be the light users described above or a result of situational conditions. If penetration is not followed as a strategy and a marketer decides to pursue its truncated base of loyal users, then the overall base of total users will fall. This is because the lapsage will not be getting adequately offset by the recruitment of new consumers. Hence, penetration

strategy covers this seamy side of unpredictable consumer movements, enabling overall growth even as consumers change hands underneath.

4. *Long tail of light consumers*: In his book, *How Brands Grow*, Byron Sharp* argues that the usual Pareto law of 80/20 (wherein 80 per cent sales accrue from 20 per cent consumers) is more like 60/40 with a long tail of light consumers who are part of the negative binomial distribution. A focused, frequency-based strategy covering the heavy or loyal users will be perilous, leaving a large majority unattended. This double jeopardy of not reaching enough people and not getting enough from those who are targeted may end up eating up a large consumer base.

A peculiar aspect in India with big legacy brands is that they tend to have a heterogeneous base of users due to their long history of consumption. In this case, the core audience ends up sharing space with secondary users in the family, much like the single TV ownership forcing consumption of all content across all age strata. Lay's chips, meant for the youth, is consumed by all, especially kids. Colas, meant for the youth, are consumed by just about everyone. A viable strategy in this case is to launch sub-brands catering to specific target audiences within the household, as per their needs. For example, Horlicks, as a parent brand has launched sub-brands like Junior Horlicks and Women's Horlicks, and Cadbury has extended from its staple Dairy Milk to Cadbury Dark Milk chocolates for adults. However, this approach succeeds only if there is a substantial consumer base of the parent brand.

For the reasons listed above, mass marketers favour the penetration strategy, and even niche ones ensure that they are well

---

* Sharp, Byron, *How Brands Grow: What Marketers Don't Know*, Melbourne, Oxford University Press, 2010.

penetrated in the targeted audience, which, due to India's size, ends up being fairly significant at any end of the social spectrum.

A more judicious approach to maximize revenues for most ends up being a mix of the two: penetration strategy at a base level of product design and consumer communication, topped up with tailored consumer engagement with a niche audience, where they naturally aggregate. Thus, you sell hair oil to all but take a variant and connect with young girls with digital and influencer marketing (details later) in niche segments.

Targeting in this manner, one can reach the massive sweep of the nation in one go and supplement it with consumer delight for specific sub-segments. Pragmarketism advocates a judicious mix of penetration and frequency to make the most of this complex subcontinent.

7

Positioning

'How do you see yourself in the eyes of your peers, Trupti?' This was quite a shock for an assistant brand manager presenting a new product launch in the boardroom. What was its bearing on the business? Fifteen people were waiting for an answer as my line manager quizzed me.

'Hardworking, committed, creative?' I answered honestly – with *some* exaggeration, since my appraisal was next week.

'That's all?'

'Also strategic, people-friendly, balanced and result-oriented.' Was I overdoing it?

'And …?' The coaxing was unrelenting.

'I am also flexible and detailed-oriented and …'

'That is exactly how your launch positioning is! A bit of everything, but nothing of any one thing. Can we be focused so consumers know what we stand for?' These lines still ring in my ears when I am working on a brand plan. Nothing could be closer to human truth and, therefore, brand truth. Everyone wants to have all the virtues, and marketers transpose this universal human desire to the brands they work for, imbuing them with all the possible benefits. But no matter how hard we try to be all good, others don't perceive us to be good at everything. Likewise, in the hyper-crowded marketplace, even our consumers don't think our brands have all the benefits. Competitive brands will also be worth something.

That leaves us with only two choices in life, the same as in brand management. One, choose what we want to be good at, making sure that it is important to us as well as others evaluating us. Second, we become the best at it, so much so that when our chosen area of excellence is recalled, our name is ahead of everyone else's.

Brand positioning is just this: choosing the right attribute for differentiation versus others and then excelling at it repeatedly.

Positioning

Positioning is the holy grail of marketing – it doesn't get any bigger than this. Positioning decides the fate of all economic transactions now and in the future. In effect, it closes the supply–demand equation, marrying need with satisfaction.

Positioning, put simply, is the expression of the eminent superiority of a company's product or services versus others in the marketplace, in the mind of the consumer. Whether or not a consumer is consuming the product at present, or even talking about it, is not important. What matters is that in the mind of the consumer, where ultimately all the battles of market share are fought, the brand's image enduringly outranks others'. Positioning, therefore, etches a brand or company's strength in the consumer's mind, granting it insularity from attacks by the competition and other market vagaries. What personality does to distinguish humans in the crowd, positioning does to brands in the marketplace.

Writing a Positioning Statement: Must Dos

A good positioning statement is worth every ounce of labour in an offsite workshop. It must be conceptualized after the vision statement to prepare the brand for its outward journey from the company's stables into the consumer's hands and must fulfil the following conditions:

- **Whom** is the product for?
- **Product** name
- **Category** within the context of which consumers will appreciate it
- **Why**: the key benefit that delivers to a consumer need and why it is so (RTB-Reason To Believe)
- **Payoff**: that bolsters the emotional benefit to the consumer

The benefit and RTB usually are the primary differentiators versus the competition and the payoff represents the secondary differentiation.

Hence, if Joy, the usual, had to beat Tarun, the torrid, he would write the positioning statement of Wonder Yoghurt as follows:

'For young girls seeking clean, glowing skin (whom), Wonder Yoghurt is the nutritious yoghurt (product and category) that comes packed with the power of Ayurvedic skin science (RTB) to cleanse the skin from within, ridding acne (benefit) and giving them the confidence to face the world (payoff).'

What are some stellar examples of positioning? Western examples can be quite instructive. Since positioning statements are companies' internal secrets, brand taglines offer a good substitute to understanding positioning and the 'primary differentiation' compared to their implied competitors.

Positioning examples:

Brand/ Company	Positioning Platforms	Primary Differentiation
Duracell	No battery lasts longer	Longevity of batteries
Lay's	No one can eat just one	Irresistibility
7 Up	The Uncola	Veritable counter to popular choice

Apple	Everything is easier on MAC	Versus IBM's forbidding machines
Nike	Just do it	Stop thinking, start acting on your dreams
Adidas	Impossible is nothing	Touch your unknown limits
KFC	Finger lickin' good	Taste that lingers on
Federal Express	When it has to be positively delivered overnight	Speed and dependability
Burger King	Have it your way	Menu flexibility with a standard taste
Subway	Eat fresh	Benefit of fresh ingredients over junk

From the above examples, the basis of differentiation starts to emerge. A firm could choose to build its positioning statement vis-à-vis a) product attribute (Duracell, Lay's, KFC), b) competition (7 Up, Subway), c) basis consumer's experience (Apple) or d) philosophy rooted in consumer resistance, like not acting out but merely thinking (Nike) or the fear of taking on difficulty (Adidas).

Positioning in Indian Companies: Ingredient, Diffused, Benefit, User Experience

The Indian experience of positioning throws up a patchy picture. Cocooned in the Licence Raj and driven more by opportunism than core competence, Indian companies have played this aspect of strategy differently in various sectors.

In the FMCG industry, there are stars as well as wannabes. Britannia has taken the market of biscuits and segmented with demographic and occasion to create clearly differentiated products within their own portfolio (the overlaps have been minimized) and with some success, versus their competitors also.

- Tiger biscuits (product and category) are positioned for (following the template we set above for writing a positioning statement) those moms (who) want their kids 'roaring' with energy (benefit), drawing from the vitamins, iron and calcium to the extent of 25 per cent of their daily recommended need (RTB). The benefit, brand and RTB are compactly held together by a unifying 'position' that also sets it apart from the generic glucose biscuit brand which sells on the street.
- Good Day biscuits bring a smile to your face (that makes a 'good day' – therefore positioned to all seeking to uplift their mood) with butter and cashews: positioned on happiness – that is non-specific and difficult to counter for rivals; as for users, the visible infusions of dry fruit at an affordable price brings the smile anyway.
- Marie Gold (not just Marie; a clever way to differentiate on a basic category name with a suffix) for women who seek to accomplish more every day, being low in fat and cholesterol. A variant, VitaMarie, comes with the extra nutrition of vitamins.
- NutriChoice: Power-packed snacks (creating a new category of healthy snacking) for people who chase a healthy way of life, with the benefit of oats and easy digestibility. A clever brand name but with a somewhat hackneyed psycho-profile of consumers.
- The indulgence segment has been tapped with cream treats, Jim Jam (at entry level) and Bourbon (for a wickedly smooth side, 'the chocolate lover's favourite guilt trip') and Pure Magic ('chocolate artistry' for the connoisseurs) positioned for wanton indulgence, overriding the linear demographic lines. Sunfeast, Parle and others have their versions too, with sometimes similar sounding sub-brand names. The

premium category is crowded with 'me too's, crying for differentiation.

- An interesting valorization of base categories of salties has been 50/50, which is a newer version of its predecessor, Krackjack (an absolutely wowing innovation) – positioning of the schizophrenic personality, both a whacky and a serious side, reflecting its contrasting flavours. In Maska Chaska, the level of innovation has been enhanced with Indian ingredients like jeera (cumin seed) and garlic.
- Little Hearts, lightly flirting between a snack and a biscuit, are 'light crunch melt-in-the-mouth biscuits for chatting with friends'. A clean and distinctive positioning, incontrovertibly complementing the product experience.

Above all this sits the brand Britannia, which some time ago was positioned as a healthy choice for invigorating the body and mind (from the Hindi *'Swasth khaayo, tan man jagao'*, rendered in English with a non-sequitur, 'Eat healthy, think better'). The parent brand works to generate trust over other categories, like snacks and beverages, at the top. Trust in the brand distils down to the sub-categories subsumed under it, increasing loyalty for the brand as a whole and ensuring constant adoption of its sub-categories, even if they are not advertised constantly. Overall, Britannia seems to have been positioned effectively in a hyper-crowded space to reach out uniquely to its diversified consumers.

Positioning is relatively easier if the company produces and sells different product categories within a single industry. Dabur has carried brand assurance across different categories. Dabur Honey is positioned towards presumably 30-plus women, with the goodness of honey providing fitness and youthful looks. Dabur Vatika oils and shampoos are positioned on the basis of their benefits, claiming 'goodbye to hair problems' with an RTB based on traditional ingredients. Dabur Chyawanprash, which is the crowning glory of their portfolio, gives the Dabur brand Ayurvedic authenticity and is positioned to improve general immunity (although it ends up being an anti-cold remedy during winters in the consumer's scheme of things) on the RTB of science and a recipe that dates back 2,500 years based on amla (Indian gooseberry) and herbs. The brand positioning of its parent brand is so strong and cohesive that it has no difficulties sitting atop vastly different opportunities finely joined by Ayurveda: 'Shilajit' for vitality (read as virility by the consumer's decryption) and the merry digestive, 'Hajmola', drawing on the differentiation of Ayurvedic ingredients like 'kesar', 'ashwagandha' or 'harh' in other products. However, ingredient positioning, that is, drawing strength from an ingredient, like in the case of Dabur, works when Ayurveda itself is a unique idea vis-à-vis the more prevalent Western allopathic practices. But when competitor brands arrive from Zandu, Himalaya or any other from the stable Indian homeopathies or Ayurvedic brands, then just selling generic ingredients may not sustain the brand.

Vicco Laboratories is an example of heightened ingredient positioning. They have taken turmeric to be the key differentiator into a host of creams and managed to expand their portfolio on the strength of one dominant ingredient.

Marico, on the other hand, has subdued its parent brand to the level of a manufacturer (barring a sign-off at the end) and kept to the classical approach of being a one-brand-one-proposition company. And it has been quite a pioneer. Revive, the brand has created a category from the starch that women in India have always used, made from leftover rice-water for creasing flimsy cotton. It has been uniquely positioned for confident, traditional Indian women without a rival. Saffola, the cooking oil with lower saturated fat, is positioned on heart-health with communication targeting women who are concerned about the declining cardio-health of their busy and stressed husbands.

The brand Parachute is positioned as pure coconut oil but lacks differentiation from brands like Cocoraj and a host of other local brands. However, it has increased its positioning strength towards hair care with propositions like Parachute Advanced and Parachute Hair clinics to enrich its core brand with more authentic hair-caring expertise, including taking steps into the service segment. And now, doing the same for men, not as an extension of Parachute, as some other companies would be wont to do, but with the brand Set Wet, it is positioned towards grooming-conscious male adults who want to move beyond the ubiquitous and strange Indian habit of oiling their hair with slick gel-like looks common in the West.

Unlike Dabur and Britannia, the disadvantage of this approach is that without a parent brand positioned for some general benefit, Marico's expenses for new launches will always be prohibitive.

Colgate is at the other extreme of the positioning continuum. All products of Colgate, save the differentiation of ingredients (charcoal, active salt), highlight the Colgate positioning of dental care directly from dentists, unfailingly every time, upon every use. The fortress-like solidity of this positioning has prevented challengers like Pepsodent or Close-up from taking a serious share of the mainstream segment, and they have managed to only dent the market around the edges.

On the other hand, Godrej, as a company, has positioned its brand with trademark quality and trust, defying any need to spell out the product/category/audience/RTB. But the diffused positioning seems to work as it disregards core competence and synergies with defiance. From home care, personal care, appliances, furniture, real estate to even insecticide, Godrej has shown great resilience in cashing in on multiple opportunities while the sun shines on its global brand. Brands like Godrej and Tata are power brands at the top with a diffused impact at the sub-brands below them; you can't have one name associated with many constituent values. You could call this 'diffused positioning', which comes with the general benefits of motherhood. A clear no-no as far as positioning games go, but it still does pretty much what positioning does, except by violating the rules and not conforming.

Reckitt Benckiser, a formidable player in home and personal care with power brands like Dettol, Harpic and Lizol, has taken disinfection, hygiene and first aid to the level of a mission (exemplified perhaps by the anti-germicidal swords on the iconic Dettol logo) so convincingly that the company has managed to register growth on each of its brands. Positioning of a brand on the basis of protection of various kinds is a great way to build trust with consumers and also continuously reinforces a company's core competence through all aspects of their business (research and development, marketing, procurement, sales). An unrivalled example of 'benefit positioning', which while seemingly limiting is actually providing legs to diversify into new uses (antiseptics for cuts to disinfecting homes and mop floors) and new categories (Dettol soap, which, not long after its launch, overtook the parent brand, Dettol liquid).

Pidilite Industries' amiable brand, Fevicol, is a great example of hyper-extolling a simple benefit – sticking well – and 'Fevi' can now be prefixed anywhere and the proposition sticks: Fevikwik, Fevistick, Fevicol, Fevicryl etc.

Where brands don't offer serious benefits, positioning can become seriously fun. Perfetti, with Ogilvy, has turbo-charged its positioning with colloquial Hindi proverbs, imparting characters to plain candies. Alpenliebe's unabashed indulgence is '*jabaan lap lapaeyegee*'. Chlormint's '*doobara mat poochna*' is unquestionably comedic. Mentos, a fresh mint flavour for perky youngsters, alights the brains or '*dimaag ki batti jala de*' with some iconic creative insight. Center Fresh, the gum with a liquid filled twist, has been sequentially advertised as '*jabaan pe lagaam de*' or '*chali hawa mastaani*' in a quirky, humorous way. A host of other impulse-driven confectionary brands – Snickers, Big Babool, 5 Star – have made us feel lighter with funny ideas and 'quirky positioning'.

Positioning can stretch beyond product fundamentals and can reflect a heightened consumer experience. The sedate category of paints handled by contractors during Diwali has been enlivened by Asian Paints as a symbol of prosperity to invite a neighbour's envy (Ultima Allura, Apex of Asian Paints). Royale, with special effects, has forced consumers to look beyond the plain oil-bound distemper (remember the ubiquitous brand, indifferently named Tractor?) and Royale Play, positioned imaginatively as bespoke finishing that brings out your individuality (*'har ghar kuch kahta hai'*). Asian Paints have elevated these expressions to a service idea where they provide tips on colour selection based on Vastu Shastra, through 'colour shastra'. This is an example of 'experience positioning'.

Durable companies, which outclass each other on newer, more updated features, strangely enough use experience positioning to amplify the impact of their brands on their consumers' lives. LG is positioned as 'Life is good', promising a better life to consumers across all product categories they operate within. Samsung offers the users an experience of futuristic technology, suitably supplemented with esoteric descriptors, like QLED TV, Galaxy J7 for mobiles and so on.

Mobile phones are falling over each other on a single insight – the importance of the camera for this selfie-crazy nation – with experience positioning too. Oppo's F3 series has features like the dual-selfie, Vivo's 24 MP has a clearer shot, and Micromax has Canvas Infinity, a full-vision display with 18:9 aspect ratio. In fact, even iPhone focuses on the photo experience of its consumers. However, when everyone converges on the same experience, positioning is compromised to work on the basis of a numeric comparison of screen sizes and megapixels.

Elsewhere, positioning is hardly used to drive differentiation among competing firms. In the case of healthcare, Fortis talks about world-class health services and so do others; in education, Amity talks about it being a world-class educational system and a world of knowledge, and the brochures of other universities seem no different. The apparel industry is famous for cloning, using borrowed models to recharge their jaded brands with non-descript imagery. Retail space is screaming with discount messages (*mahabachat*, *acha din*, mega saving) between Big Bazaar, Spencer's, ABRL and more, although Fashion Big Bazaar (FBB) is patriotically claiming to make India beautiful: *Aaao banaye India Sundar*. Banking is again marked by a host of 'feature positioning' methods. Yes Bank claimed to be a bank for professionals and wanted to be the finest bank globally by 2020; but they were unable to specify why or how. HDFC is somewhat differentiated with their promotion of house financing, but the others talk, in various words, about a relationship of trust and ease, scantily hiding real drivers like interest rates and ATM locations. Eventually, these sectors are just monoliths with many lookalikes lurking, with no real difference between each other.

Pharmaceuticals and other heavy industries abound in feature positioning, spelling out their multiple offers with multiple words, loosely held together with a semblance of positioning ideas. Aurobindo wants to be the leading generic pharma and Cipla is positioned on caring for life, authentically led by the visionary, Yusuf Hamied, but it lacks the sharpness that positioning requires to stand out from the crowd and galvanize its employees.

The real estate companies and public sector behemoths aren't positioned based on feature but on political appropriateness. Words and phrases like 'make in India', 'nation building', 'trust' and 'promises' have a hint of positioning but only reflect what can be uniquely Indian: 'political positioning' – a fallout of the *mai-baap* relationship with a government that is often both the client and the consumer in the final analysis.

Positioning: Pain Points and Opportunity

Companies and brands are wary of committing themselves to a specific positioning because they fear that if consumer demand changes, they will be left with a proposition that has no takers.

To navigate the uncertain waters of business, therefore, it helps to position as widely as possible – even if it is vague and ordinary. Then, whichever way the wind blows, there will always be something to offer.

However, there are a few considerations that argue for staying grounded with regard to positioning, even if the current environment isn't entirely conducive.

First, trends which reflect how a need-state is being approached come and go, but a need-state doesn't. The basis for need-state, which may just have been heard less because of the reduced noise of advertising, hasn't yet disappeared. The Beetle, after many years, incontestably stands for safety in the whole gamut of automobiles. If anything, with time, it has also become stylish in itself. Therefore, what needs to be dispensed with is not the brand's positioning but its articulation, a bit like in the case of Titan Sonata, which is reorchestrated and revisualized every year, but its core is unmistakably the same. So, before a certain type of positioning is abandoned, it should be recontextualized to the prevailing setting and period.

Second, embracing the dominant need in favour of one's time-tested need pushes a company towards creating me-toos and lookalikes. The expedience may lead to some initial cash, but it soon runs dry as others elbow you out with better deals. Otherwise, the Maruti Swift would have been no different from Hyundai i20 or Ciaz and consumers would choose on the basis of a technical detail, like torque or the shape of the taillight. Eventually, the whole category suffers as consumers stand on a highway of misinformation.

Third, positioning is based on sound selection and quantification of a segment. Usually, there is plenty of room within one's own segment if it is conducted by covering all the aspects of positioning (benefit, RTB, need and so on), precluding any need to look to external circumstances. For instance, Ford Figo can position itself as 'the ultimate safe car for the responsible family that values tough cars that can weather Indian roads, eliminating discomfort inside, because it comes with the finest technology – balancing on suspension, air bags and a toughened body'. The Swift could position itself as 'the car with speed and economy that makes the urban Indian dominate on difficult Indian roads because its powerful engine ensures maximum speed with minimum fuel consumption'. Both positionings have their strengths and appeal without overlapping or sounding the same.

Fourth, minor changes in the consumer's perception of need-states can be integrated through brand communication, by highlighting relevant features without derailing the overall positioning. Sporty looks and cool chrome features can be highlighted without making a safe car into a sports car.

Fifth, if dramatic changes are sweeping the consumer base, then a good alternative would be to launch a variant or a whole new brand. It's always preferable to entrench your positioning and the need-state you own with it, rather than diluting it to accommodate a current fad, which may or may not last but which has the potential to damage the longterm equity of the brand that has been built on consistent positioning.

Positioning of the Company Brand and Product Brand

Could there be a way to integrate changing trends of the global world while still keeping the positioning consistent?

The answer to the above question can be understood in the context of Indian society. Our identity contains three elements. Let's understand this as if we're peeling an 'identity onion'. It has the following layers: *naam*, *upnaam* and *upadhi* (name, surname and title). Since brands have a lineage, we can construct them from the outside to the inside and embed within them specific as well as general needs. For an individual like me, Arvind is the *naam*, Bhandari the *upnaam* or surname and Verdia, my gotra or jati, becomes my *upadhi* or the class to which I belong.

Identity rings

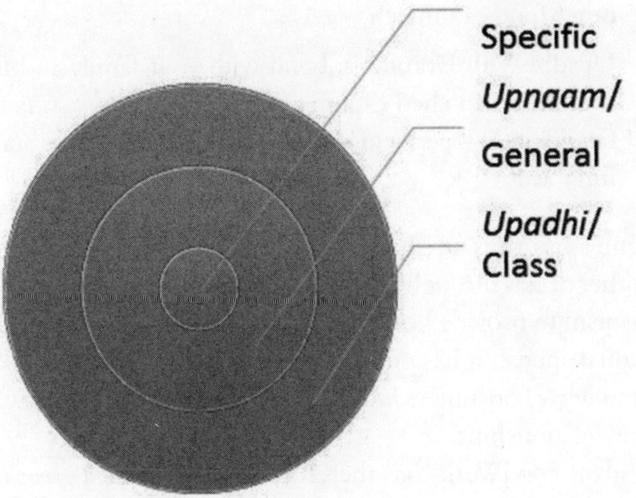

Source: Authors

Accordingly, a brand like Domino's can operate at three levels. *Naam* is their cheese crust pizza, *upnaam* is the pizza, the food category, and their *upadhi* is a larger category, such as fast food. The need-states vary at different levels as consumers reject as much as they select. At the *naam* layer, the organoleptic delight of a cheese crust pizza is chosen over a thin crust or other forms of pizza. At the *upnaam* layer, the need of a quick, cheesy and heavy meal of a pizza over noodles or Thai curry. And finally, at the *upadhi* layer, it refers to the need to eat something wholesome rather than drinking or going out.

Now, positioning can be written for all three levels as follows:

- *Naam* Domino's cheese burst pizza doubles for a pizza party for the hungry at home; it comes loaded with stringy cheese inside the crust and is layered with the choicest toppings.

- *Upnaam* Domino's pizza is the yummiest, hottest pizza for the hungry who won't have to wait with assured fast delivery, with the most delicious crust and toppings that no other food can match.
- Upadhi With Domino's, bond with your family and friends over an unmatched experience – 'Ye *hain rishton ka time*' (it's family time) – perfect for products like Pizza Mania and their fun meals.

Domino's has thus strengthened its positioning as the best pizza over other pizzas through product attributes and an instant delivery mechanism to provide hot, yummy and cheesy bites. And through emotional appeal, it has entrenched its position beyond other fun foods to draw consumers who are looking to rekindle the warmth of their relationships.

Jubilant FoodWorks has therefore demonstrated a great mix of an alluring product positioning that consumers can't refuse and an expansive positioning of the brand at the *upadhi* level to stand for family moments instead of just another meal.

Positioning, therefore, can both sharpen the lure of its product and also encircle the consumers with a larger idea beyond the product. The *naam*, *upnaam* and *upadhi* levels of positioning allow the brand to zoom in and out, thereby tapping consumers at different need-states and demand moments (as detailed in the chapter 'Demand Plasticity').

Similarly, companies can position their parent brands or corporate brands at the level of macro need-states. For example, the promise of Ayurveda for Dabur, commitment to simple and everyday conveniences through innovation for 3M, achieving empowerment through communication for Idea cellular networks and so on. And within this umbrella positioning, constituent brands can be positioned on more specific need-states pertinent to the period, thus fruitfully managing short-term and long-term benefits of positioning.

Enduring Positioning through Secondary Differentiation

Indian companies have abstained from sharply positioning their brands to avoid committing to a position that might stop them from availing new and emergent opportunities. To inspire growth and go beyond primary differentiation based on brand features, they would be well-placed to explore secondary differentiation. Iconic companies like Apple, Google, Facebook and Amazon are known for their simplified visions that reflect in their positioning. They draw from the categories they operate in, but equally, they refer to human values. This not only guides their huge corporations through business trammels but also draws employees who chime in with their philosophy.

Secondary differentiation is not based on mere RTB but on human and emotional truths, which answer to universal need-states. It's about how a brand connects with the larger community and how it seeks to contribute to it. Staying away from clichés and unrelated hyperboles, it must sincerely spell out how it intends to serve its consumers.

Secondary differentiation drives the purpose of the brand at all levels. Nike believes in supporting athletic activity so dreams can materialize, as epitomized in its slogan – 'Just do it'. This not only justifies its apparel and shoes business, but it also gives them room to expand into sports training, equipment, adventure sports or any exploration-related product or service. Wipro appeals to the innovating side of consumers and is positioned as #bethenew, egging everyone to connect ideas and innovations for creating excellence. Engaging consumers emotionally will also enlist their brand loyalty far more than any product feature or promotion pricing.

Embracing secondary differentiation can sharpen positioning for Indian companies while consolidating their large operations under a powerful call-out. The following are a few suggested and best examples of how Indian corporates can position themselves or are currently positioned:

- GMR infrastructure: 'Reducing barriers to togetherness'
- Amity: 'Expanding potentialities of its students'
- Fortis: 'Pioneers of life – enabling, nurturing and growing'
- Star/Zee: 'Best family friends forever'
- Paytm: 'Financing and building dreams instantly'
- Raymond: 'Complete man'
- Femina: 'Woman of substance'

Infusing positioning with secondary differentiation is hugely energizing as it reminds and goads employees and customers towards the human purpose that underpins their sterile everyday operations. It also indicates that there are new opportunities in the segment of the need-state they are committed to serving, in the widest and most responsible sense. In doing so, positioning doesn't bind, but liberates.

Positioning: Focus Essential

Positioning works well if companies and brands stay focused on what they stand for. Day after day, they must commit themselves to excelling in meeting that one need-state they are resolved to defending and growing with, while stoutly rejecting temptations that distract and don't build towards that chosen and singular path.

Great companies know it; small companies either don't or they ignore it. The seduction of quick gains takes them into side alleys of unrelated work, which blunts the image-driven consumers' hold over them. It is the same for a bright child or a swashbuckling sports enthusiast who must repeatedly keep up that image to stand uncontested and above all the others. If the bright child indulges in a bit of sports or the sports enthusiast begins to study, we would struggle to associate them single-mindedly with any one area of excellence. Brands are no different from people. They need to speak the same language of mastery – day in and day out, so consumers will privilege them.

Al Ries and Jack Trout*, in their iconic book, *Positioning: The Battle for Your Mind,* decry the tendency of marketers to infuse a brand with too many features or values through line extensions (same category but different usage, like Colgate Dental Cream and Colgate Sensitive) or brand extensions (different category and different usage, like Bournvita milk food drink and Bournvita biscuits), because this dilutes the brand's core equity, making them vulnerable to an attack from me-toos. Against this, single-minded positioning reinforces the consumer's positive experience of the brand, making them oblivious to other brands.

In the same spirit, companies and brands have to first wisely choose their positioning methods and then assiduously commit to refining that method and that alone. For only by doing so can they breed huge value-creating companies and become like Apple, Google or Facebook. With the exception of some companies in IT, India has a long way to go before it can have globally wowing companies. Positioning – the battle in the consumer's mind – has to be the starting block for that charming destination.

---

* Ries, Al, and Trout, Jack. *Positioning: The Battle for Your Mind, London*, McGraw Hill Education, 2017.

8

Communication

'What's the "Big Idea"?' We have spent hours labouring over the right answer in a typical client-agency standoff.

'What is the objective of this piece of communication?' the agency answers back in defence.

'Let's see the creative.' Sometimes, the brief can be modified if the creative is kickass. We have even felt guilty for keeping the brief somewhat loose, either by not being sure about the real consumer insight or by hoping that the ambiguity helps creativity to get something out of the world (or out of the brief).

'We have already presented three!' the agency reminds.

'But it's not working: the product is incidental and the copy has no emotional impact either,' the adjudicating client tries to dominate.

'The brief is confused,' the agency retaliates.

An everyday conversation for many, this is the usual agency–client impasse. Though it's usually blamed on people (lack of talent, right attitude and so on), the conflict is more fundamental. In the art of creativity versus the science of consumer persuasion, let's take a deep dive into the process before the creative leap is taken.

Business, Marketing and Communication Objectives

As the business idea develops, a great amount of confusion arises between the business objective, the marketing objective and the communication objective. Without being pedantic but also while exercising rigour, much clarity and direction can be achieved for generating communication that works hard without merely amusing our consumers.

It is therefore highly useful, even if a little tedious, to know what the business and the consumer want and, therefore, in what language and tone we need to speak to the consumer.

Source: Authors

Business objective details how outside opportunities will be utilized with internal capabilities to produce value for consumers in keeping with the company's vision. The output is higher revenue and profit for the firms.

If you are Asian Paints, while exploring the unexploited ceiling-painting option (a whacked out idea) with myriad colours and themes while utilizing the idle emulsion plants, the business objective is to generate additional revenue at incremental margins by developing and owning the ceiling-painting category. Or if you are in the ice-cream business – eyeing the gargantuan sweets market in India – then your business objective is to create additional sales for your manufacturing facility by building a portfolio that is as appealing as sweets. Or if you are an e-commerce player, then your business objective would be to take a share of the large dairy and vegetable market to supplement your growing grocery business.

Business objective puts the firm in a commercial relationship with the outside world, optimally connecting existing capabilities with future potentialities.

From here follows the **marketing objective**, which looks closely at the segment and target audience to connect the consumer need with its appropriate solution. Marketing objective cuts the cloth to the size of the consumer's needs, thereby alluring consumers. The sharper the cut, the better its offering as compared to its competitors.

So, for Asian Paints, the marketing objective is to connect the need of seeking distinction in one's homes (in keeping with '*har ghar kuch kahta hai*') with the innovative idea of ceiling-painting with myriad colours. For the ice-cream company, it's linking the craving for sweets with ice cream through related flavours and imagery. For the e-commerce player, it's to trigger online purchase over offline for all home shopping needs.

Marketing objective clarifies the consumer's need and then introduces the company's product or service as the optimal satisfier of it.

From here, the **communication objective** comes into play. Communication objective drives awareness or consideration or purchase amongst target consumers through a functional reason and an emotional appeal. It takes the marketing objective of connecting need with the consumer one step forward by defining what change in belief or behaviour needs to come about in the consumer to lead to brand adoption.

Following our examples before, Asian Paints would state its communication objective as 'driving awareness of a whole new idea of doing your ceilings with chic designs, so that it mirrors your distinctive personality'. Since the idea is new to the world, it's important to spread awareness first before trials happen. For Mother Dairy ice cream, the objective is to 'drive trials of ice cream amongst experimental sweet-eaters with a unique concept and taste, guaranteed to surprise and delight incomparably'.

For the e-commerce player, it's 'driving preference for Flipkart in every grocery purchase in households because of sheer convenience, range and value, thereby setting you free from daily chores'.

From here begins the chase to zero down on the single overriding communication objective (SOCO) so that the client's desperate laundry list of demands is pruned to that one thing that will set the consumer running towards the brand's consideration or trial. Since this cannot be researched, a battle of 'cold' strategy and 'warm' creative ensues, with the client and the agency taking position on opposite sides. To resolve this amicably, one last academic step needs to be invoked: this is the advertising brief that will bring peace to the office so that the market can be set on fire.

Advertising Brief: Positioning Exploded

Most agencies and clients have secret advertising brief templates that are zealously guarded as intellectual pills of great value. But very often, they simply spell out the following ground rules before the creative acquires escape velocity. As can be seen in the details below, elements of the advertising brief lay out the positioning of the brand with a microscope.

- The landscape and brand opportunity: What's happening to other brands in the category that is leaving a nice gap in the need-states for our brand to mop up gleefully, in a manner better and bigger than others?
- Communication task: From the above, what must be said that links the gap in the consumer's need with the brand's answer? And in doing so creates a reaction which either drives awareness of the new product/service of the brand or causes the trial of the new idea for the first time or affirms an existing behaviour, thereby entrenching loyalty.

- Functional reason: The specific product benefit that makes brand adoption/retention compelling.
- Emotional reason: What tugs at the heartstrings, enchaining consumers with positive emotions.
- Brand essence: How this ties up with the core of the brand promise (more in the chapter on brands), ensuring that consumers are delighted with the quality and consistency.
- Big Idea: This sets all the elements chiming in unison with a succinct expression that –
    - is up the consumer's alley, reflecting his life and his expression of it without being make-believe.
    - is insightful, says what the consumers truly feel, even if they are not able to articulate it themselves; sometimes it even invokes universal human values, thereby making it deeply resonant.
    - is distinctive, tells the familiar in an unfamiliar way or tells the unfamiliar in a familiar way, either way resulting in a delightful discovery.
    - is a solution to the current tension.
    - is sticky, makes you want it again.
    - is actionable, causes a desirable change in behaviour.

If a brief is written well, is the Big Idea a fait accompli? No, a clear brief just clears up the clutter of confusing noises so that a clear answer has no choice but to emerge. The diamond is yet to be crafted but the unpolished stone is gleaming in sight and the creatives have the tools to go after it, fully focused and without distractions.

Even though the process above is tedious and stressful when creative is wanted 'as of yesterday', its academic intensity ought not to be short-changed. When all things are considered, funnily enough, only one thing remains to be said. Not because it's one of the many things, but because it's the one that sums up the many. Now, the fluffy cotton ball of whirring business ideas at the beginning of brief writing has become a taut thread, ready to be merrily tossed into the warp and weft of a creative pattern.

Big Idea

The Big Idea is the seed of the above processes, rearing to be thrown into the soil to branch out into a resplendent tree. What are the best examples globally? Below are a few inspiring call-outs:

Google: The world's information organized so it's universally accessible and useful.

Amazon: A place where people can come and discover anything to buy.

Southwest Airlines: The low-cost airline.

Nike: Brings inspiration and innovation to every athlete in the world (from Nike's perspective, if you have a body, you are an athlete).

Facebook: Empowers people to share and make the world more open and connected.

eBay: Provides a global online marketplace where practically anyone can trade practically anything, enabling economic opportunity around the world.

All the Big Idea examples empower consumers, enabling them to reach a place in the future where unrealized dreams may be realized. They provide consumers with tools, ideas or just inspiration to connect with their desirable experience.

The Big idea has overlaps in part with the vision and positioning statements of companies and brands. This can happen when objectives of a company get refined and its expression becomes succinct. These are a few Big Ideas that we have figured or constructed based on their work:

Bingo: Brings comic disruption to life's mundanities with zingy tastes.

Parachute: Gives everyone a chance to groom beyond themselves.

Pepsi: Gives the youth the confidence to stand and live for what they believe in, notwithstanding the world.

ACC cement: Brings solidity to construction no less than the bond that cements Indian relationships.

Britannia: Creates healthy food that enriches the body and the soul.

Dettol: Assures protection against outside threats to physical well-being.

Johnson and Johnson: A mother's partner in raising her infant.

Dabur: Provides Ayurvedic benefits to modern living.

Samsung: Ushers in future capabilities today through the gift of technology.

LG: Enhances life with easy and reliable tools for good living.

Mentos: Sparks new ideas even where it's least possible.

Fevicol: Provides sticking options that are, well … simply irreversible.

Some of the Big Ideas above will set the creative juices flowing at the mere start of the briefing, some will lead up to multiple requests for a coffee break. And when creatives do come out, a client-agency impasse follows, relived by Ogilvy's lines: *

'If the client groans and moans, show his logo.

* Ogilvy, David. *Ogilvy on Advertising*, USA, Prion, 2014.

If he is still refractory, show his factory.'

Following the rigorous briefing session as outlined before ticking the box on stickiness, uniqueness, truthfulness and actionability – the attributes of Big Idea as explained before – the child is ready to be born.

Creative Expression

Creative expression is subjective as hell. However, there are some dos and don'ts that ensure that maximum people are turned on by the creative output of the communication. A skeleton on which creatives can be mounted emerges. It has the following elements.

It begins with the condition that whatever is creative has to seem real, so much so that that the story must feel personal. It must speak to every individual seeing, hearing, reading or remembering the creative expression, even though it is broadcast on mass media.

The next breakthrough for creative expression happens when an emotional block in the consumer is opened, leading to a release of emotions; even a gentle tug will do, but the path of impact is invariably through the consumer's heart. So when the competitors come calling with a superior or more logical proposition, it makes no impact because consumers have transcended beyond logic to cavort with you already.

To release the block and usher in the brand (as relief and the antidote), it needs to unearth biases and either support them or counter them. But for resonance, it must dive deep with the consumers first and at all levels.

- *Individual bias*: That fairness has a correlation with confidence (tackled by Fair & Lovely), not going for made-up appearances but natural beauty (for those who advocate natural beauty, like Dove) or a counter against flamboyance as an essential trait to win over the opposite sex (like in the Sprite campaign, 'Clear *hai*').

- *Cultural bias*: Insistence on low costs of maintenance (adverts around the fuel economy with respect to bikes and cars) or painting the outer walls of your house to impress your neighbours during Diwali (Asian Paints campaign).
- *Social bias*: Against political apathy (*'Jaago re'* campaign of Tata Tea, which uses its brand proposition figuratively to build towards a brand idea), or countering female infanticide (done by the same brand). Idea's recent campaign upholding the rights of women to defend themselves and the rights of LGBTQ+ groups to express themselves uninhibitedly.

Insight, both mined and expressed, by great creatives must look at various departments of creativity to craft their stories with distinction. Here, Bollywood and popular folk culture start to peep through because they reflect and shape the experience of consumers in celluloid. It's no surprise then that a battery of elements in the creative bouquet are mixed and matched for delighting a consumer.

- *Music*: Soft, reflective, lingering, melodious, uplifting, strident, jarring, disruptive or silent to complement the copy.
- *Casting*: From good-looking people to everyday people to weird people to forgotten actors to celebrities.
- *Visuals*: Retro, chic, contemporary, aspirational or western, ethnic, techno-futuristic, limbo, stark, sunny, dark and brooding or diffused, a panorama of lights, locations, camera filters and camera treatment (high-speed, candid-jerky, slick-cuts). The options are mind-boggling.
- *Post-treatment*: Once the film is made, editors and special effect folks gleefully descend to cut computer graphics (CG) for product shots with seductive appeal (use of glycerine drops on Cola bottles to make it look dew-dropped and frosted to uncooked rice for Basmati brands to the use of

potato paste posing as ice cream under heat-generating lights – the bag of production tricks to create what is sublime from absolutely nothing is unlimited).

- *Voice-overs*: From sweet canoodling to gruff to admonishing to baritone male to assuring female to child-like to folksy – it's amazing how consumer responses differ dramatically with different renditions of the same dialogues.
- *Editing*: The packaging of it all into a nifty 10/20/30/45/60 seconds, designed to touch the consumers' hearts while also reminding them of the functionalities of a brand. Now, with digital GIFs, statics and carousels, the creatives have fragmented, and speaking to an attention-challenged consumer has become even more demanding.

However, even if these are all top class, marketers and creative heads may end up with a dud. The storytelling, much like in the case of a feature film, has to be impeccable.

The best and the mightiest creatives were chosen and the following patterns emerged.

All-time Creative Greats

Creative agencies and marketers routinely huddle together to wow their consumers. Statistically, however, they fail more often than they succeed. Analysis shows that the fuzzy method to winning hearts falls under following categories:

Twisters: These ads tell a simple tale but add a twist at the end, turning the ordinary into a riot. Advertisements like 'One black coffee please' (a lecherous executive getting his due when he is mistaken for a waiter by a sophisticated lady in the Ericsson TV creative) or '*Dimaag ki batti jala de*' (twisting an entry into a classroom as an exit by a smart aleck student walking in backwards, made by mouth freshener, Mentos) lead to consumers looking forward to the ad – this is the ultimate high.

QQ factor: The higher the 'quirky quotient', the more the people will notice it and the more it will be recalled. From '*Beta sweater peheno*' in the commercial for Polo, the mint with the hole (exaggerating a pointless feature, endlessly), to the over-emphasized huffing of the pug from Hutch to the 'ZooZoos' of Vodafone – choosing one odd aspect of a creative plan and cranking it up delivers thumbs up from viewers, time after time.

Exaggerators: Consumers are won over with unabashed hyperbole. Happydent, with its gleaming human teeth lighting up the royal corridors to Fevicol's claim of sticking anything together to the romantic conquest of Axe – they all remind us that the greater the exaggeration, the greater the mirth as consumers feel as if they have connived with the advertisers.

Jingly tunes: Consumers follow jingles like a spell if advertisers stay loyal to it – ad after ad. From Maggi to Titan Sonata to 'Washing powder Nirma' or '*Hamara* Bajaj' – these jingles have to just begin with a few notes and consumers chime in; a sheer client's delight because they deliver more for less.

Cause hunters: Think of '*Jaago re*' of Tata tea or '*Kya idea hai, sir ji*' of the Idea telecom service – these campaigns promise to change society. Because the cause is bigger, the attention from the consumers is disproportionate.

Emotional teasers: Whether it's fear that's triggered by the heart-friendly Saffola oil, backed by the holy and pious science of polyunsaturated fatty acids (PUFA) and monounsaturated fatty acids (MUFA), or whether it is the 'neighbour's envy, owner's pride' of Onida, or romance as in '*Kuch khaas hai hum sabhi mein*' in Cadbury's iconic Dairy Milk advertisement, which is easily the most-recalled advert to date, basic human emotions, when deftly scratched, can drive brand choice beyond reason.

Celebrity dazzlers: Bollywood casting works. Top it with a celebrity's acting prowess and the small screen turns into a cinemascope. Be it the multiple renditions of '*Thanda matlab Coca-Cola*' garnished with the acting prowess of Aamir Khan or the '*Filmi sitaron ka soap*', featuring the who's who of Bollywood, nothing glues eyeballs to the screen like celebrity presence.

Cheeky counters: As competitors slug it out, brilliant creativity sprouts. 'Nothing official about it' from Pepsi to the 'All taste, no gyan' of Sprite – cheeky ads invariably tickle consumers and cause the intended brand change.

Cute capers: Just pure and spontaneously cute – the kid from 'Petrol *khatam nahi hunda*' of Maruti to the Johnson's gurgling kids to the '*Jab mein chota bacha tha*', viewers just love the endearing lens.

Functional bashers: The benefit-espousing, brand-in-a-second kind of creatives pelt our screens like shooting body pain. But they are no less valuable because they drive the message of the brand clearly even if they are not fun to watch.

Flipping through pages of history, it would appear that adverts have a high chance of clicking with the consumer if they fall into one of the ad archetypes above. If not, consumers are going to use the advertisement break for their convenience, wasting millions of the client's cash. To raise your noise above the clutter, everyone has to rise above, queering their pitch on one of the above creative levers; even if in the process, they end up adding to the noise rather than making others redundant. This is advertising-very cluttered yet offering scope for brands to stand out.

Storytelling With a Brand

There is an emerging consensus that brands should be communicated like a story to one's consumers and customers for creating an impact and promoting empathy. This notion could not have come at a more opportune time than now because it amalgamates the history of Indian art, which is pivoted around the elaborate tradition of '*nautanki*' or a song-and-dance show, with the necessities of modern commercial realities.

While Indians are naturally good at storytelling, some mandatory steps have been delineated here to maximize success. Storytelling is as much about saying what is required as it is about leaving out redundancies. In India, where there is commotion everywhere and noise is a natural part of the environment, creating room for empty space in one's narrative becomes critical to making a consumer pause, look and register the import of a brand's message.

How do we make a powerful message with only a few words and pictures? How can we imply more by saying less? In other words, how do we achieve a good story, which Alfred Hitchcock defined as a 'life with the dull bits cut out'.

Donald Miller, in his book *Building a StoryBrand,** has detailed the features of good storytelling. These are,

1. **Character**: This refers to the sharp reason for telling a story. Here, the consumer's ambitions have to be pared down to the focusing areas since, sometimes, even the consumer or customer is not clear about his/her needs. Various needs that have been identified in the previous sections must be clarified. For example,

   i. Insurance: trouble-free retirement plans

---

* Miller, Donald. *Building a StoryBrand: Clarify Your Message So Customers Will Listen*, USA, HarperCollins, 2017.

ii. Restaurant: big on an eating experience, big on frills, surprisingly short on bills

iii. Nutrition bars: better nutrition with no hidden negatives like fat, salt and sugar

iv. Real estate: houses that look as good on paper, delivered as committed on paper

The winning character definition grabs the primary purpose of the consumer's search and addresses it squarely, over all the piffling distractions. Also, whether it exists or not, good storytelling requires that a 'story gap' is opened or a need is created, which craves the attention of the brand to redeem it – much like the misery exaggerated in Indian films, which necessitates the arrival of the hero.

2. **Problem**: The story gap as identified above needs to be exaggerated to create dissonance to make the indifferent consumer face the grave prospect of ignoring a must. It gives the consumer frustrations a focal point, like the exaggerated prickly germs in their toilets or fuzzy mothballs lingering in the air for air purifiers. Donald calls them 'personified versions of conflict or villains'. However, the villain should be real, relatable, the root cause and singular to be effective. If you spread too many small irritants across the story, you lose the result of a single monstrous enemy. However, the villains are not always external – they can be internal problems as well, like the consumer's self-doubt or apathy. In the case of Saffola cooking oil, the helplessness of a wife in addressing her husband's rising cholesterol is the chief villain that needs to be decimated. In some cases, brands may even take on a philosophical problem, like feeling distinguished and sophisticated in the thoughtful pursuits of their daily struggles in the cerebrally piquing environment of a Starbucks.

3. **Meeting a guide**: Where a brand steps in with empathy and authority to understand and address the problem. Diapers that understand the requirements of baby skincare step in to resolve the mother's deep anxiety about her newborn against the horrifying back side spectacle of eczema. Here, testimonials, statistics and awards come in handy to establish the brand as a trustworthy guide.
4. **Plan**: It encourages the consumer to walk into a brand's world through trial packs, scheduled appointments for a discussion to know the plan, as in the case of insurance or financial processes, test driving a car, a payback or a return policy in the event of dissatisfaction. This serves to remove doubt and mitigate the risk of a wrong decision.
5. **Call to action**: Could be a direct call, something that screams a 'try me now' or 'buy now' button on e-commerce sites. Or it could be a transitional call for free demonstrations, free samples or a trial day at the gymnasium. This allows a brand to build its stature as an authentic partner and create reciprocity with the consumer.
6. **What helps them avoid failure**: Brands ought to explain what would happen if their help is not taken to address the consumers 'so what' question. This is based on the deep-seated consumer insight that consumers are driven by the principle of 'loss aversion'. People are more likely to be driven by what they could lose rather than what they would win, as per the 'prospect theory' argued by Daniel Kahneman in his book *Thinking, Fast and Slow*.* In other words, people hate losing $100 more than winning an equivalent amount. Accordingly, a bit of roused fear is acceptable to change a consumer's attitude, 'Get your home treated for termites to avoid losing your furniture', 'get your heart checked before

---

* Kahneman, Daniel, *Thinking, Fast and Slow*, London, Penguin, 2011.

it's too late', 'drive slow to prevent your dears from waiting forever' and so on are the kinds of stories that could trigger instant action.

7. **What ends in success**: A great story includes a reward after enduring the travails at the end of a story. The typical images of hair being restored or fat-destroying products or services depicting the consumer situation before and after are the best examples. Storytelling must make consumers or customers feel empowered, enhanced, emboldened and closer to their potential than they were at the start of the journey. The brand becomes the focal point of conversion-enabling consumers, from being anxiety-ridden to being confident alongside a shampoo brand, or from being confused and ill-equipped to smart and in control with a home loan. Brands thus emerge as champions.

Advertising Evaluation

Is there a simple way to evaluate advertising? A straightforward grid evaluates an advert with respect to the quality of the impact it generates – ranging from indifference to contagious conversation.

Negative	• Consumers turn against the creative idea • Brand impact is negative
Indifferent	• Advert is recalled, but message recall is faint to nothing • Brand metrics don't move up
Stimulating	• Consumers react with a positive opinion • Brand shows a positive uptick
Change-agent	• Consumers respond with high sales • Brand world-view is embraced and echoed
Contagious	• Deep impact on a loyalist • Contagious conversation is created

Source: Authors

Depending on the quality of the creative, advertisements shape the course of the brand. But are the changes so easily detectable? How long should advertising continue and what impact does it have on the brand's long-term revenue and equity?

How Advertising Works

'Advertising troubles both sociologists and financial directors: the former because they think it works, the latter because they think it does not,' says Byron Sharp. Unfortunately, this can't be directly measured since advertising has a long-term impact and the drop in sales is not immediately noticeable – over a period of time, it impacts a consumer's ability to recall. Advertising works like the engines of a flight: while the engines are running, everything is fine, but when the engine stops, the descent eventually starts. The bigger the brand, the more it has to spend to appeal to a larger number of consumers across various occasions to keep a threshold recall for their market share to hold.

Also, continuous advertising refreshes, reinforces or builds the memory of the brand in the consumer's mind, often subconsciously, and eventually nudges the consumer towards purchasing. On other occasions, it might just work to nullify the impact of competition.

There are a few subtle reasons why advertising works.

It builds stature. Consumers respect advertised brands when compared to those that aren't. In fact, the premium charged by brands that are visible on TV and other media is usually recovered by way of higher consumer disposition to pay more for them, although they may enjoy no functional differentiation over the less visible brands. People also assume that if a brand has the power to advertise, it must be of good quality. Research also shows that people don't believe the explicit messages that the advertisers capture, but decode a general message of quality. Over time, with usage and continuous message being deployed, consumers start to trust the brands as well.

Advertising also builds an image, which makes the products aspirational. For this reason, even luxury brands are advertised on mass media to build desirability in society so that those who can afford to buy them feel truly special in the eyes of those who couldn't. This also creates a long list of potential consumers for premium brands. Those who want an Audi or BMW are far more than those who drive them, but these non-user consumers are not worthless.

Continuous, small-intensity advertising subconsciously predisposes the consumer to purchase. Unfortunately, the gap between seeing a brand and purchasing its product defies all determinism, and this leaves advertisers with no choice but to be omnipresent and continuously seen. Use of a range of brand assets – brand colour, symbol, taglines, consumption visuals, topical messaging linked to call of action, brand ambassador's associations, influencer and blogger reviews – all these help brand recall.

Considering the above, there is a pressing need for distinctiveness, which is to build a set of distinctive assets for the brand that are identification triggers in a crowd and which help to grab market share when the consumer is navigating the category. This helps attract the long tail of the light/occasional consumers who have a weak affiliation with the brand. But for this to happen, the brand should be consistently communicated across different platforms, and repeatedly. Digital marketing requires this even more as brand creatives multiply across various platforms.

Media

When a story is well made, it's as critical that it is also broadcast well. And options of broadcasting have expanded manifold: from the simple TV, radio, print and outdoor bouquet of yesteryears to include various digital formats. How do you cross-compare between options and decide on the best medium? For this, a quick run-through of media fundamentals is warranted.

Reach refers to the total number of audiences that will be delivered a message at least once during a given period of time, through one kind of medium. *Frequency* is the number of such discrete and separate exposures that happen. If you multiply the two, you get a *gross rating point (GRP)*. So, if you cover fifty per cent of your audience five times in the first week of the launch of your new campaign, you achieve 250 GRPs. Across industries, this is a standard way to start a campaign to ensure a 'threshold reach'. With sparse budgets, you can reduce the average creative duration (ACD) of the commercial and reach desired GRP, but the quality of brand recall is adversely impacted.

Through scheduling, you can vary the intensity of the campaign or distribute it evenly. Generally, the campaign is opened with high GRPs – over 200 – and it reduces in the subsequent weeks, before pulsating to a closing high, thereby achieving optimal reach. Once about sixty per cent of the targeted consumers have been reached with a frequency of three to four times, a campaign can be considered to have delivered optimally. A campaign can be run continuously for four to six weeks, or with a gap after four weeks to prolong the life of the campaign, sometimes coinciding with the buying cycle of the product.

But this is just the tip of the iceberg in modern times given the rapidly fragmenting media and even more distracted eyes of the Indian consumers.

Indian Consumer and the Media Options

The Indian consumer is a varied species, appearing diffused and concentrated: of the ninety million urban households, nearly fifty per cent are in the top ten metros, split across different socio-economic classes and family types (joint families are still significant). And being a young country (compared to Japan, where, for simplicity, sixty per cent of the people are above sixty), we have kids and tweens who are not only huge consumers but also significant influencers regarding the purchase of categories they don't directly transact with. The complexity increases exponentially when you consider the massive rural strata.

With so many types of consumers to cater to, it's no surprise that media is fragmented, both horizontally (many of the same kind) and vertically (many of different kinds), grabbing eyes every living minute of a consumer's life. Below are the number of media touchpoints consumers are swamped with.

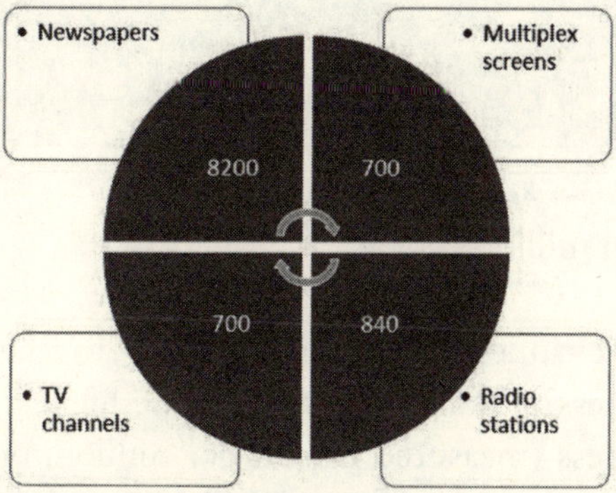

Source: Indian Readership Survey (IRS), 2019 Data

While no single consumer will face all these media vehicles, the increasing penetration of all the media and the fluidity of information among viewers (like seeing print content on TV or watching your favourite TV show late at night on YouTube) means that content is raining – literally everywhere. The current penetration of different media (approximating figures for better comparison) is simply staggering. While there are soon going to be as many phones as the number of people in the country, TV covers nearly half the population and the pay channels – cable and satellite (C&S) and direct-to-home dishes (DTHs) – are about 25–30 per cent of it. High definition TV is increasing rapidly and as a result, smaller or niche brands are often able to satisfy their reach targets without going to standard definition (SD).

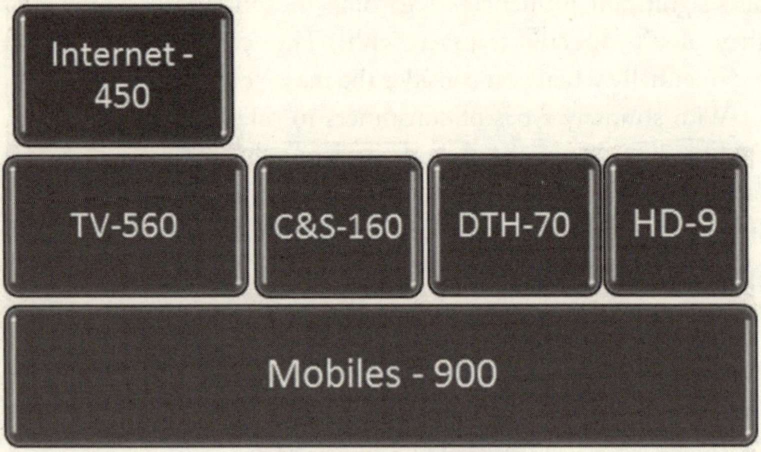

Source: Indian Readership Survey (IRS), 2019 Data

* All figures in million people

How do these channels compare with respect to reach, affinity and cost effectiveness? TV and digital score the highest on reach and cost effectiveness (measured in cost per million, or CPM, views by target audience). Magazines and dailies, though lower on reach, score better on 'affinity' (this refers to the quality of consumer engagement with the media) than TV because readers assimilate more in print as compared to the distracted nature of watching TV (which is indexed at 100). Cinema scores the highest, indexed at 150, considering the exclusive attention of consumers that it demands, followed by digital at 143 (due to the intimate nature of the medium) and radio at 125 (because while you are stuck in a traffic jam, you have no option but to listen to it).

However, a new kid on the block has been rewriting the media script furiously over the past few years. Digital is shaping the new economy in ways that few can catch up to, even as we barely come to grips with the reality that sits in our rooms, unacknowledged. Sample some of these factoids:

- Facebook has higher reach than the biggest TV channel, Star Plus, as per the graph below (from BARC, FB, YT).

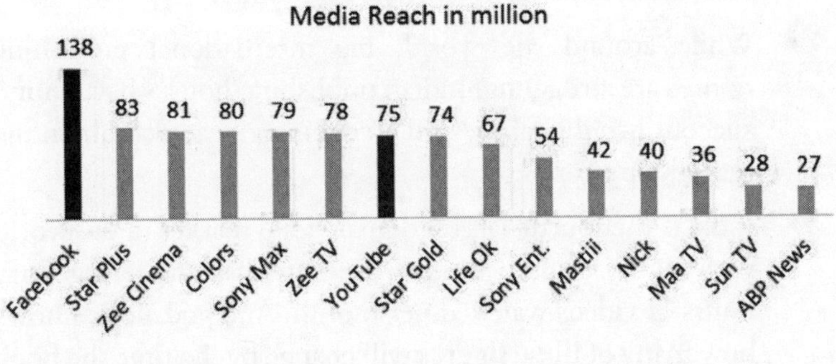

Source: Broadcast Audience Research Council (BARC), 2019 Data

- India has 375 million users, second only to China, growing at 40 per cent.
- India has already become the number one market for Facebook around the world, and others are soon to follow, keeping in mind their already huge consumer base.

Source: Broadcast Audience Research Council (BARC), 2019 Data

- India has over one billion mobile connections, which means that the penetration gap is narrowing.
- Online shoppers are expected to be around 175 million by 2020. Amazon already has a monthly user base of 38 million.

- Mobile TV has over 12 million consumers, even though this baby has just been born.
- Radio has 47 per cent listeners on mobile.
- While around the world, big international publishing houses are struggling, Indian publishing houses have found succour in a digital age and are seeing a steady climb on the readership of apps.
- India is the fourth-largest digital video market in the world with eighty million unique users, with a staggering forty hours of videos watched per month. And god alone knows how many of these figures will change by the time the book goes into print and is read by you.
- As per the TRAI: NASSCOM report 2016, the Indian digital market is slated to grow exponentially as the figures below reflect the future.

Figures in million users	2016	2020
Internet users	375	730
E-comm. consumers	75	175
Online transactions	618	2000

While mobiles drive the growth (smartphone usage is up from 160 million in 2013 to 640 million in 2016) and connectivity poses problems (not in remote towns like Shimla, but in dense urban epicentres like Nehru Place, Delhi), Wi-Fi is now spreading beyond Starbucks and regular office internet.

Wherever you go, whatever you do, time spent away from a screen is increasingly getting more and more scarce, and media houses, while they decry the fragmentation and the associated uncertainties, privately confess that they have never had it as exciting as it is now.

Digital, as a medium of communication, is now driving content and even creative strategy. For the new fragmented India, digital offers the boon of context and behaviour marketing that was never possible before, but not before morphing marketing into a whole new science and art, as we will see on the chapter on digital marketing.

9

Brand

I remember my brand manager asking me once, frustrated on seeing that odious buy one, get one (BOGO) sign of our competitor: 'Can we do anything against this slaughter? Brands hardly matter to consumers these days.'

'We have to stay focused on how we meet our consumers' needs better,' I answered. 'We will last longer,' I added, feeling my voice fade away.

'But all that consumers care about is the price. A good deal. They love it.' His voice only thinly disguised a cry.

'We have slipped up on our need-satisfaction to become vulnerable to pricing. It's time to revisit our proposition from scratch.'

'It's tough. We're getting commoditized. Now only the price matters.'

'Brands are built on differentiated benefits – irreplaceable opportunities for consumers to enhance their lives, and finally even fulfil their higher order benefits, if brands are insightful and empathetic towards their patrons.' I offered a host of possibilities we could be exploring instead of getting into a price war on the retail shelf.

'How are we ever going to start a new conversation when competitors are pulling down the value of the category every day,' he protested.

'Brick by brick – building brands is like that.' I put on a wan smile of encouragement, without deluding him in anyway. Big brands do outlast alluring promotion winds, but it takes a lot of investment in the brands.

Brand, Brand Everywhere, but Is There One Really?

What a stethoscope is to a doctor, a brand is to the marketer. It measures how the consumer's heart beats for his product. From a company's perspective, if you listen closely, you might hear the cash registers ringing. If you listen intently, you might even figure out for how long it will ring.

Understanding a brand requires determining what it isn't. It's a bit like the way Krishna explains the nature of the soul in the Gita by choosing to spell out what it isn't over what it is to dispel all mis-impressions, ultimately leading Arjun to the truth.

Brand isn't a commodity: It's not another pack of rice or phone or facial cream – it's Kohinoor basmati rice or an Oppo phone or Boroline. Brands deliver so consistently on what the consumers expect that they can't be replaced by another brand from the category easily. Whether in terms of quality, trust or utility, brands eliminate the repeated evaluation of products to instil blind adoption so that there is only a thrill and no surprises at the end of the consumption.

Brand isn't benefits: If brand benefits are replicated by another proximal brand in the same category or a distant brand in another category, can the brand be replaced? Not really, unless the brand is weak. There is a legacy of usage, a history of experience and a trail of association that soaks brands with inexplicable stickiness, making severance difficult. Other brands may shave beards as well or soothe your throat just fine, but would a consumer switch just because he has understood the generic benefit of the category?

The answer is no, because new alternatives have no history, whereas brands have highs, even lows, having grown up with the consumers.

Brand isn't a form: So, if benefits are not the real deal, does brand power sit in the form and its iconography? Take, for instance, the iconic bottle of Coke or Perrier, the Parle-G or Amul kid, the Air India mascot, the timeless bottles of Hamdard's Safi or the trademark stinging smell of Dettol. But logos change, glass bottles turn into plastic and the brand still persists. In fact, when Oreo goes into a milkshake and loses its shape, the brand gets blessed with extended usage. When Dettol gets extended to soaps with neither the sting nor the familiar dissolving cloud in the water, you know the brand substance is beyond form.

Brand isn't an association: A brand often becomes associated with a ritual, a partner or an occasion accomplice. Snickers is associated with hunger, Fair & Lovely with an indispensable aid to manage a good impression during an interview or a date or Dabur Chyawanprash as a preventive intake during the first whiff of winter – these are seminal to the brand but do not become equable with it.

Brand isn't irreplaceable: Even with high market shares, brands don't become completely irreplaceable. Consumers do occasionally dabble with alternatives, but that doesn't mean that their brand loyalty is dead. You can come back to it or relegate it to a more preferred usage, and the brand health only moves a notch up. You may try a beverage other than your favourite Cola or another shoe polishing format that is not available in Cherry Blossom or Ola versus Uber on a few occasions, but would it mean that your favourite brand is becoming a commodity? Not necessarily, unless you consider meeting another friend a threat to an existing friendship every time. Consumers will and do flirt with other brands, but *what they favour and identify with most often* decides brand loyalty, not an eternal choiceless relationship.

Brand isn't trust alone: It's much more than that. Trustworthy brands may come to stand for a set of rigid values, allowing little flexibility to change in accordance with evolving times. Brands must be able to surprise, delight and occasionally trump consumer expectation, and that is just not possible if every manifestation of it can be predicted and, therefore, trusted. You cannot trust if you don't know what you are trusting. Brands that are very linear can be better trusted than those that keep turning up with new variations. Since variation is important to stay relevant, trustworthiness on a set of known usages and attributes can become a serious handicap. Hush Puppies can launch a leather wallet or purse as conveniently as shoes and needn't be distrusted. Or, on a slightly more provocative note, Fevicol can launch relationship-binding counselling and have consumers line up expectantly. Trust is tied to a form and usage, and strong brands will challenge that because their strength comes from being able to delight consumers with better and bigger solutions to need-satisfaction – not predictable solutions which lead to the atrophying of consumer interests.

Brand isn't a friend only: Friends make us comfortable because they help us connect, relate to and make sense of our lives. But for the most part, they don't drag us where we are not comfortable. In contrast, brands show up in areas where we least expect them to because they often know our needs better than us. They are like our friends in listening to us, but they can also be like our parents in providing for our needs even before we feel them or are ready to express them. We don't imagine the apps that crowd our smart screens, but we still find them immensely useful. Caramel ice cream with sea salt or chocolate with chilly is unimaginable till we taste them. Brands that think ahead of consumer needs have an edge and transform from being friends to guardians, parents and counsels.

Before we decode the core kernel of the brand, evaluating the brand market and typifying it will help us tag it with appropriate labels. Then, we might be better placed to sift the gold after ridding ourselves of the dross.

Types of Brands

Heritage brands: They owe their equity and raison d'etre to being around for long. We have quietly reasoned that if they have survived for long, they must be good. Think of Colgate Dental Cream, Dabur Janam Ghutti, Hamdard Rooh Afza, Charminar cigarettes or LIC's Jeevan Dhara policy. They are trusted for their core functionality, often becoming synonymous with it, but, like grandparents at home, they can be taken for granted. If a more fashionable brand positions them as fuddy-duddy, they may be abandoned with ease. Unless they translate the heritage into a virtue, like Dabur Chyawanprash, or have product propositions that require stubborn sameness, like Safi and Boroline, they will become antiquated. Outside India, Tabasco and Marmite are excellent examples of how heritage can be cast in stone even for the future, without the threat of falling into oblivion.

Edgy brands: They are at the forefront of embracing change. MTV and Pepsi are brands that adapt constantly, reflecting the changing aspirations of their target audience viz. youth. They are choice-driven by the people whom they are bound to truthfully represent. However, too frequent a change without being fulcrumed on a core set of beliefs can create schizophrenia, making change not a productive reflex but a hapless twitch. Changing occasionally is fine, but when the balance is lost, the tell-tale signal is the ever-changing logo or the packaging of a brand.

Stolid brands: They stand for only one thing and nothing else, irrespective of the winds of change. Bata shoes, Indian Oil and Indian Railways will give consumers the comfort of tradition and constancy even if they are imperilled to extinction due to this. So long as there are consumers who like that, no problem is expected. But there is no guarantee that the number of such consumers will not decline.

Wannabe brands: They seem to try hard but don't quite have the stature to gain respect – these are me-too replicas and brands that mushroom during festivals, seasons or around events. Over time, consumers will prefer them but will not accord them the stature that regular brands command with ease.

Marquee brands: They strut the high streets of shopping with arrogance, sparking envy amongst the uninvited – premium and extravagant brands that are not necessarily expensive but represent peripheral needs rather than basic ones. From Swarovski to grooming parlours for males (as an extreme example) to cufflinks, these brands are maybe known to many, but are only used by a few. Through their exclusivity and inaccessibility, these brands often choose their customers.

Pedestrian brands: The pedestrian brands for the masses (which are watered-down versions of the main brands and not necessarily customized for the popular section they represent), such as Nirma, Dabur Red tooth powder, Lifebuoy, Parle-G and Tata Salt – these brands satisfy many, and in doing so, walk perilously close to being the commodities they narrowly differentiate with respect to.

Opportunistic brands: These expand into the next most attractive segment, disregarding what they are good at – Tata Salt to Tata Realty, Godrej locks to Godrej soaps. 'If they are in so many categories, they must be okay' is the feeling that invites the implicit faith of the consumers they draw their usage from. A lot of Indian companies with cash, but no long-term direction, end up falling into this cash trap.

While marketers aspire to create iconic brands, they find their brands belonging to one of the above types. So, what makes successful brands iconic? Taking a few examples, such as Dettol, Big Bazaar, Haldiram's and Fabindia across a broad spectrum, we can uncover the basic DNA of iconic brands.

Ensuring Success with Brands

Owning category prime benefit: All iconic brands over-index on the core benefit of the category they reside in. Dettol is for uncompromising protection against germs, Big Bazaar is for value grocery purchasing, Maruti for dependable and economical private transportation, Haldiram's for varied Indian snacking and meals, and Fabindia for quality and a fashionable Indian take on apparel. If you took a poll regarding what in the categories of infection-prevention, organized retailing, mobility, eating out and clothing mattered the most, these brands would rate high.

Benefit singularity: These brands have not only gotten the core benefit right, but, through constant innovation and communication, have stayed right on course without drifting towards other attractions. So Haldiram's, like McDonald's, has stayed on top of its core values of cleanliness, service and value. This is despite their huge expansion. It has also not expanded its menu beyond some seasonal favourites, thereby consolidating the back-end supply chain like McDonald's and providing consistency. These companies know their core competence and prefer to stay entrenched in it, rather than flirt all over.

Quality commitment: This seems obvious, but it cannot be emphasized more – top brands are obsessive about meeting their consumers' needs – Maruti with its rugged, dependable fare across all sections of cars; Haldiram's with sublime palate satisfaction; and Big Bazaar with one value-related offer after another, tiding the rough retail winds, including e-commerce. Quality may be the hygiene factor and gets taken for granted, but is an absolute must to get started.

Stretching core benefit: Iconic brands know what they stand for and extend it to their other areas with ease, without losing their focus. Dettol moves from antiseptic liquids to soaps and shaving creams and gains not just additional business but enhanced equity as well. Big Bazaar extends from grocery to apparel, benefiting the common man with value here as well.

We have seen what brands are not and what they are. But what is it that attracts the right elements and repels the avoidable?

At the heart of the brand, much like a human being, stands its values – what it stands for at all times and what gives it that certainty and solidity, that we recognize in humans as a basic and unalterable personality. Values are driven by a core philosophy that drives a brand's endeavours to create products and services, capitalizing on opportunity after opportunity, overcoming difficulty after difficulty and dodging what doesn't add up to the need-state – it is committed to serving its consumers fervently. This is the gist of the brand and its essence.

Brand essence: This sits at the intersection of what companies can do well and what consumers want. What consumers want has to do with how brands help them come out on top against their emotional, everyday struggles. Some examples of words that help consumers better their environment are the first part of the brand essence, and can be called enablers. Typical examples of enablers that fire the brand essence are as follows:

- To empower
- To give confidence

- To help overcome
- To change
- To manage
- To win
- To grow
- To accelerate
- To instil
- To inspire
- To create

From enablers flow the need-states that consumers can hope to meet through access to brands. If we refer to Maslow's grid and its manifestations on either side of fear and delight, we come to a range of emotions that tend to be universal. They work across cultures and can be subdivided into the following:

- Individual–basic
    - Hunger: satiation, indulgence
    - Safety: physical well-being, feeling of being at ease
    - Physical: attractive, fit, impactful
    - Family: caring, giving, protecting, providing, belonging
- Social
    - Status: recognition, awards, titles, fame, respect, admiration
    - Influence: power
    - Domination: aggression, winning (even when it is vindictive)
    - Romance: love, sex, desired, lustful

    - In-group: bonding, fun, relationships (at work, social), community member
    - Out-group: exclusivity, distinction
- Individual–advanced
    - Exploration: discovery, creativity, self-expression
    - Ideals: equity, justice, probity, freedom
    - Meaning: purpose, goal-seeking
    - Order: beauty, security, stability, self-assured
    - Peace: tranquillity, harmony, relaxation

Brand essence must *enable* the need-satisfaction of consumers along the above lines. A few examples, but without referring to brands yet, could be as follows:

- To empower one to achieve a certain status
- To provide the opportunity to satisfy cravings
- To encourage the building of communities
- To explore one's creative urges
- To support the bringing about of stability
- To help lead growth
- To enable one to find freedom
- To provide avenues to live fuller lives

One can spot the clear brand opportunity that consumers truly care about. If companies are able to cater to what consumers want, instead of trying to retrofit themselves with contrived needs, they will have a better opportunity to click with their consumers.

This is how the brand essence comes into play:

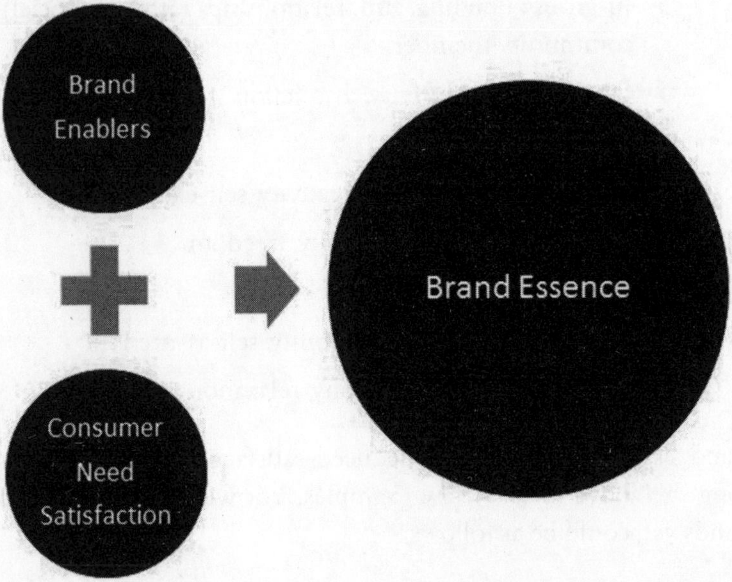

Source: Authors

As an example, we could now add brands to the above statement and imbue them with a particular meaning, thereby building a brand essence. To empower one to achieve status, through *the way you look and feel*: Raymond. To provide the opportunity to satisfy cravings through *unbeatable chocolate desserts*: Cadbury's Dairy Milk. To encourage *communities of the like-minded and the striving*: Bajaj Pulsar (like the Harley Group). To explore one's creative urge with *writing instruments*: Camlin. To bring stability through *structures that makes the bedrock of relations*: ACC cement. To find freedom, with *nothing to hold me back*: Stayfree. To live fuller with *my best look forward*: Nivea.

Now, there are a few clear advantages in writing the brand benefits in this manner, as outlined below:

a) It's written in keeping with the consumer's interest. All statements above could have been written directly as, to achieve status, satisfy cravings, build communities and so on, but that would be an exaggerated claim that lacks authenticity. The thought, on the contrary, is to empower consumers with the opportunity of meeting their need-states with the brand in tow. This way, the consumers can sit at the front wheel and the brand takes the back seat, happy to support the consumer's aspirations.

b) The need-states are not operating at the feature-benefit level of Maslow, but are operating at the higher order, going all the way to the top rung of self-actualization. In the above examples, the italicized portion refers to what the brand is currently focusing on with their given product range. But should it decide to go beyond the existing product range, the same philosophy should enable it to do so with ease, without any internal conflict or external consumer dissonance. Thus, Camlin's core need-state is satisfaction, which is aligned with expression and creativity. Its brand essence allows it go into curating and promoting art from a brand that produces writing instruments. Nivea is about living fuller lives – whatever that may entail – and not merely selling creams. If it desires to expand into grooming parlours, that should pose no difficulty. By focusing on the core need-state that forms the brand's bullseye, its enablers unshackle the business from the existing product format and allow it to look beyond.

To come back to our earlier question – what are brands all about? The answer tends to become somewhat abstract in the final analysis. Brand essence, then, is the philosophy of the brand, which helps the consumers meet their desired need-states at all levels. The greater and more completely it satisfies the need-states, the stronger it becomes. But for that to happen, the brand should connect at the core need-level and not walk away when its basic product or service level need has been met.

Now that we have a good brand, how do we create brands that receive love? What is the road to becoming iconic, cult-like brands? More importantly, how do we create brands that are made in India or adapted in India for our tricolour nation? As we delved deeper, we realized that a whole new brand building framework has to be made for India, rooted squarely within India.

10

Cult Brands

'Can we make our brand into a cult? What is the next big step to greatness?' He looked at the dipping sun against the jagged Gurugram skyline, feeling philosophical after a month of good sales. This was the same brand manager who had earlier been frustrated by dipping sales, following the competitor's BOGO.

'Time to think beyond products, benefits, even emotions. Time to dig deeper.' He exhorted himself without waiting for an answer from me.

Success creates its own momentum and brands acquire their own velocity when consumers love them.

When brands become dear, how do we make them so close to consumers that they start to represent them? Like when our daughter, Rishni, remarks about her favourite bag brand: 'This is very me.'

Brands Are Us

Brands are, in the final analysis, an interaction between the manufacturer and the consumer with need-satisfaction as the bridge. With the brand's claim plotted on a y-axis and the consumer response on an x-axis, we get four levels of the brand. Also, since brands in India are increasingly speaking the language of their consumers and not merely retro fitting Western labels, we have chosen an Indian nomenclature, as shown below:

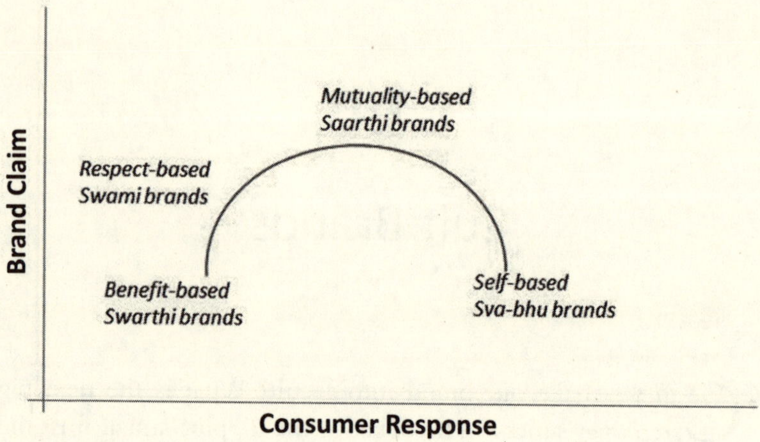

Source: Authors

***Swarthi* brands**: Brand > Consumer. Emotion: apathy

These brands are based on feature-benefits, where the brands are bigger than the consumers and in an unequal relationship. Most brand noise that catches your ears would fall into this category as it constitutes a one-way monologue from the manufacturer's trumpet into indifferent, and even annoyed, ears of consumers. Brand communication (like 'buy now', 'try me', 'don't miss out', 'first use, then believe' kind of statements) and products that continue their one-way communication from the brand, sit in this quadrant. As the consumer's will is poorly represented, these are, in a sense, selfish or *swarthi*, and the quality of emotion between them and the consumer is asymmetrical, like in a traditional Indian household led by a dominant male, apathetic to his partner. Staples, textiles and construction material are the categories where these brands slink into our homes unguarded, utilizing our indifference to them.

***Swami* brands**: Brand > Consumer. Emotion: respect, and sometimes admiration borne from it.

The brand continues to be superior to the consumer in a sense, but the earlier one-sided brand relationship tends to acquire some respectability and receives the first blush of love, as in old Indian marriages, where the husband (*pati-dev*) is respected as a lord (*swami*) before he is loved. Monolithic Indian brands, like Tata, ITC, Aditya Birla Group, Maruti, Lifebuoy – these formidable brands make you look up to them in awe and respect. In fact, the mere labelling of these brands on the categories they are not remotely associated with receives trials, like Godrej real estate or Tata Salt. They are hugely beneficial for launches in new categories and are an absolute media delight since they lend themselves to so much synergy in communication; the brand custodians of these brands are also corporate affairs managers.

***Saarthi* brands**: Brands = Consumer. Emotion: love, mutuality

Inequality is replaced by equality and respect gives way to love and admiration, as brands romance the consumer and bear their love marks, becoming what is called cult brands or iconic brands. *Saarthi* means a pal who walks with you. Brands become 'our brands', as consumer and manufacturer are in perfect equality. Like a couple in love, there are moments of cosying up and also moments of feeling ignored, but never moments of estrangement. Conversation between the two is frequent and unconditional – think of the avid fans of Apple queuing up during the wee hours before the store opens, the Nike fitness club members sweating out, T20 aficionados and so on. When things go wrong, they feel cheated and need to be placated and romanced, like a friend.

As the brand grows, consumers get comfortable, tagging themselves as though they were related to the brand or embracing it with full gusto – wearing its t-shirt, displaying its merchandise and memorabilia (Ferrari jackets and denims). Think further of exclusive brands, like Patek

Philippe, Chanel No. 5 or Montblanc pens, and you are entering the haloed portal of brands that make consumers glow. Few Indian brands, like Charagh Din shirts (in olden days), Hush Puppies shoes or Fabindia fabrics, are making a tentative entry into this passion-filled club, but timelessness is another facet of this relationship and many brands fail to create that enduring distinction. Another recent entry into this club could be Chumbak – a stylish brand of apparel and accessories, capturing Indian art with panache and drawing consumers who closely identify with its imagery.

***Sva-bhu* brands**: Consumer > Brand. Emotion: self-expression

Now, here the equation flips. Consumers supersede the brand and lead it, rather than being led by it. In a sense, consumers move from their intense love of a *saarthi* to the need to self-actualize, as in Maslow's hierarchy, as the divide between them and the brand vaporizes. Brands then become the mode of self-expression for consumers as they start to craft the brand's destiny, like it is their own: *sva-bhu* (born by self, not through another).

Brands like Facebook, Instagram and Twitter are the avatars of this new consumer need which seeks to express itself openly, unabashedly and fearlessly in ever growing communities, defying the old groupings of caste, class and religion. In a deeper sense, brands that have embraced this technological leap have co-created the impossible – being hugely individualistic and vastly social in the same breath. From the innards of your being you emote and, within no time, publish and generate empathy. The best of modernity and primordial essences coalesce in one collective whoop of joy – as consumer becomes the master and the brand only a facilitator.

While brands with a technological edge over other, enjoy an inherent advantage in this category as they are able to give consumers both cupboard anonymity and global publicity, this aspect of a consumer relationship has just been revealed to consumers. And the best is yet to come.

The equation between consumer and brand can be summed up like this:

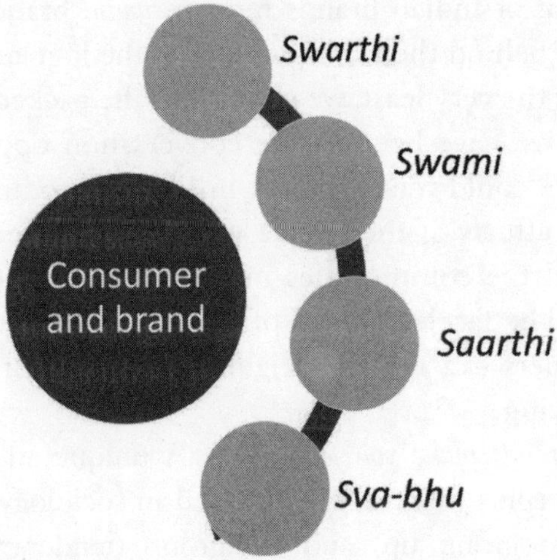

Source: Authors

Let's explore how we can upgrade our brands from *swarthi* to *swami* to *saarthi*, and then from *saarthi* to *sva-bhu*.

From *Swarthi* to *Swami*

This is the easiest transition and can be seen in the move from a brand being a commodity to becoming a packaged brand. Think of the open gunny bags of salt, wheat and rice and compare them with their upgraded versions in plain polythene bags, with a slip of the manufacturer's name and address, and a basic ingredients list. This mere effort, where you declare who you are as a manufacturer and what you have put inside your products, makes the first jump into the branding ladder, from a selfish commodity producer to a brand owner – *swarthi* to *swami*.

From Boss to Pal, from *Swami* to *Saarthi*

Swami brands sit on a pedestal higher than their consumers, demanding their respect like a typicall dominating Indian husband, not a doting one. How does one convert the respect into love and admiration that *saarthi* brands exemplify?

Why a lot of Indian brands remain *swami* brands is because the concept behind their brands stops at the logo and packaging graphics. At the very least, we could turn the packet and see how indifferent we have been to the conversation opportunities at the back. We could travel further inside the product and reveal the earnest efforts of the people who have worked behind the curtains and the communities impacted within the vicinity of the brand. The faceless world of the brand has just opened up and consumers can feel the frigid indifference of these *swami* brands thawing.

Saarthi brands make you feel special: A unique and paradoxical insight underpins this reality, explained in sociology by in-group (tendency to group up) and out-group (tendency to exclude others) tendencies. All of us like to be different from the masses. Yet, if we go too far with that idea, we would be isolated maniacs. So, whether we realize it or not, we also want to be in the same space, participating in like-minded communities. *Saarthi* brands help us both segregate from the rest and aggregate with desirable feel-alikes. Oprah makes a club of book readers and divides people into those who read and those who don't, but not before creating a huge aspiration about reading and empowering yourself. Apple's Macintosh allows you to look and feel different with funky translucent plastic cases. The Beetle looks more human from the front than its sleek, aerodynamic peers, at a price which proudly spells out, 'I only paid so much.' Or consider the Linux operating system, with a cute and friendly Penguin as its mascot against the overbearing techie logos of Microsoft.

Saarthi brands, by virtue of being vastly and insanely different, grant their adopters a glow which puts others in a shade.

How many Indian non-luxury brands do this? Titan's Raga collection for him and her draws couples in. Tata Starbucks gives you an environment to be yourself at leisure, yet feel very special with jazz and a whipped-up glass. Fabindia excites you with the possibility of redoing your home and your clothes while celebrating India. Amazon opens the global galleries so that you can be different, while having the option to return your order if it turns out to be like everyone else's. But the list soon starts to dry up.

Saarthi brands are interesting: Like best friends, they not only make us feel secure but also push us to aspire for more. Beetle cars and the iconic Star Trek series had a lousy start, but they stuck to their guns till the people they reached out to became brand evangelists and started working for them, almost bailing them out of their initial teething troubles. How often do Indian brands get into conversations with their early adopters and loyalists? How many Indian brands are truly unique and popular, and how many are just well known because they deliver the basic minimum at the lowest cost? In a country where the spending power was initially low, we have gotten used to making brands that deliver a basic minimum to the maximum number of people. In the future, this approach will do little as consumers look for interesting brand ideas, refusing to smile at the obvious benefits. And when brands do start with new ideas, they must seek the support of their early patrons to get the word around.

Saarthi brands have fun and make a life statement: They help consumers fulfil the dream of self-empowerment and self-expression, which is the higher order of Maslow. Apple turned computers from a forbidding number-crunching machine into a platform to plan your work and have fun with friendly virtual repositories for storing music, pictures and doodling with your creativity. Oprah's show, while greatly empowering, was also great fun to associate with, because it felt like every person's story with a positive twist. In fact, they have so much fun that they make monuments out of it. Disney's theme park is a good example of how cartoons have been given a real-life destination. Whispers connects with teen girls through their 'Like a girl' campaign, allaying fear and providing self-assurance during the crucial years of puberty.

Popular brands like Lay's and Bingo could extend their fun franchises with restaurants or parks that enhance the brand experience while also creating great opportunities for live interactions with them, like Harley's managers routinely do at the rallies sponsored by them.

Saarthi brands have evangelists: Consumers enter into a relationship that is so strong that they become brand champions, almost pre-empting the need for the brand to communicate in conventional ways. But for this to happen, companies would have to pamper their loyalists in exciting ways. Meetings, free tickets to concerts, parties, blogger meets – all that we do to entertain our friends is what brands have to do to kickstart 'influencer marketing'. In the long run, it may even cost less than mass marketing, where communication and response is averaged out.

Apple had set up regional liaisons and the Apple User Group Advisory Board: people who used Apple products and gave feedback to the company. Volkswagen organized innovation summits to interact candidly with their patrons, admitting their mistakes and constantly improving to win consumer relevance and love. Linux, with its open community of users and the motto 'Do the unexpected', put power back into the consumer's hands. But companies have to go the extra mile – how many companies in India do that? OLX tried user testimonials but soon dwindled to traditional advertising. Uber is luring riders with the proposition of seeing the city with a proud resident who is also your taxi-owner. Marketing to evangelists is by and large an accidental procedure rather than part of a well-planned marketing strategy.

Saarthi brands create communities: Like relationships that expand on gaining strength, the brand's area of influence expands with increasing popularity. The Milwaukee-based Harley-Davidson, with the Harley Owners Group, stays unbeaten for 'tribal marketing'. But it didn't secure wide acceptance initially, only consolidating itself when it started participating in rallies and when it started the 'try and buy', concept, after which a deep involvement with dealers took root. World Wrestling Entertainment (WWE) used to organize large meet-and-greet sessions to provide its fans an opportunity to meet wrestlers, selling tons of merchandise and associate sponsorship rights.

Has Mahindra evaluated doing the same for their range of Scorpios? Has Maruti, with its sweeping presence, given any opportunity to its consumers to speak for themselves and the brand? If the large number of its followers seem difficult to manage, has it considered working with a more exclusive club so that the positive word goes around? In India, the dependence on big TV creatives with contrived acting seems more significant than the endorsement of the large number of actual users.

Saarthi brands advocate a higher purpose: Apple champions education, Bill Gates has a foundation that does charity work worth over five billion dollars and Oprah's charities are a part of her campaign – the mantra 'You receive what you give' is applicable here. How many Indian corporates see corporate social responsibility (CSR) as a brand opportunity to rally their consumers – who truly care but cannot participate to the same extent as a corporate – around their causes?

Saarthi brands are inclusive: This stems from the above. Consumers want a chance to not just be different but also aggregate around a loved cause. Brands that bring consumers of different ilks under the umbrella of a noble rally build a unique opportunity for loyalty. Corporations that are faceless may find it difficult to have consumers queue up at their stores. In fact, Oprah, with her apparent vulnerabilities (sexual abuse, cocaine addiction and obesity), drew more fans than svelte models because consumers could link themselves to an authentic person more easily than with plastic glamour dolls. Brands that smell of authenticity get invited to consumers' living rooms.

Saarthi brands utilize a heritage of imageries (covering all five senses) and nostalgia: They even have arch enemies that ultimately affords them great unity (Pepsi vs Coke, Samsung vs Sony). A lot of brands today just rot in lifeless packs without breathing in a history of struggle and growth. Brands that do have heritage succumb to the lure of being contemporary, ignoring the solid weight of their history. Rooh Afza, Keo Karpin, Nirula's and Coffee House are formidable powerhouses waiting for self-pride to valorise their antiquity as heritage, reversing their march to oblivion.

Saarthi brands stand for a larger cause: This is now gaining currency as 'cause marketing'. If brands identify and promote a cause in the public domain which expands beyond the benefits that the products embody, cause marketing is born. Resultantly, consumers don't merely connect with the brand at an emotional level but also reach out for its social concerns, thereby impacting brand consumption.

Through its campaign that advocates for cleaning '*mooh*, *haath* and bum' (mouth, hands and bum), Unilever advocates national hygiene while promoting its brands Lifebuoy, Domex and Pureit and also drives awareness of life amelioration through simple hygienic practices. Procter & Gamble ran a campaign wherein the purchase of its products was linked to contributing to charity, targeted at benefiting mothers. Or, more recently, a Mountain Dew campaign showcases real life examples of bravery to enliven its Big Idea around *darr* or fear.

Sva-bhu Brands

As brands climb up the ladder of intimacy with their consumers, going beyond being 'love marks', the gap between them and their users narrows so much that they become the surrogate symbols of the people they represent. Consumers consider these brands to be their own creation, or a part of them – hence, *sva-bhu* or self-created.

Now, brands are not thought of as distant, as mere products of consumption, but inseparably tie up with consumers' personalities. Since they replicate the consumer, these brands are steeped in such truth that there is no place for superficiality. They are what we truly believe in: not our public posturing, not our convenient selves that we put up for public gains, not the socially acceptable face we put on to mingle, but what we privately think about in the private chambers of our hearts and minds.

Very few brands achieve this level. Harley Davidson represents one such brand whose evangelists are happy to replace their names with the logo of the mere bikes they ride. The ethos of exploring the world on your own terms, at your pace and in its raw form is such a germane expression of the individual urge that consumers clamour to be like the brand and, in doing so, find a bunch of people who feel like them, thereby opening up the possibility of forming a tribe. Oprah's show is watched with complete surrender when it starts to mirror the viewers: their aspirations, travails, despondencies and, most importantly, their power to change in spite of their vulnerabilities. She enriches the conversation with a brutal admission of her failures as a struggling teen succumbing to obesity and still coming good at the end of it. When Oprah speaks, her voice distils the emotions of the millions standing invisibly behind her, and their huge undertow of anxieties and hopes of alleviation find expression through her. At any point during the show or after it, Oprah and her viewers are walking in each other's shoes. Self-expression brands are the gut, the heart and the mind of the consumers, not merely their shadow. Self-expression brands are 'me brands', reflecting the consumer.

Talk shows in India have not touched this truth. When they do, however, like in the show *Satyamev Jayate* hosted by Aamir Khan, they swiftly moves to being preachy. *Sva-bhu* requires reflecting the consumers as they are so that a genuine conversation can follow.

It would appear to require an awful lot of work to get there. Should the brands attempt the arduous climb? Most are content with healthy revenues and a positive uptick in brand health scores. Well, the benefits go beyond the cash register. Just as the final measure of everything is us, similarly, the final goal of brands is to be so close to a person that they almost become a substitute for him/her. In the business sense, it means unimaginable loyalty. Consumers don't just interact with the brand – they become the brand. You don't have to sell the brand to them; they are addicted to be your patrons for life. Forget about great pricing, extra benefits or lucrative promotions to wean away your consumers, because other brands are not even taken into consideration. Even flirting, which can happen in the *saarthi* brand stage, is a non-option because you can leave your friends but not yourself.

What's the downside of being a *sva-bhu*? Hypersensitivity. Anything that a brand does, if it happens to fall out of favour, invites extreme reactions from consumers. Moreover, just as you talk to yourself, the brands also have to be in constant conversation with their consumers. Often, the products or services they represent are a very small part of it. The lifetime revenue that comes from self-expression brands is huge, but the responsibility is no less. But on balance, the rewards outweigh the travails.

How do you craft a self-expression brand if you want to baptize your consumers for all the products, now and in the future? First, be *authentic*. As a matter of fact, you can't even baptize consumers – you have to win them over because contrivance makes them run away, since they can smell an inauthentic brand just from the logo. If consumers are going to trust the brand to represent them, they need to know it's not phony. This means that all the grand stuff that companies write about themselves – about being the best, most-caring, human-oriented, excellence-driven – should move from being mere hype to reality. If the company's people and policies are not in sync with its philosophy, the company has to get up and believe in it. If it means recrafting, they need to do so to bring it within the realm of credibility even if that means confessing your fallibility in the interim. But make it *real* – not superficially laudable. That itself is baptism by fire because a few companies actually believe their own gilded letters of intent. And fewer still will admit to their shortcomings. Ironically, though, if it is well-intentioned, consumers buy it. Woolworth, the retail giant of South Africa, came out with a public statement about how they would be unable to offer lower prices in the recession due to their business model of sustainable practices. Consumers not only appreciated that but turned up at the stores to buy more. The result was that Woolworth bucked the trend of downturn by being, well, honest.

Once the company has become real, soak the brand with *transparency*. What you are doing today, including your shortcomings (in fact that helps it make human and relatable), has to be in the public view. If you aren't what you are supposed to be, make plans to get there and work hard to share your progress. Lower salt in food, higher reliability in automobiles, better experience in vacation packages – whatever you sell must become transparent; no hidden surprises. For *sva-bhu* brands, being fair and transparent sits ahead of being ruthlessly successful.

From 'dibbi' to self-expression: Even if our brand is a mere shoe polish *dibbi* (box), there is a story behind it – how we apply fair procurement policies, how we treat our stakeholders, the community we engage with, how we give back to them and the preventive steps taken to save the environment. Such mega issues seem to radiate out from the innocuous little *dibbi*. Normally, these are relegated to the bucket of CSR, but now it becomes centre stage as the persona of the brand starts to take shape. Now that the wax polish box seems to reflect the persons working behind it, it's time to bring in the soul.

All of us, whether we realize or not, have a point of view about the world: what it is, how hostile or friendly it is to our dreams, how it can be exploited or leveraged and where it lets us fit within its scheme of things. This is the world view: a perception about something as distant as the world, from a view as close as our eyes. It extends far but it connects deep within.

Our world view is, therefore, a philosophy; a rough aggregated compass that aligns the whimsical outside with the opinionated inside. Brands, too, need a world view that explains their position vis-à-vis the outside world. If it's authentic, giving consumers a reflection of their own lives, a connection is established instantly. If, on top of that, the world view is also desirable, the brand becomes aspirational, moving closer to the consumers to represent them. Apple is forward-looking and disarmingly simple, Google demonstrates the power of access to knowledge and Nike invites action over protracted deliberation. Each of these carry a sliver of who we are, encompassing even the weaknesses by making them real. More importantly, they provide a hope for things becoming better – a bit like our everyday self and the aspirational one that we cast every year with our new year resolutions. Brands have to do just that – present themselves transparently but also espouse a cause they aspire towards. It's not about being perfect, but about seeking perfection.

Indian brands have a big opportunity to become like real people. Often, when you conduct personification studies to fathom brands as people, vague and uninteresting people emerge. Consumers don't really know who you are, and when they guess, they often get led onto the wrong path. That is a sacrilegious miss. Hence, Indian brands have to start finding a world view if they don't have one, and if they have one, they need to start spelling it out because consumers are waiting to join them.

Tata Tea started well by becoming the consciousness of social awakening. It could be more visible in real life, taking its creative commitment to ground with '*Jaago re*'. ITC could communicate and expand its world view of enduring value by inviting consumers in the value-creation process from e-Choupal to e-responsible consumption – encompassing plastics and cans. Big Bazaar could link its brand of quality access and affordability with the world view of inclusiveness by extending its private label into women empowerment, like Lijjat Papad has done.

World view needn't be all serious, and it definitely needn't be too abstract, talking of things far from the brand functionalities. In fact, it can humanize the benefits, making them characters we would love to be. Mentos is not merely a mint, but it embraces a world view of making light of everything by the ingenuous intervention of humour. Fevicol could have a world view of being a great integrating force – binding things and people into a whole. Asian Paints could focus on being as good-looking on the outside as on the inside, and so on. Once the world view is established, brands should take up larger causes that chime with their world view so that the breadth of their vision and its seriousness can be seen in action by consumers. Mentos could be seen where de-stressing opportunities exist – stand-up shows and *haasya sammelans* (comedy gatherings) – choosing content that is light-hearted and purposeful, not frivolous. Fevicol could be a part of nation building and Asian Paints could be associated with charity-driven art forms. With a bit of abstraction and personification, the brand can be tagged to a relevant, larger cause in the society, wherever relevant and to win consumers like Harley followers. But for that to happen, brand custodians have to take conscious steps.

Once the world view has been cast, brands must literally step aside and let consumers take over. Like mature parents that provide the platform for growth, they must not lead with their diktats. The role of the brand changes from leading the conversation to enabling and fostering it. One way to do this is to provide consumers technological enablement, like Facebook, LinkedIn, Instagram and Twitter do for its members. This creates great communities, where your brand champions draw more people like themselves, enlarging the brand's area of influence. Another way could be to congregate brand evangelists in offline interactions around causes that the brand advocates. Tata Tea could organize debates on social change. Idea could cocoon innovation hubs by enabling conversations amongst like-minded people. Moreover, companies could even chaperon their *sva-bhu* brand champions from the back by providing them opportunities to connect with celebrities and notables in that field, occasionally even funding some activities that translate their world view on the ground. The scale of the activity or its financials are less important than the intention. Once brands start to widen the scope of their engagement with consumers, new roads emerge for them. And companies needn't be making it at all.

The consumer and brand circle of life thus concludes as shown in the chart below. As brands mature from top to bottom, they move from merely familiar to the smugness of being the reflection of the consumers themselves. Along with it, the distance collapses and the power in the hands of the consumer multiplies. This is the consumer and brand circle of life:

Consumer-brand circle of life

Brand	Brand-consumer Relationship	Distance	Power
Swami	Respect	Far	None
	Fear		
Saarthi	Friends	Close	Shared
	Love		
Sva-bhu	My reflection	None	Full

The Indian consumer–brand circle of life has just been put into motion, the Pragmarketism way. With the expanding sway of technology and the concurrent urge amongst people to talk and connect, brand champions are looking at a unique opportunity to turn their brands into the hands of the consumer, towards the elusive *sva-bhu* brands. With digital marketing, this dream might be closer than we imagine.

11

Digital Marketing

'Boss, we will understand the data signals, optimize our search, do some data management, integrate AI, set an evaluation metric …' a young trainee exults as I look on, wondering whether he can connect the dots.

In another context, I hear a colleague say, 'Digital marketing will either outdate us or recast us.' At a CMO meet recently, we nodded our heads in sombre agreement.

'What's going to decide which way we end up taking?' somebody asks.

'If we are able to synthesize classical marketing with the new emerging tools of digital, we will lead the change, if not …'

'We will be led,' the others echo.

As members of the Internet and Mobile Association of India, who are seeing the digital reality unfold, we have felt two contrasting tugs. One towards the exciting new world marked by new technology, and another that confuses managers as they struggle to reconcile digital marketing ways with classical marketing that they have grown with. It's like putting a square peg into a round hole.

That's what digital is like: too vast for anyone to comprehend in its entirety, yet too intrusive and pervasive to be ignored.

Digital Disruption

Earlier, we consumed TV alongside some radio news and magazines. Now, we incessantly gaze at our mobile screens, and this isn't just the urban consumer anymore. Breakfast is had with WhatsApp 'good morning' greetings – the only one of its kind – with spiritual admonitions (blame it on continuity and transcendence, as referred to in the chapter on Indian society earlier) and work or college hours are dotted with frequent visits to Facebook, Instagram or Twitter. During long commutes, we snack on YouTube videos, and after a brief interruption for dinner, we start swiping at the screen for online shopping, in between Amazon Prime and Netflix shows. This is the hugely transformed consumer's life and marketers have to shadow this digital overreach.

For a while now, digital strategy has been the residue of mainstream strategy. When the advertising brief is written and executed, and media monies saturated on TV, the leftover money is allocated for digital presence. However, we need to repurpose our strategy by considering the consumer realities, as given below:

- Consumers aren't anonymous anymore. We need to wake up to their strong digital identities. They interact with brands and often want to be in the driver's shoes.
- Consumers are seeing deeper and further, worldwide. Not only is this raising their expectations but also their frustration if/when products fail. With a rise in e-commerce, ordering globally may not be so distant. Empowerment of consumers is happening at a blistering pace.
- Information is gathered in seconds and opinions dart around in nanoseconds. Doctors have to contend with global experts while Ola and Uber have to constantly submit to the tyranny of user experience. Brand loyalty is now the result of the last experience, and is not built on the habit of quiet brand usage.

- Passive consumption is becoming a thing of the past as consumption activism rises. Consumers are demanding: 'What's special for me?', 'What's the promotion here versus somewhere else?', 'What else am I getting?', 'How are you making my life choices better than your competitor?' and even, 'How are you helping me get more out of life, improve my health, express myself better, get fame and money?' Brands that delight have to pander to all this and still surprise with more.
- Reactions take place in real time. Irate consumers can whip up a storm through a mere tweet with a few characters, or horrify with a graphic on Instagram. No algorithm can predict how viral it becomes and how it spins out of control. You can't do an ABC analysis of consumer response and template a satisfactory answer. Answers have to be customized and provided instantly.
- Consumers are also cross-connecting with communities around the world, asking questions that were otherwise kept in remote files of CSR. Information can't be closeted if it concerns the consumer – they decide what concerns them.

Welcome to the age of consumer tyranny or consumer celebration. Which side you are on is determined by how you view digital. Before the consumer turns indifferent or hostile towards a brand, they must be integrated with a full-blown **digital strategy**.

The first problem with digital is the jargon, which confounds us completely. However, can it be seen as the old world, only clothed in new garments – differing in some respects but fundamentally behaving like the old one, familiar to most marketers. A closer look unfolds more opportunities than confusion.

Bridge to Digital Country

For a long time, digital was seen as inadequate, since it could not reach mass audiences required for mass marketing. The truth, however, is changing so fast that even the graphic below might change dramatically in the next few months. If you consider those above the age of fifteen of the 260 million odd active urban internet users, then across different platforms, the reach of digital is closer to traditional media, as illustrated below.

Digital platform flywheel

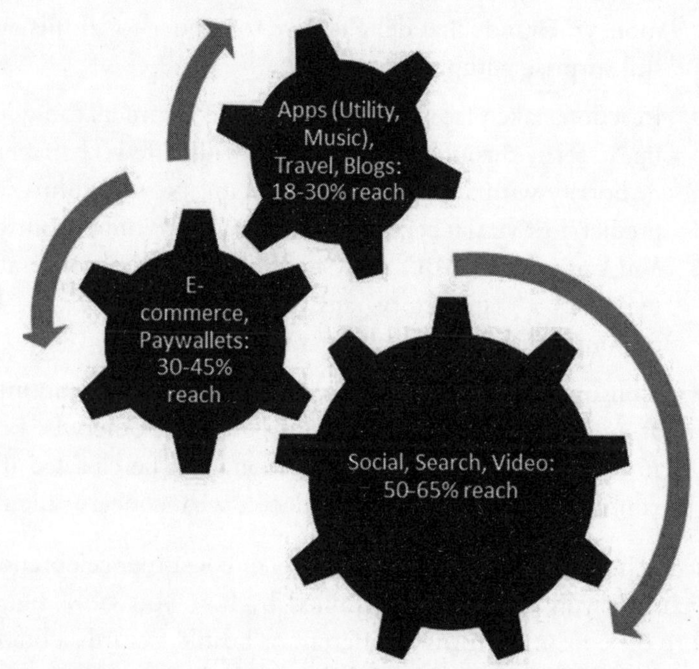

Source: Authors

However, the way we measure consumer response to marketing campaigns changes a little with new metrics. A simplified table of the digital world seen through a conventional lens looks like this:

Conventional/ Digital	Awareness	Interest/Decision	Action
Reach	Impressions/page views/unique user/video views	Click-through rate (CTR), watch duration, likes, comment, share	Buy now, CTR

However, there is no digital presentation that doesn't bamboozle us with funny-sounding words. To make sense of the terms above, the bumps of digital ignorance need to be flattened.

Digital Decoding

- Page views: Viewing the page a single time is called a page view. However, it doesn't mean the consumer has read your page – a view is counted as soon as a page loads.
- Video views: Once a video begins to play (regardless of how long it is played for), it's counted as a video view.
- Lead: When a site asks you to fill in your details, which then becomes a lead.
- Unique user: The number of unique or solo users who have visited a site during a particular time. Any duplication is removed for this purpose by software.
- Measurement terms:
    - Click-through rate (CTR)%: Total clicks on a unit/total impressions served of the unit × 100.
    - Video-through rate (VTR)%: Total video views on a unit/total impressions served of the unit × 100.
    - Click-through lead (CTL)%: Total leads on a unit/total clicks received of the unit.
    - Cost per thousand impressions (CPM): The cost per thousand impressions bought. The most common term used for buying online inventory.

- Cost per click (CPC): Only when a user clicks on an advert does the advertiser pay. Used on biddable platforms like Google, Facebook, etc.
- Cost per view (CPV): When a user views a video for a certain period of time.
- Cost per engagement (CPE): When we expect the user to engage with our tweets, through likes and comments, is when the advertiser pays. Primarily used on Twitter.
- Cost per lead (CPL): For getting the information of the surfer.
- Cost per acquisition (CPA): The cost that is charged to the advertiser after the lead is converted into a sale.
- Search engine optimization (SEO): This allows you to make your page stay on top of a search engine through the use of specific keywords and lead over other brands.

Now that we are somewhat equipped to face the brave new world, it is time to stretch the canvas of digital strategy with an adapted STP (segmentation, targeting, positioning), which is a 3D framework that allows digi-signature, digi-shooting, digi-petaling/fugaling.

Digital Strategy

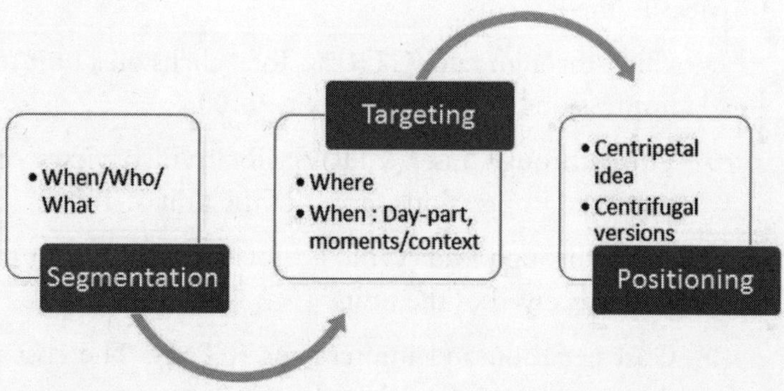

Source: Authors

Digi-signature (segmentation): Consumer segmentation in the digital world multiplies depending on how it is used; it either confounds or it rewards. The segmentation options based on demo-geo-psycho-graphic filters can now be converted further into more dynamic filters and intersected with the consumer's behaviour, as evidenced by the digital signature he/she leaves after signing in and out on the net.

Criterion/Behaviour				
When:	Breakfast	Pre-noon to lunch	Lunch to Dinner	Post-dinner
Where:	Social, messaging, news	Search, shopping	Social, shopping	Mails, apps, social
What:	Browsing, engaging, participating	Events, prescriptions, apps	Moments/ occasion, video platforms	Blogs, forums, website

Now our consumers appear as people, not a lumpy set of data. Better still, we know them not only by their exact coordinates but also know what they are thinking on the basis of their behaviour. Whether they are interacting with their friends through social platforms like Twitter, Instagram, Facebook, LinkedIn and WhatsApp or browsing the news or websites or prescribing to sites for help, buying products via apps, e-commerce sites (Amazon, Flipkart) and indulging themselves with videos (Netflix, Amazon Prime, Zoot, Hotstar) or being influenced by bloggers – the consumer's digital signature is strewn all over the net for marketers to gleefully swoop in on and capture.

Digi-shooting (Targeting)

Digital targeting or digi-shooting is sharp because it is directed towards a person, not a group, and is more effective because it happens when the person is in the mood, not when he is disinterested.

Following from the above, the simple SEC A consumer classification changes to: a consumer living in south India with a propensity to consume diapers, but currently using cloth. Someone who loves ordering biryani, shops for expensive cosmetics from Amazon, who follows DIY tips for YouTube, gets her information on parenting tips from the parenting blog Momspresso. Suddenly, the multivariate segmentation from the initial chapters not only becomes more real but also more elaborate.

Not only do you know her, you can also target her when she is shopping on BigBasket or browsing for parenting tips or meeting at socials as Facebook tells you everything. If even after all this, she has spurned you, you can retarget again – when she goes to buy her favourite magazine and lipstick, clubbing it with an irresistible deal and other user reviews that makes leaving your brand an insane choice. Targeting is precise, a lot like surgical bombing.

Segmentation and targeting are developed to place the erstwhile static and lumpy consumer into many categories, doing many things, which may be classified as follows:

- What is the consumer's exact inclination?
    - Google Pixel 2 conducted psychographics and came across the following segments:

      From Facebook: Photographers, musicians, cyclists, gadget lovers and filmmakers. Make a master copy, with about six seconds dedicated to each consumer type so it can be broadcast as a whole or in sections adapted to the media, appropriate for the audience.

- Where are they likely to engage?
  - Nike and Google launched HyperCourt – an app-based interaction service, wherein consumers can choose to train like their favourite basketball icons, based on defending, shooting and dribbling, and can be scored and used to earn cards, which they could then flaunt on social media.
- How to appeal to them?
  - Ikea created a buzz with its new catalogue when Yanjaa, a girl, memorized the entire 300-page catalogue and recalled the pictures of people and items when asked randomly. The intrigue it created led to the company considering the old idea of catalogue launches (running for over sixty-seven years), which drove up the awareness about the catalogue in 124 countries, driving up footfalls and sales. It reached seventy-three million people with an estimated earned media worth of USD 5 million and with a return on media investment of 1:18.
  - To make the content travel further and faster, *The Tonight Show Starring Jimmy Fallon* ran a feature where it played misheard lyrics through the twitter hashtag #misheardlyrics. The ensuing hilarity of misheard lyrics of popular songs ('those bastards' instead of 'ghostbusters' for example) became digitally tradeable – interviews, hashtags, name-that-song contests and lip-sync battles were created to spread the popularity of the show.

This is the power of digital marketing when it is unabashedly used.

Digi-petaling/Digi-fugaling (Positioning)

With sharp segmentation and targeting, positioning needs to be detailed so it leads to multiple conversations and engagement opportunities – not a single large-format TV commercial. A plain banana is passé, but banana shakes, banana flavourings, banana toppings, banana crust and so on are the new consumer demand. But how does one multiply the offer of a brand in the digital age, where proliferation at all levels is inevitable, and yet, stay entrenched in a unifying core idea that doesn't let multiple versions blur the nucleus of the brand? The answer is subjecting the brand positioning to centripetal and centrifugal forces and creating digital versions, which we have named digi-petaling and digi-fugaling.

- **Digi-petal** in the digital world stands for the core idea of the brand or brand essence which represents the brand. It's that unchanging identity which pulls together the diverse manifestations of the brand. This is linked to the core of positioning.
- **Digi-fugal**, on the other hand, stands for the vast representations of the brand which allow it to surround consumers in multiple ways, connected to the core digi-petal identity.

For example, Uber, which is positioned as 'enabling people unlock the full potential of the city through shared service' has a centripetal or digi-petal idea to 'unlock or discover' one's city. The centrifugal or digi-fugal ideas are contained in the phrases 'full potential' and 'shared services'. Therefore, all creatives that are made must finally deliver on the topic of unlocking the city, but must also explore myriad ways of doing so. Hence, you could explore the city to travel for work, leisure, eating out, hanging around with friends, reaching home or watching sports ... from this idea was born the Uber campaign, where it became the central point that could collect and disseminate information about the city's best places for eating, tourism, street life and all sorts of experiences that were then brought out by Uber. Flashed through Instagram visuals and Facebook posts, users found the Uber brand to be like an exploratory friend that came with myriad possibilities, making it a true *sva-bhu* brand.

Likewise, Red Bull, which stands for energy to realize the best in your world, has a digi-petal idea of energy with digi-fugal possibilities of realizing interests like sports, adventure, fitness, biking, cricket and perhaps even gruelling office hours.

Digi-fugal possibilities make the message relevant to everyone, while a digi-petal idea ensures the consistency of brand deliveries across all people, places and experiences. Just to comfortably understand the two, below are a few more examples.

Bingo chips: Bringing comic disruption to life's mundanities through its zingy tastes. Digi-petal: disruption. Digi-fugal: mundane ideas, situations, people jolted by the twisted, the weird, the fun, the unexpected and endearing dabs and nudges. This allows the making of various creatives around digi-fugal ideas, which are always consolidated through disruption as the central theme.

Dettol: To assure protection against an external threat to one's physical well-being. Digi-petal: protection (iconic sword). Digi-fugal: external threats (flies, mosquitoes, strangers, returning from sports, outdoors) of infection, disease (food poisoning, cold, other air and touch-borne diseases). Again, several creatives centre around various kinds of threats and the resultant diseases that may occur at various times of the day or the seasons, solved by the Dettol promise of protection – the unifying factor across multiple creative versions.

Dabur: Providing Ayurvedic benefits to modern living. Digi-petal: Ayurvedic science. Digi-fugal: perils of modern living.

In fact, by applying the above method, one can modify one's existing asset (TVC, print advert, etc.) or create entirely new ones.

Since digital messages (self-containing, forwards) bear the imprint of the consumer, it must be relatable and help them project themselves as smart and as being able to reflect things they truly care about with their views and emotions. Digital creatives differ from the conventional ones because of this singular reason.

Digital Content Creation Process

Digital content creation is iterative and conducive to creating excellence by taking measured steps as in the following:

Digital content creation waterfall

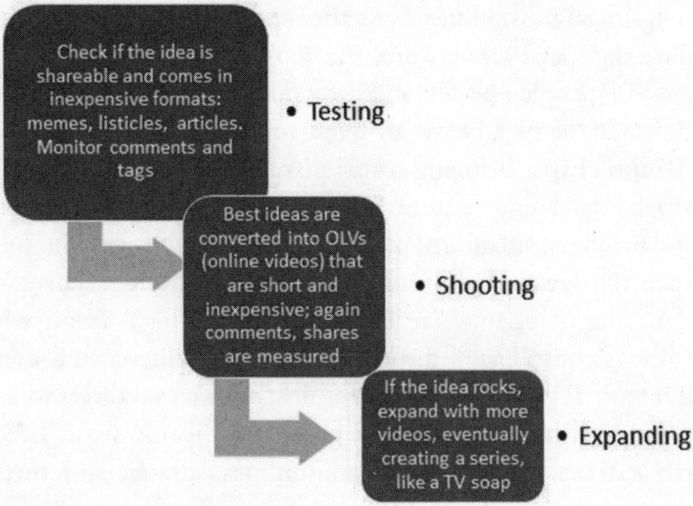

Source: Authors

For example, Kurkure had done a campaign where it put the consumer first by taking digs at the famous misconceptions prevalent in India. Like the unfounded hope that your roommate would return what he or she borrowed from you. This kind of approach, referring to real-life truths, generated huge shareability.

It could go further, taking its positioning of '*Tedha hai, par mera hai*' and extending its brand relevance into areas that are endearing, despite being offbeat – articles and videos on errant but lovable husbands, painful but well-meaning friends, caring but intrusive wives, informative but annoying subordinates, helpful but over-involved bosses. The potential to amuse their consumers with real life content, packaged through the brand's point of view, is huge.

Touching the consumer's nerve at the right point can yield huge multipliers, as explained above.

Digital Media

The last mile of digital gets exciting, delivering its fruit for the painstaking digital marketing effort. As the content becomes consumer-friendly, there is, for the first time in the brand's history, desire amongst their consumers to share content without being paid for it, becoming what *saarthi* brands truly ought to aspire to. The media proliferates to:

- Paid media: media that you have paid for, as in conventional advertising and media buying
- Earned media: by virtue of consumers sharing, liking and 'viraling' your content
- Owned media: when consumers land at your assets (websites, apps, e-commerce links) triggered by an interest in the brand

The cycle of marketing now comes full circle, as the brand has acquired its own momentum, which requires little supervision and expenditure from the manufacturer. This is the dream. Advertising gets the consumer while becoming pocket-friendly.

So now that we have slotted digital marketing into the traditional world, here is a full plunge into making the most of it – replete with the best examples from the industry.

Marketing Objective

To start digital marketing for our brands, it is worthwhile to step back and ask what our **marketing objective** is (refer to previous chapters) so we can make a big leap through this new technology.

- To sell the same to more – or penetration
- To sell more to the same – or frequency

Then we plot them on to two axes and we get four quadrants, as shown below:

Digital objective grid

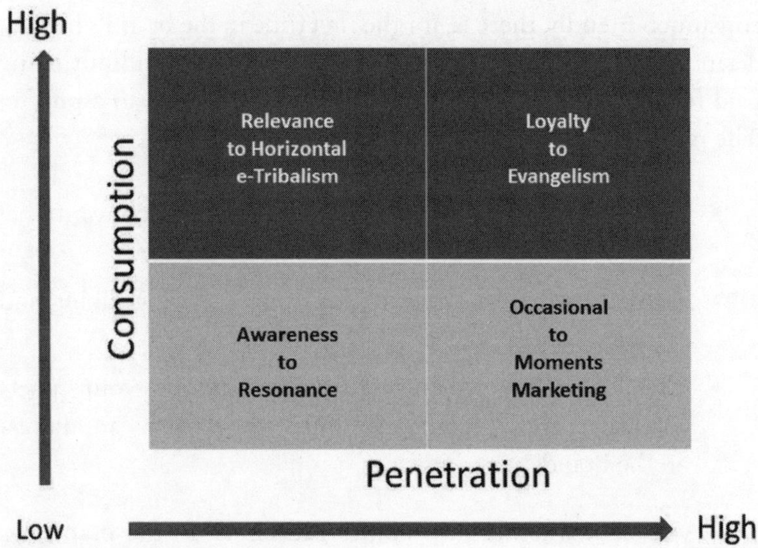

Source: Authors

1. Low penetration, low consumption: The brand suffers from low knowledge when its consumers are ignorant of the brand. Hence, awareness needs to be spread, but given the precision of digital, we can move from awareness to the resonance of the brand.
2. Low penetration, high consumption: Some people have embraced the brand, but there is an opportunity to get to more people. Therefore, the brand's relevance has to be disseminated wider and horizontally.
3. Low consumption, high penetration: Many consumers are using it, but only a few times. The marketing task is

to increase the usage. Digital can convert the occasional to 'moments marketing'.

4. High consumption, high penetration: The brand is well entrenched and well on its way to becoming cult-like. Can digital help turn the loyal consumers into brand evangelists, thereby multiplying brand ambassadors on the ground?

Let's consider each of these opportunities:

From brand awareness to resonance: With traditional marketing, the approach towards awareness is much like striking a nail with a sledgehammer. The nail is wedged in, but an awful lot of work is wasted. Likewise, a general message sprayed across by a single standard TV creative across national channels works with the implicit assumption that all consumers are endowed with equal amounts of interest and capability for consuming content.

Digital, by contrast, targets consumers with content that is not only specifically relevant to them (even traditional marketing can do that) but what *resonates* with them. Hence, you don't have one message for many, but many messages for many. E-commerce has demonstrated how to do this. ShopClues, which draws its consumers in with the lure of price first, rather than brand first, serves various adverts with price discounts on the categories that the consumers are looking for. If this doesn't work, they retarget the same consumer through offers on other associated categories, which they have shown an interest in (via analytics), and follow again with lucrative offers that are hard to not fall for.

Intent targeting refers to approaching consumers when they are most disposed to picking your brand. Unlike plain display ads, where the features spread brand awareness, intent targeting uses search engine marketing (SEM) to tap into consumers when they are prepared.

Ford, which has a low number of online searches for its cars, used a digital strategy effectively by targeting and retargeting consumers looking to buy automobiles on the basis of their intent, customizing creatives each time to convert them, while gathering leads from even offline queries.

From Occasional to Moments Marketing

When a brand is consumed by many, only during an occasion or two can digital step in to deepen this consumption. When the consumers are seen through the lens of a) their need-state (functional or emotional), b) the activity they are engaged in at a given time (general behaviour – watching TV, socializing) and c) other categories being used at the time (cross-category behaviour), new opportunities emerge. When this is superimposed with existing knowledge of brand segmentation, new moments of consumption surface, which are more intensive than communication of single consumption. This '**moments marketing**' steps in and captures the mind of the consumer and offers a brand in the way it ought to be at that very moment.

Livon's hair serum was targeted for higher growth, but consumer usage studies showed that women were using it very occasionally. Further research revealed that there were various stages where the women needed their hair fixed, but they weren't necessarily considering Livon's hair serum. They were classified as a) for college party, b) monsoon haircare, c) salon look, d) to avoid helmet hair, e) perfect selfie look, f) first day at work/college look, g) get ready for a date and so on. Around these moments, separate videos were made, where Livon was seen as the perfect solution for each state. The result: not only was the brand compellingly contextualized but its presence multiplied manifold. The video-through rate (VTR) for these creatives was about 40 per cent, using mobile interface with a positive uplift on sales.

Moments marketing moved the focus from product benefits – smoother/glossier/disentangling/salon finish – to the consumer's desiring mindset. With digital allowing for an intervention at the right time, with the right offer, consumer conversion becomes a breeze.

From Relevance to Horizontal e-Tribalism

When a few have embraced the brand and the brand manager desperately depends on word of mouth to endorse his brand, digital helps to create an online community of likely and well-placed adopters to spread the word. Enter WhatsApp, Facebook and endless other social media interfaces where conversation spreads like wildfire in a matter of hours – if the content is appealing.

Momspresso, the leading parental platform, disseminates countless online videos (OLVs) on content relevant for a community of mothers. They now measure at an impressive thirty-two million monthly visitors, interacting over subjects like motherhood and parenting. Mothers are opening up to them like never before, demolishing many myths of the past when conversation tended to be socially pleasing. As honesty reigns, the conversation goes viral and brands see an opportunity to participate.

One-to-one (O2O) consumer engagement, the digital equivalent of 'path to purchase', uses data analytics to target consumers more sharply, selecting consumers who are interested and then by following them through and maximizing conversions. An O2O consumer journey involves choosing your consumers and targeting only the chosen ones at the right time (during a festival or marriage, when consumer interest is high) and leading them up to the point of a sale. Along the way, creatives are varied to generate, sustain and converge the interest towards a sale. Below is the process flowchart of O2O.

O2O flowchart

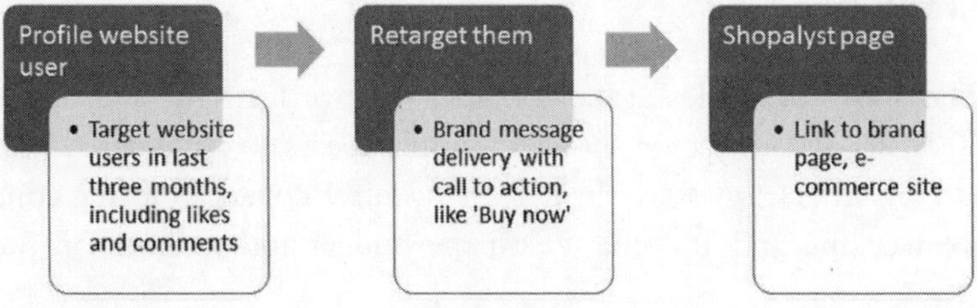

Source: Authors

The result of conducting a campaign with O2O not only provides better returns (CTR, engagement rate) but also better economies (CPV).

From Loyalty to Evangelism

When consumers are in love with the brand, digital enables them to act as the champions of the brand. No longer do marketers need smaller edits, or the main or functional films, because the job is now passed on to the brand evangelists who replace their display pictures with a picture of the brand (on the higher side) or rave about its usage on social media. Brand managers can rest back contented – they have set their idea ablaze.

Without our realizing it, all of us, through the mere usage of LinkedIn, Instagram, Facebook and Twitter, have become evangelists of these brands. This is the space of *sva-bhu* brands, where the consumer is the brand or the other way around. So, when anything goes trending as a hashtag, consumers are evangelizing the brand. It is the same with Snapchat or Instagram. This unique swap between the consumer and the service provider has resulted in crowdsourcing as a way to generate content. Unlike conventional media houses, like Star or Zee, that create content, YouTube merely scouts for what's viral, selects it and rewards the content creators. Zoot and Hotstar are hosting mainline content on mobile platforms, but YouTube is where consumers are empowered to create their own content – this is redefining the rules of content.

Creatives

The above examples argue for new creative formats. The large, 60/30 seconds director showreel stuff appears to have dated fast, as consumers are now turned on by nifty copies. Shorter edits are working and are smarter on the budget and tougher on the consumer's psyche. Data pulled from a FMCG brand shows that both YouTube and Facebook view rates and CPV improves with shorter edits.

The new creative formats are: carousel ads (sliding static ads that unfold with the swipe of a finger), banner ads (static) and even GIF files. While these are less glamorous than their larger versions, their utility can be drawn from their sharp features and multi-messaging ability that befits the attention-deficit consumers.

Skippable ads give consumers a choice and, therefore, creatives have to grab the consumer's attention in the first few seconds, before they take charge of the cursor and skip. Forced views disempower the consumers and brands don't want to be watched by an irate consumer either. Another way is to place the advert not in the beginning, when the search has ended and consumers are all agog to watch, but in the middle, when they have already seen their chosen media for a while. This is the mid-roll option and it often comes without the choice to not watch it. Usually, the CPV of both forced and mid-roll adverts are cheaper than skippable adverts (since viewing is somewhat assured). TrueView is a YouTube feature that charges advertisers only for the adverts that have been watched.

Other options are banner adverts, mastheads on YouTube (like the masthead of a leading publication, which is often sold for a hefty price), which gets high visibility but are viewed with disdain or indifference by consumers looking to hurriedly navigate on their small screens.

What makes a good video? Short edits (one to three minutes), a powerful video thumbnail (the opening shot of the video that decides if you will be watched at all) and vivid subtitling (since most videos are watched silently, to protect the consumer's privacy while streaming) go a long way in increasing video click-through and the time spent viewing it.

Which creative formats and media best work for the objectives above? Below is a prescription:

Brand Task	Nature of Creative	Media Choice
Relevance	Carousel, banners	Search, display (keywords, content)
Moments marketing	Small edits	Mastheads, Hotstar, Voot
E-tribalism	Usage-led, social media friendly	Facebook (geo-target), YouTube
Evangelism	Testimonials or user-generated content, personalized engagement, advocacy, CSR	Blogger meet, YouTube (geo, affinity)

Using Google SEO, one can find the keywords associated with one's category and cause one's brand to feature more over the others when consumers are searching for answers. Display adverts around searches that are related to one's category is yet another way to spread the relevance of one's category, considering that the consumer is already in an appropriate state of mind. Now, Hotstar, Voot and other over-the-top (OTT) platforms have become strong alternate mobile TV channels for consumers to watch their serials at a chosen time and destination. Placing one's creative there, through pre-rolls and mid-rolls (in the middle of the content), in a non-skippable format ensures sufficient exposure to achieve the reach we expect from traditional media.

Geo-targeting is possible with Facebook and YouTube to target consumers where your brand's products and services are going to be available, allowing marketing to be focused. Affinity allows your adverts to be served when the content is closely associated with your category – like serving a Horlicks creative when a consumer is looking for nutrition solutions. Lastly, where loyal consumers are expected to be turned into brand evangelists, brand owners must provide the forum for consumers to embrace. Blogger meets for positively disposed bloggers, conferences to get brand loyalists to act as advocates and, finally, the dissemination of CSR initiatives (like Dettol's participation in the 'Swachh Bharat' campaign by the Government of India) through digital initiatives propels the brand's philanthropy outwards for brand evangelists to publish it further.

That leads to the last step in the consumer journey: a purchase. Digital initiatives have a distinct advantage – they are able to reduce both distance and time to create brand awareness that leads to a brand purchase. The decision traversing through the awareness-interest-decision-action (AIDA) model, which requires at least three or more exposures and a high probability of losing consumers along the way, has been reduced; now, it only takes the time to move the finger from one click to another.

As an indicative example, through a search which stretches across YouTube and Facebook, one gets an offline store visit of around 30 per cent, which is a significant rise over the reaction that is generated by traditional media. Consumers may conduct offline checks with the actual product and maybe even check the brand page, and finally, only 2 per cent are converted to a sale. Certain other food brands get a higher conversion of 4 per cent. However, a better way to secure conversion is to bombard consumers with different messages continuously, and to get them to fall into the arc of purchase more often, thereby generating more revenue per click.

What is the future of digital marketing? Prashant Sinha, who has founded the hugely successful Momspresso, highlights the three Vs to watch out for: video, vernacular and views. Video is the medium through which time-starved consumers lap up content as they also tend to believe the authors, who they can see and hear up close. 'Go local,' he admonishes, as smart phones become affordable to a whole bunch of new eager consumers from the lower socio-economic classes. Already, Hindi speakers have a click-ability six times that of English speakers. And to top it off with views – let people articulate what they have to say about brands, and refrain from talking down to them in the manner of classical communication.

Maximizing All Aspects of Digital Case Studies

The following examples highlight how digital media has been used by advertisers in unimaginable ways and across all marketing platforms. Examples have been taken from many brands that we have judged or seen across various digital presentations and seminars. We have dissected across these examples to see which aspect of marketing has been enhanced with digital innovations.

Changing behaviour:

- In spite of the blurring of gender roles and increasing women's participation in the global workforce, women still do all or most of the household chores. Ariel ran a campaign, 'Dads #sharetheload', urging fathers to assist in loading washing machines. Over two million Indian men pledged to do the laundry, increasing consumer engagement by four and a half times and Ariel earned two billion impressions, which is worth ₹75 crores. To supplement the idea, an odd/even pack was launched for men and women – the sales exceeded the target by two and a half times and the video was endorsed by Sheryl Sandberg (CEO of Facebook) and Melinda Gates, with a positive social media spin-off.
- Nicotex started an ambitious campaign to make not smoking, but quitting smoking fashionable through its campaign: #UQUITIQUIT. Eight celebrities from the Indian Super League urged fans to quit through 100-plus videos seeded on social media.

TV innovation:

- An Audi TV campaign, '#GreatnessStarts when you don't stop', led by Virat Kohli, asked people to share their tweets on greatness, and then played the best selected tweet live on TV – in real time – on Audi TVC. The selected few were notified of their tweets. The first ever TV innovation on the campaign multiplied on social media as twenty-seven live tweets were diaplayed on TV, generating 27,000 tweets.

Mobile innovation:

- Castrol CRB Mini Truck lubricants launched a campaign based on the overheating that happens during in-city driving. It was called '*Engine thanda toh dimaag thanda*', reaching a million-plus drivers through mobile phones while they were on the move (with smart targeting using location cues of transport centres as the base and layering with average revenue per unit, or ARPU, and usage habits). It was led by a few drivers who propagated the message to the entire community. It increased brand familiarity to 75 per cent and doubled the market share in the campaign period.

Content innovation:

- Mountain Dew crafted the 'real heroes, real stories' campaign with the real-life stories of unsung heroes who were identified through social listening. It created content for Hotstar and Saavn. Reaching through mobile platforms, it cut the clutter with the youth, increasing TOM (Top-of-mind awareness) and Mountain Dew share as compared to Sprite.
- Storytelling in cause marketing: Dove collaborated with Terribly Tiny Tales (TTT) – a leading storytelling platform –

to capture, on International Women's Day, the social, cultural, political and economic achievements of women through punchy ten-seconders. These were published across Instagram, Facebook and Twitter. Ten such tales reached over 3.5 million people, with almost 0.2 million plus reactions.

- The apparel brand John Players launched #JPJFlipographs on Twitter, featuring five graphics that depicted five different people in their usual jobs and all the other things they do as you tapped closer on their image. It trended organically at number one on New Year's Eve.
- Kalyan Jewellers created the first ever 'Truly Bridal' campaign in digital space with social influencers and stylists, focusing on jewellery, fashion and beauty with more than seventy-five videos and 200-plus dedicated blogs across YouTube, Facebook and Instagram pages, driving Kalyan Jewellers' image across the country.
- Tata Sky launched a thirteen-part TVC through its movie *Daily Dillagi*, which began with a teaser and a trailer that introduced the characters and finally, a music launch. Fans engaged and participated through social assets and microsites and over eight million people were reached, through 20,000 Twitter followers.
- TataSky also launched a unique innovation, where it notified its consumers about great moments during a live telecast that they may have missed, through their Everywhere TV app.

Media innovation:

- Himalaya Herbals designed an alternative media strategy to target the consumers who had not watched their TV advert. The video ad played on the mobiles of people who hadn't seen the TV advert by exclusion mobile targeting, creating an incremental reach of over 30 per cent.

- Himalaya's sparkling white toothpaste made a web-based magazine with content that evoked emotions like joy, by capturing moments that triggered happiness and launched them across multiple screens.

Intent modelling innovation

- L'Oréal launched the campaign 'No colour, no fashion' to establish hair colour as a necessary fashion accessory. Partnering with Amazon's search engine, it created two segments: hair colour intenders and fashion forwards. The first group was caught through ads when they searched for keywords, including the consumers of competitors like Godrej, and the second segment, when they searched for lateral terms (shoes, clothes, fashion accessories, etc.). Fashion forwards was served personalized ads. This exercise led to a lower CPC and a higher CTR.
- Garnier Men Facewash worked on the insight that 85 per cent of men used soap on their face, and, unlike women, they don't talk openly about personal care. Using voice recognition technology, Garnier created a virtual personal advisor who would comprehend various accents, which could be activated by enabling the microphone on one's phone. After triggering the intent for using facewash, Garnier converted these prospective consumers with a special promotion on the pack.
- Lakmé tied up with Yash Raj Studios to drive preference for the 10,000 crore wedding season with a campaign, 'Band, Baaja, Baaraat'. Videos on beauty were played in a five-part web series, especially cut for topics such as meeting the

parents, bachelorettes, sangeet, pre-wedding and a bridal image, registering a whopping increase in their brand conversion by ten times.

Targeting innovation:

- Lava partnered with Zapr as a technology platform to identify TV audiences who were exposed to Airtel and Vodafone ads, specifically during IPL matches. They served interactive banners that were synced with TV ads and had a topical campaign: '4G can't run fast enough without the right device.'
- Lava also ran a campaign to capture sports enthusiasts with the a campaign – #Nevermissashot – highlighting the slow auto-focus feature of the Lava V5, reaching out through the Indian railway catering and tourism corporation (IRCTC) portal with sharp five-second skippable creatives.
- The Muslim community was targeted by Lifebuoy with campaign, 'Before Iftar is Lifebuoy time!' by using multimedia messaging service (MMS), served up on their feature phones with an 'infection alert system', targeting the group just five minutes before Iftar.
- MotoX targeted those who had experienced broken phone screens by asking them to share #myshatterstory. Then, they selected influencers with a high clout score who specialized in technology and mobile phones.

Celebrity innovation:

- Consumers got a chance to talk to Aishwarya Rai through L'Oréal; they could give her a missed call and hear back from her (though it was a genuine sounding pre-recorded conversation). The campaign elicited an audience of four million.

- Lufthansa, in an attempt to drive its Indian-ness with its high-end users, drove a strong word-of-mouth campaign via key opinion leaders (KOLs), like Twinkle Khanna, Atul Kasbekar and Rahul Bose, on Twitter. They followed back via email to users who expressed an interest.

Cause marketing innovation:

- Red Label is all about 'apnaapan' (togetherness). By extending its invitation to the transgender community with the debut song *'hum hai happy'* based on the Pharrell Williams hit 'Happy', the nobility and uniqueness of the cause touched a chord, taking the brand's consideration score up to 69 per cent.
- Unilever's *'haath, munh, bum, bimari hogi kum'* campaign used social media and YouTube to spread awareness about personal and public hygiene, which could be combated through its products, like Domex, Lifebuoy, Unilever water filter Pureit, aligned well with the government's 'Swachh Bharat' campaign.

Digital marketing has, therefore, extended marketing to a level that exceeds in intimacy and sweeps traditional marketing in innumerable ways. Playing by the old rules in the new reality can transform need-satisfaction, the holy grail of business, to a level where *sva-bhu* brands can mushroom up in unimaginable ways.

Integrated Marketing

Digital is exploding, but traditional media is still formidable with its reach. Deploying them together becomes an interesting ploy in the new age. How does one maximize the best of both? It can be done by using them to supplement each other at various points, leveraging their strengths. Below is an integrated marketing circle that shows the linkage between the old and the new ways to market.

Integrated marketing circle

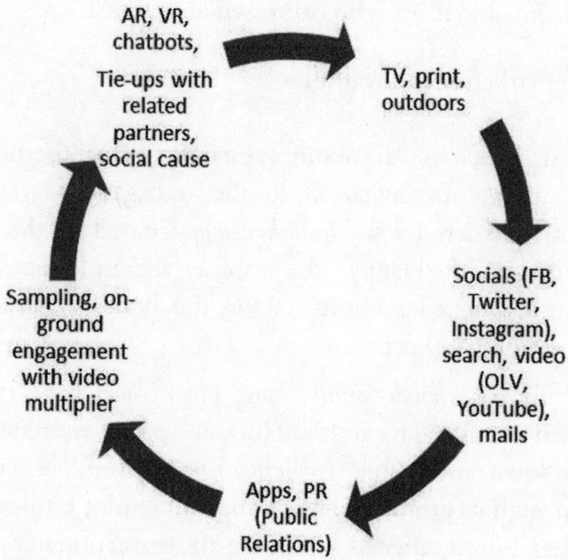

Source: Authors

Let's look at some examples of integrated marketing that we had the privilege to judge.

- Saffola Oats repositioned itself as a tasty snack for weight watchers from being a mere counter to junk foods. Apart from the main TV commercial, it supplemented the campaign with the following activities:
    - Conducted recipe tie-ups with Fitfoodie.in to extend their product usage, as well as a product delivery integration with Holachef.
    - Collaborated with Facebook Messenger for recipe dissemination with a chatbot.

- Cued brand relevance through fitness apps, such as MyFitnessPal and MyPlate.
- Wet sampling at high traffic destinations, especially during breakfast.
- Had a tie-up with chef Kunal Kapoor to create two new products, Chinese and Italian flavours, and it came with the surrounding PR noise.
- A campaign on Instagram, highlighting the superiority of Saffola Oats versus the usual tempting and sinful foods.

- Ceat ran a campaign called 'For the game called road' to bring the consumer's attention to the relatively low involvement category of tyres, establishing the importance of having a good grip on unpredictable roads and traffic. Apart from the TV commercial, they contributed to filling potholes with the help of authorities, promoted it through PR, social media and messaging.
- Raymond ran a campaign, 'Metamorphosing the complete man', taking its original idea of the complete man further by launching products with techno-stretch fibres. Apart from print and TV, it demonstrated the capacity of the techno-stretch fibre through a game in its store windows – rivals across the table would stretch the cloth using their power, which was unleashed through a fanciful AI interface. The buzz generated through such a ground level engagement was played up using social media and searches, which reflected in the positive increase of sales.
- Kaya Laser Hair Removal used bloggers and influencers to relay the message of low pain, low cost and a lifetime of ease where you are able to wear the clothes you want. The campaign was supported by the tweet #wishwearflaunt and had reposts from people who dumped the old

conventional technique of hair removal in favour of laser removal.

- Paytm expanded its presence to 12.5 million people through stickering several participating accounts with its quick response (QR) code, overtaking Mobikwik, as the battle extended beyond traditional advertising. 'Paytm *karo*' became the unifying war cry across various creative renditions that were unleashed simultaneously.
- Infosys expanded its brand recall and new business leads taking a completely unconventional turn. In partnership with the Association of Tennis Professions (ATP), it analysed the performance of top ATP ranking tennis players through a campaign, 'See more, be more', making statistically counted leader boards by analysing the data on players' strengths. It then offered various engagement zones viz. gamification to fans, where they could play against their favourite stars, or 360-degree virtual reality (VR) and augmented reality (AR) and talk to robots in tennis stores – all to help fans play and coach themselves alongside their idols. By demonstrating its technological might in a completely unrelated space, Infosys became a recommended and preferred brand, taking competitors by surprise.

Finally, in staying on course with the marketing objective, various touchpoints can be explored across traditional and new media to not only increase a brand's awareness but also multiply it manifold in ever-increasing spirals, inducing consumers to buy. A country with a billion people is waiting to be delighted by marketers who champion the digital ecosystem.

Pragmarketism overlays the fundamentals of traditional marketing on top of the evolving digital landscape to satisfy consumer needs with more precision and relevance. In doing so, old frameworks of marketing are optimally deployed to capture current opportunities without losing direction.

12

Innovation

'American Style Cream & Onion is our biggest success to date.'

'Sensodyne is going to change the dental landscape in India.'

But these successful launches sit over the debris of many failures. They involved the same people, the same teams and the same enthusiasm; yet, the results spawned could not have differed any more.

Innovate or perish. This has been our hard-earned learning over the years. There is no choice. It turns out that this is where managers crash into their Waterloo or ascend to Mecca.

So, what's required is a magic pill, the five effective ways, the hitchhiker's guide to ... a catapult to failure-proof new ideas.

If it was easy to cast into a formula, set into a mould or embed into a blueprint, it would constitute a veritable competitive edge for companies. So, we drilled through examples and caged this elusive animal into a framework that guarantees success.

The Innovation Paradox

Innovation can be summarised as follows: doomed if you do, perish if you don't. Innovation succeeds in less than 2 per cent of the cases. Dishearteningly, it may take anywhere between 30 to 40 per cent of the brand manager's time (the rest may be spent on justifying why he doesn't need innovation); it actually gives very little credit to his stint. Yet, he is likely to be rewarded more for his failure in attempting an innovation than for saving the company's time and effort by staying away from it. Why do successful companies hanker after innovation so much, when in fact it yields so little?

Innovation has a real benefit and a perceived benefit. If even one in several innovations click, the future of the firm is insured. Not only does the company become futuristic but it also acquires the tenacity and financial muscle to support the growth. The perceived benefit is that brands that constantly innovate stay relevant and contemporary for consumers and customers. Moreover, it imparts dynamism, purpose and consumer orientation within the company, leading to constant growth.

So, the question is not whether or not to innovate, but how to innovate infallibly. Knowing in advance that failure is statistically inevitable, how do you dodge it so that you don't share the fate of iconic companies like Kodak or Nokia?

Innovation Waterloos

To succeed, the reasons for failure must be made transparent so that recurrence of what's mentioned below is eliminated.

Boss is the consumer: In a worse scenario, the consumer is the boss's wife. Surprisingly, we found that innovation is often an attempt to please seniors. Internal feelings often masquerade as consumer insight. A story is often narrated about a boss feeling that the thick deposition of tomato solids around and inside the cap of tomato ketchup bottles was ugly and that research and development (R&D) should find a way to remove it. After intense research, the product was improved and launched, but it met with instant rejection. The reason? Consumers found the deposition to be a sign of naturality. Failure is inevitable when the consumer is kept out of sight.

Lack of differentiation: Old wine in older bottles. Endless flavours, aromas, colours and shapes as extensions of existing brands with fanciful new taglines don't count as innovation. Line extensions rarely enrich brands because a brand works best if it's based on a single proposition. Pushing too many ancillary features without any real differentiation dilutes the core equity of the brand without the joy of additional revenue.

Poor presentation: A great product that is clumsily packaged attracts dust instead of consumer intrigue. The concept of a product that precedes the experience must draw the consumer with the right expectation. The Tata Nano car was an engineering marvel at a wonder price of ₹1 lakh (INR 100,000). But positioning it as the dream of the miserable two-wheeler hopefuls robbed the potential owners of much pride in the eyes of the club of car-owners that they were waiting to join. Unless the concept of the product inspires hope of novelty, consumers simply don't show up. Often, the graphics and packaging (a ruefully undeveloped industry across all categories in India) discourages rather than entices consumers, leaving many great products within untried. For that reason, Paper Boat's entry with a flexibly contoured bottle, reminiscent of childhood paper boats, moved consumers towards quick trials.

Insufficient follow-up: The hoopla and hysteria around a new launch product is rarely sustained afterwards. Availability becomes patchy, stocks become old, visibility a nightmare and replenishment and channel selection thoughtless. Consumer perception takes a knock, and any chances to improvise any aspect of the launch (product, placement, promotion and price) is lost sight of. In reality, a lot of uncertain starts can be corrected mid-course to yield infallible results if managers continue to follow up on the response during the initial days. However, often, the management takes a premature call, dismissing a failure or extolling a success too soon after the launch, ignoring opportunities to improvise.

Perfection paralysis: The tendency to dot all I's and cross all T's of innovation means waiting too long in the green room even as competitors are stealing the march on you. The idea of first-time-right overplays the importance of fixing everything you know before the launch versus things you don't know subsequent to the launch. In hypercompetitive fluid times, it's better to get into the market with 90 per cent readiness on time rather than 100 per cent readiness after the consumer bus has left. Some answers emerge as real action kicks in, while some can be answered with the learnings post the launch, but that can happen only when 'improvise as you go along' is the motto along with servicing consumer needs promptly.

Return-of-investment (ROI) anxiety: Corporates love to check ROI against an imagined and unrealistic ideal. New products need time to take root. The cycle of AIDA needs to go round for returns to follow. Yet, we imagine our consumers waiting at the bus stop to better their lives with our deodorant. And if they are not there when we want them to be investments are reviewed to be cut, diverted or withdrawn, cutting short the basic gestation period of the idea.

Innovate to Succeed

When do you innovate? It's important to identify the root motivation of the project, because that often determines the latent energy behind it, which in turn has a direct bearing on the likelihood of its success downstream. Innovations take root when:

- There is a situation of threat. Growth is embarrassingly low, the market share indicates imminent extinction and panic has gripped the office. In a conciliatory response, projects are compromised in intent or execution for result management, often to save someone's ass (as the office grapevine goes). Innovations in this circumstance come with a short shelf life.

- Sustenance is the mindset. Brands are ticking along nicely – the performance measures are healthy and mild nudges are required to keep the ship sailing smoothly. The environment promotes incrementalism in the garb of innovation: a change in the logo design with a new look 'n' feel, the incongruous addition of an Ayurveda herb to a toothpaste or changing the tail light of the car and relaunching it. This works fine when competitors are stagnant and there is no serious challenger to the category from outside.
- Innovation is the DNA: Companies like Ikea and 3M innovate with practical affordable utilities that make life simpler and faster, saving precious time. However, even these companies face the risk of getting typecast unless they find ways to disrupt internal motions.
- Propelled by a leader's vision: A leader's dream or vision propels change. Disruption follows and markets are reconfigured to make room for the new. Ratan Tata's dream of a car priced at ` 1 lakh (*lakhtakiya*, as an aspiring owner called it), Steve Jobs' vision to propel computers, mobiles and even films in his brief helming of Pixar Studios to the next generation of technology or Varaprasad Reddy's (of Shantha Biotech) launching of the Hepatitis B vaccine at less than ₹30-40 per dose, down from the prohibitive ₹2,200 paid for earlier imports. What drove these guys into the deep abyss of the unknown before they emerged at the far end with breakthrough solutions? The dream to 'put a dent in the universe' for Steve Jobs (as he further inspired Sculley, the Pepsi marketing wizard, to choose selling computers over selling soft beverages) or bringing mobility within easy access of millions of families in India riding on shaky scooters or eradicating Hepatitis in India.

While innovation may differ on the outside, within, its triggers could be vastly different: threat, habit, aspiration or even an affront. Innovation tends to be energy-demanding, so understanding the triggers helps estimate the velocity of a new idea and the barriers to it. Companies have to understand what drives them routinely towards innovation and constantly find ways to elevate it. Taking the reasons for innovation from above and improving on it – threat should be turned into a pre-emptive strike, habit should be given more teeth with truly disruptive innovation, while the aspiration and affront of leaders should be turned into a collective vision.

The word innovation is usually associated with marketing. However, there are as many, if not more, opportunities in supply chain, finance, sales and logistics, as later examples will verify. If the mindset to improve and make better prevails, there is no knowing where the magic wand of innovation can usher in unforeseen benefits.

Also, innovation shouldn't be confused with its distant cousin, renovation. They differ substantially. Renovation revisits an old product or process to improve its delivery to consumers in aspects where it has trailed behind due to the changing times. It seeks to make better, not transform the old. The change is not radical and does not lead to the creation of something new that is entirely dissimilar to the old, either substantially or entirely. In renovation, communication to consumers of enhanced benefit is not elaborate, and merely mentioning it suffices. Innovation, by contrast, requires full-fledged need identification, commensurate benefit explanation and RTB. Companies can kid themselves by passing off renovation as innovation, but innovation stands proven only when consumers are willing to pay extra because they appreciate the inherent value in the offering.

Without disparaging renovation, what are some quick wins available to product or services managers to improve without setting the arduous cycle of innovation in motion? If we look under the skin of the brand, the easy opportunities are as follows.

- Ingredients: Increase the positives and decrease the negatives in what goes into making your product. Reduce sugar, salt and fat, and add more organic, natural, sustainable and authentic ingredients along with transparency in food; reduce chemicals in creams and shampoos, cheap plastic in cars, extra hidden costs in banking; switch from synthetic fabric to cotton in apparels, medium-density fibreboard (MDF) to hard wood in furniture; and multiple features rather than simple usable ones in electronics – every category has an opportunity to be simpler and better. Embracing these early gives competitive edge and sustainability. The world is changing from the earlier industrial production that favoured scale and standardization to environmentally responsible supply that wins consumer appreciation, ensures longevity and allows a firm to charge a premium.

  However, where cost consideration is important for being affordable to consumers at the bottom end, removing frills but enhancing the quality of existing products is the answer from a renovation standpoint.

- Packaging: Try new packaging formats, from rigid to flexible, from hard outlines to soft packaging, from cuboid packs to zany shapes, from opaque surfaces to see-through materials, from large to multiple single-use packs and from smaller portion packs to monster party packs. The options to re-chop, resize and reimagine brands are limitless. As David Ogilvy said, imagery transforms user's perception. Packaging is the most significant working variable of image for brand managers.
- New graphics: Current graphics include the logo and a product or a pretty consumption picture that is artsy. The

minimalism of Apple, the celebration of the Haldiram's gift pack, the authenticity of Forest Essentials, the heritage of Dabur or the simple functionality of Su-Kam inverters catch the eye, but after a quick glance, we return 'empty-sighted'. For a country that has a festival every other day and with almost twelve new years in a year, our graphics fail to mimic the vibrant life of our consumers.

- New payment options: Provide consumers the option to pay through instalments, subventions, payment portals with discounts, e-wallets, loyalty cards and clubbed deals on cards. Financial renovation can touch any aspect of our lives if we look beyond the usual schemes.
- New delivery mechanism: Shift from general trade to organized trade, from category counters to new out-of-home occasions and from brick-n-mortar to e-commerce.

Renovation helps delight consumers and entrenches brand essence. It minimizes cost and risk because its return is calculated on the denominator of the base business. High returns come with high risk – this adage is truest when innovation is spoken of. How do we reduce risk and minimize gains and innovate well?

Innovation Funnel

The common route to innovation in most companies is through the 'Stage-gate' process or its adapted versions. Whatever the name, the process resembles a funnel. Ideas are located at the broad end, and as we progress towards the narrower end of the spout, the concept generation, prototyping, commercialization and industrialization stages follow. At the narrow end of the spout of innovation, only 10–15 per cent of the ideas may precipitate into final products withstanding technical, consumer and commercial scrutiny along the stem of the funnel. Below is the graphic representation of the innovation funnel:

Innovation funnel

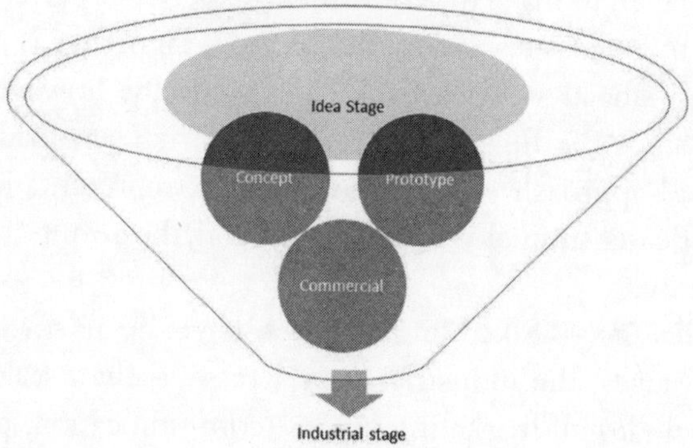

Source: Authors

Idea stage: This is where several opportunities are identified. Ideas are allowed to fly and commercial considerations are held at bay. Consumer needs and creative ways to segment them are encouraged amongst team members. Energy is high and creativity is valued.

Concept stage: Targeting of consumers, benefit exposition and RTB is constructed as the first P&L considerations start to take shape. Stakeholders widen as the technical and the sales community may be brought in to obtain their views before consumer testing – with or without the product prototype – is set afoot.

Prototype stage: If sufficient endorsement is achieved internally, a rough mock-up of the product that mimics the performance of the final product is introduced. This is followed by the concept and product testing (details in the chapter on consumer insight). The result is a go/no-go input. Hard decisions at this stage can help prevent wastage of resources later. Weak ideas should be weeded out ruthlessly or beefed up to be considered alongside strong contenders for commercial scrutiny to sift the golden ones.

Commercial stage: If the product or proposition is liked and the financials are deemed acceptable, the innovation is ready to go. Feasibility trials happen in actual production conditions, and all real life considerations – shelf life, stress test, performance measures – are undertaken to make the consumers' experience perfect. If there are fundamental issues, going back to the design stage is preferable over going ahead with the launch. Practically, however, this is difficult, since the financial commitment has been made. Often, a mid-road approach of modifying a weak representation of the original idea is mutually agreed upon and the results reflect the compromise.

Industrial stage: Since most issues have been sorted at the previous stages, the industrial stage is essentially a scale-up plan which includes all marketing inputs (communication, placement and sampling) and channel plans in order to achieve the desired objective.

Stage-gate works fine for the most part. Ideas are generated and refined, stakeholders are engaged and review meetings are undertaken to achieve progress against carefully calibrated steps. Where it fails is in delivering really disruptive and path-breaking innovation within its straitjacketed structured process. Stage-gate also makes a sweeping assumption about people's buy-in. If multiple stakeholders aren't convinced, they can dilute the project with lip service and mere process adherence without striving to make a real difference. For truly disruptive innovations that bring huge value, stage-gate needs a fair deal of mental and process restructuring.

Evaluating the best innovations in the market and sometimes going beyond corporate, a different framework is suggested here. It includes the following:

- Understanding the problem accurately to recontextualize the situation: REFRAMING
- Rallying resources to bolster support for securing escape velocity against resistance at every step: BOLSTERING
- Correcting midway to maximize the winning potential and eliminating dampeners: REGROOMING

- Capitalizing early wins by scaling up and branching out: EXPANDING
- Making every step of the process down the stream innovate and not merely stopping at the first step: BRANCHING

For simplicity, we call it the R-B-R-E-B model of innovation.

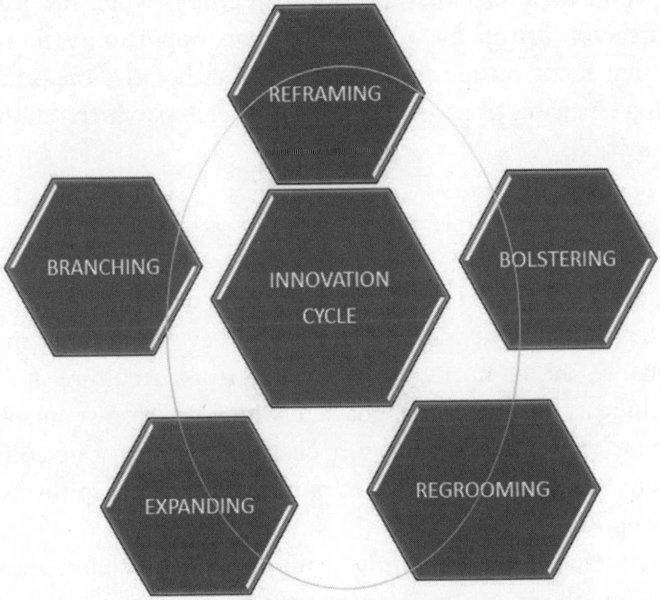

Source: Authors

As we explore each of these steps, it also becomes apparent why success is so difficult to come by – the skills required for each step are varied. While reframing requires objective assessment, it also cranks out most of the creativity to make a real difference. Bolstering depends on eliciting the support of varied people with different styles, making human resource skills paramount. If reframing requires audacity and determination, regrooming requires flexibility to not only accept what's not working but also bend backwards to accommodate the bigger cause. Finally, expanding is about enterprise and boldness to convert early gains into substantial wins to make the difference count, and branching is about embedding innovation in the DNA, forever. Below is the detailed run-through of the processes.

Innovation Circle from Rigid Linear Funnel

Innovation requires either a problem framing (when it's goaded by threat or driven by a process) or an opportunity framing. Let's first focus on the problem definition, because opportunity framing emanates from vision-setting leadership, which cannot be standardized.

Reframing

The problems we see in our heads are often, without our realizing so, the result of some framework. The framework may rest in our personality, the company's culture, the nation's culture or even something as small as the language in which we express ourselves. Below is an example of how a change of words can conjure different images to the mind, reframing a challenge to throw up fresh opportunities.

The mere selection of words, with or without the intention to frame something, can have grave implications, as seen below. If you count the places where you see a clock, the statistic depends on how the question is framed.

a) The number of clocks at home? People usually count both, the wrist and wall clock.

b) The number of devices that show time? Now you can include the microwave, mobile devices and laptop.

c) The number of devices that keep time or a rhythm? Even bodies can be counted as having a rhythm, or the events in the day that help you estimate time, such as the milkman's delivery, the sun's rays hitting the wall of your room through the curtains and so on.

Sometimes, the framework we live in is so deep-seated in its cultural context that we don't even realize it. Consider the following riddle: 'Three doctors say that Robert is their brother, but Robert says he has no brother.' How is this possible? Who is lying? Nobody gets the answer right until the quizmaster discloses, 'Nobody is lying, Robert has three sisters who are doctors.' We don't get the answer right because of our gender bias – in this context, we imagine men when we think of doctors, not women. Reframing things forces us to look again so our known or unknown blinkers are removed.

Reframing helps us lay the framework and define the problem before a solution is sought. Reframing allows us to a) extend the scope of the inquiry, and b) contradictorily enough, circumscribe the limits of the inquiry by attaching it to a purpose. This has its origins in a psychological reality, where it so happens that when we approach a problem, our ability to find a solution is restricted by the subconscious framework within which we think. Unless we are challenged, the framework does not become apparent and neither does the solution flow. A besieged brand manager would typically state his problem, therefore, like this:

- My category is declining and my brand is losing shares and it seems to have no future.

By asking a few questions centred around the rate of decline, relative category growth, competitive challenges and so on, the same problem could be reframed in less bleaker terms.

One of the ways in which the problem could be reframed and answered is:

- The category of washing soap is seeing an increasing trend of decline for the last three years and my brand is declining at a rate less than the category because my brand is strong, but consumers prefer the new format of liquid gel, which my competitor is offering.

The first statement defining the problem would lead to a defensive strategy with an eventual plan of withdrawal. The refined problem statement leads to the following innovative opportunities:

- Reformulate the product and launch a brand extension of liquid gel.
- Relaunch the existing product with enhanced features and reinstate its inherent benefits through new communication; refer to its usefulness such as economy, ease of handling, etc.
- Tide over the current downturn and do not make hasty exit decisions, and instead, focus on expanding your usage to a new target audience at the lower end of the socio-economic ladder. The product can be repackaged or reformulated with better value for consumers.
- Considering that the brand is strong, conduct a study to identify the core brand essence, and while forging ahead in that direction, explore new categories for the brand.

Rajiv Narang and Devika Devaiah, in their book *Orbit Shifting Innovation*,* and Porus Munshi in his book *Making Breakthrough Innovation Happen*,** have discussed the value of reframing to achieve breakthrough innovation. Inspired by their work, we have captured some examples of reframing that have yielded successful results. Reframing can be done at various levels, starting from within the core proposition, but also extending far from the proximal to the distant areas.

---

* Narag, Rajiv and Devaiah, Devika, *Orbit Shifting Innovation: The Dynamics of Ideas that Create History*, India, Random House, 2013.

** Munshi, Porus, *Making Breakthrough Innovation Happen*, India, Collins Business, 2009.

Reframing the Core

Here, the very basis of a brand promise is taken and the assumptions inhered within are restated to generate radical alternatives.

- CavinKare challenges the mighty Unilever in the shampoo market by reframing the problem: shampoos are not for the rural masses because they are expensive and come in larger product formats, and upcountry consumers don't care about hair health. This breaks the reference frame of pricing and the expensive bottle format. Mr C.K. Ranganathan, the founder-pioneer of CavinKare company, reframed the opportunity thus: shampoos can be sold to rural masses at the right price and format if these consumers are educated about the utility of shampoos with respect to hair-health. Running contra to the prevailing limitations, Reddy framed the new opportunity and launched Chik Shampoo at ₹1 and then reformulated another recipe to penetrate the market further at ₹0.50.
- *Dainik Bhaskar* launched its newspaper in Rajasthan to extend its sway from Madhya Pradesh, at a time when no one would give it a chance against the formidable *Rajasthan Patrika*, By framing the situation as, winning against the topmost is impossible because of its size and reader loyalty, *Dainik Bhaskar* countered it by launching on a formidable scale, building reader loyalty even before the launch. This was done with a unique approach: they hired a committed, well-trained and motivated team (researchers would start the day with an inspiring Hindi jingle – '*Man mai hai vishwas*' – and meet later to share and celebrate their experiences, much like a cohesive army out on a mission), establishing direct contact with 200,000 consumers directly, co-creating content with them and checking for its likeability at the same time. By doing this, they countered the scale and the loyalty of

Rajasthan Patrika. Because they identified the core limitation, acknowledged it and challenged it, they were able to launch and carve out a number-two position for themselves, inching closer to the leadership in no time. The same experience continued when they launched in Chandigarh against a leading English newspaper. By framing the challenge around the lousy content and layout of the preceding newspapers, they restored quality in both segments and took leadership in no time with a Hindi newspaper.

- Internationally, a wine's authenticity depends on its place of origin. However, California challenged that years ago with a scientific and technological application that provided global consistency of industrialized output, which scored at par in blind tastings. A fundamental assumption of the industry had been countered by challenging the core frame of origin and replacing it with determinants like processing and technology.

Framing the challenge truthfully and acknowledging one's limitations with reason (rather than not seeing or denying it) points towards a direction for the innovation that is planned, improving its chances of success.

Reframing the Need

In this case, the need of the consumer is reframed through a different lens to arrive at solutions that are unimaginable.

- When there is a need for providing power backup for computers, why can't the same technology be used to provide reliable power backups for electricity? Su-Kam did just that. By framing a known malaise – power cuts – and overlaying it with the framework of UPS inverters, Kunwer Sachdev delivered the solution to meet the need of continuous power backups, like in computers. He innovated ruthlessly in every part of his ambitious mission: from its appearance (using a plastic body with specially imported plastic from GE) to power output (the models in the east are used for outdoor power backup and they are charged through a continuous power supply, and not erratically, as is the case in India) to resourcing his team (professionals on this new technique were unavailable, so he hired people from disparate industries. For instance, a person with missile technology background became head of R&D) to distributing (containing his competitors of cheap battery manufacturers by making them his distributors) to, finally, advertising (advertised in unconventional classified ads section with unusual creative sizes, consistently) to revolutionize electricity. By doing so, he truly ushered in innovation in the bottom-most quadrant of the grid of innovation.

- At a time when the highest rating was reserved for cricket matches, it was unimaginable that another category could be crafted to wean eyeballs away. Yet, led by Peter Mukherjea (former CEO, Star India), the challenge was reframed from a different angle: who can bring the country to a halt for an hour? And a new need was created – marrying the power of a Bollywood celebrity with a simple lottery, in the format of a quiz. Thus *Kaun Banega Crorepati* was born in India. When a need is reframed, alternatives emerge; this has potential to even beat the earlier reference.
- Who would think that the period of waiting for a standard ringtone could be a source of revenue? Well, it was. When interesting ringtones were invented, they received such a huge acceptance that consumers were buying it for a piffling amount. But when multiplied by the high number of users, they became a veritable source of revenue from a completely idle market.

- The flattening revenues of one-day and five-day test matches were revived by reframing an old need through the cracking pace of modernity – the T20 format – and framing the challenge by including time as a critical problem, and, therefore, this consideration led to the creation of new cricketing content.
- In the early years of the dot com, content was made readily available online to seriously coach MBA aspirants through sites like Saarthicool.com or egurucool.com, which made online coaching and administration of tests in a way that was superior to classroom coaching.
- Revolutionary needs can be created. At the launch of a leading mobile telecom services provider in Delhi, research returned with a paltry estimate of their sales potential, as potential consumers felt that they wouldn't need phones outside their homes, since they already had phones at home and in their offices. Reframing the need in the context of critically looking at out-of-home usage paved the way for mobile phones. Eventually, the market became so big that it took away share from landlines as well.
- Dr Reddy's Laboratories spearheaded solutions that changed not only the drug but also the delivery system, like in the case of a nasal spray, which delivers the drug without the pain of an injection. Other innovations include a combined drug for the elderly who have to take many medicines or a Zembrace SymTouch injection, which migraine patients can take via injection with faster results. All this is possible through reverse translation or an approach towards design that works by keeping the patient at the centre of considerations.

Reframing by Fusing Adjacencies

Sometimes, framing a problem by coalescing adjacent categories can create innovative hybrids.

- 'Chips are great and are a convenient snack as finger-foods, but they don't sell as much as "namkeens". How can you get the benefit of both?' This problem-framing led to the creation of Lehar Kurkure, India's first finger-food namkeen. The familiar base, gram flour – a staple of all namkeens was fried, much like Cheetos cheese puffs that used rice. Thus, the fun and random shapes of Kurkure was created, sprinkled with the universally popular masala.
- Nimbooz launch by Pepsi: 'Cola is popular, but it lacks the fresh and energizing cues of the omnipresent nimbu pani.' This framing could have led to improving Pepsi by launching variants with the freshness of lemons, but the problem definition was so clear that the innovation was already apparent in the problem framing stage. Out came Nimbuzz, an unabashed name with the taste of nimbu paani, fizz and the marketing razzmatazz of cola: a thumping success from day one.
- 'Credit and debit cards have great utility, but they lack merchant acceptance and are not as useful as cash during small transactions.' This led to the creation of e-wallets, like Paytm. E-wallets are now becoming so big with technological advancements at the front (smartphones) and even at the back end (encryption and the speed of image identification, payment processing, etc.) that retail banking is under threat. How long before they integrate further investments into mutual funds and equity for you? After all, they further fuse the benefits of banking, framing their nets of opportunity wider and wider.
- Freddie Mercury composed a song fusing a ballad, an operatic section and a rock ending in his genre-defying album, *A Night at the Opera,* and the famous 'Bohemian Rhapsody' a track that ran for an unprecedented five minutes and fifty-five seconds. An instant hit!

- Medical tourism, a hugely profitable venture, is based on the unique fusion of a dire need like medicinal care with the luxuriant world of tourism, which until it was executed, seemed even strange to think of. Fusing can work at radically different levels if challenged well.
- Reframe the benefits of two adjacent categories, create a new holistic frame and double the consumer's benefit – as in the case of shampoo-cum-conditioner or a TV with inbuilt internet browsing features.
- Bosch India was struggling to modify their expensive engine so it would synchronize with high-pressure pumps. They reframed the proposition, stating the difficulty of modifying their engine, which caused them to evaluate whether it was possible to modify the pump itself to meet the stringent emission norms that were emerging for diesel engines. Once the paradigm was shifted, the solution, however awkward and painstaking it may have initially been, came through faster and cheaper than it would have through the original framework.
- Microsoft acquired the idea of an e-reader from a fictitious one, from Michael Douglas's *Hitchhiker's Guide to Galaxy*; a fusion of fiction with reality, by reframing imaginatively.

Reframing the Business Model

If it isn't sufficient to innovate parts of the whole product/service, recast the whole in a new light. The innovation is thus born and is truly transformative.

- When Yogi Deveshwar (chairman of ITC) challenged S. Sivakumar (head of IBD) to create an agri-business department that could stand on its own feet and grow, ITC's e-Choupal programme was born. For that to happen, the framework centred around the fact that farmers could not get the best rates for their produce because they possessed an imperfect knowledge of market conditions had to be challenged. Farmers simply did not know which *mandi* was offering the best rate. As a result, farmers incurred inconveniences and higher costs to move their produce to the nearest *mandi*, and were manipulated and had to give in to sell at the lowest rates, since they could not return to the farmland once they had arrived with the crops at the *mandi*. If their limitation was the lack of information, the challenge was overcome by using technology that informed farmers of the best rates in the neighbourhood (a kind of Google Maps, guiding them through the least-trafficked route), giving them a chance to get maximum returns. The intermediaries who benefited from the earlier regime resisted, but were placated as their volume of business increased, even as their oppressive control on farmers reduced. Furthermore, the advantage for ITC was their backward integration into the rural hinterland which enabled them to launch their own brand of Aashirwaad Atta and staples (since supply and traceability of inputs was assured); they could also set up their shops in e-Choupals to sell other goods, giving farmers the benefit of quality products right next to their homes. By framing the problem correctly, the IT solution (Sivakumar was inspired by a Tata Consultancy Services, TCS, stall in 'India Internet World Fair') emerged and its execution on the ground delivered many collateral benefits too. These included the use of solar energy to power the IT kiosks, empowerment of farmers who became the *sanchalak* (operator) and dissemination of knowledge to farmers regarding the best farming practices and soil management through 6,500-odd e-Choupals.

This case also illustrates the successful integration of the frequently lip-serviced aspect of CSR as the keystone of a business structure.

Reframing the Mental Challenge

- Sometimes, the biggest challenge is nowhere else but in the deep recesses of our minds. Sometimes, it's not exposed because it's too obvious to be spoken; sometimes, too ridiculous to even bring up for discussion. But through reframing, such lurking realities can be exposed and innovation opportunities can be realized. Xerxes Desai, the CEO of Titan Company, reframed their challenge to counter the widely held mental framework that Indians can't make the slimmest watch in the world.

  The idea instantly knocked against the walls of mental bias – how could Indians do it if even the Swiss, the legacy watchmakers, could not? Well, the reframing included mounting the insurmountable plan – beating the Swiss. This meant that no references could be used and everything had to be done afresh – from designing the thinnest movements to the frame that held it to the glass that in spite of being the thinnest, complied with Swiss resistance parameters and could weather tropical wet Indian conditions, to the thin lug and the strap and finally, a battery smaller and more powerful than ever before (a difficult challenge, which often becomes a source of monumental inspiration). Yet, with supreme gusto and teamwork, the solution was found and the monumental launch of Tata Edge, the slimmest watch in the world, happened with a majestic piece of communication creative – India's glory through trademark Titan communication style. The framework was both the constraint and the source of inspiration. Through reframing the mental barrier against beating the best, it was a David-Goliath kind of saga.

- On odd occasions, reframing creates outlandish ideas when logic is turned on its head. George Lucas, of *Star Wars* fame, made the subsequent films of the franchise as prequels to the first film. The new instalment, therefore, was the fourth film in the series. The result was an epic success.

Reframing with Altered Eco-system

- When Dr Govindappa Venkataswamy (popularly known as 'Dr V'), of Aravind Eye Hospital, wanted to eliminate blindness that occurred due to a problem with lenses, the current medical framework did not work. He reframed the problem as 'maximum good for maximum people', which was within his objective to come up with standardized, almost assembly line-like operations similar to the McDonald's to cure the maximum number of patients. Breaking burger-making and serving into standardized items and by creating service flow charts that are easily scaled by specialized employees, McDonald's restaurants are able to offer quality, service, cleanliness and value (their four pillars) with unfailing consistency. Dr V increased the number of patients an ophthalmologist could operate on from 250 to 2,000 by prepping patients through conducting procedures that required less skill and could be done by the support staff before the treatment, so that the ophthalmologists could focus on their core job and operate on more patients. Other changes in the ecosystem included paring down all costs, other than just the cost of the lens and instruments. Even these costs were reduced later by paying for the technology to be transferred to India and made here itself, with high quality sutures. Support staff were hired for their motivation, not always for their intelligence or skill – this ensured that people, once trained, worked diligently (considering that Dr V himself had to modify his instruments to suit his disabling arthritic condition, this incidence also goes to show how solution-searching is germane to the founder of new ideas).

- In the Murugappa Group, the Chola finance team set up dream targets for vehicle financing, chasing impossible numbers when non-banking financial companies (NBFCs) were struggling for growth. They did this through many firsts: differential interest rates, depending on customer profile; autonomy at branch level to decide whom to grant loans to, while adhering to an average interest rate; and even tractor financing increased the ambit of vehicle financing with easier qualification norms for the debtors (like changing the norm of the minimum acreage under each farmer). All these innovations, along the entire spectrum of business, led to astronomical growth rates for Cholamandalam's finance.

Reframing with a Vision

- This is a wild-card innovation entry. It starts with an aspiration, then it finds people who can support it, and then, the idea appears, yielding to the doggedness of pursuit. There is little precedence here and the only thing that is certain is the goal. It's led by a vision and framing is done, in a sense, by disregarding everything else. The Hepatitis B vaccine of Shanta Biotech, led by their visionary founder, K.I. Varaprasad Reddy, falls into this league with their launch of an inexpensive vaccine, made possible through a series of record-making efforts, encompassing product formulation, team resourcing, acquiring funding, rallying a community of doctors to reduce margins in the business and, finally, launching it. The end goal was non-negotiable and everything that blocked the way was modified.
- Apple's computing devices and phones are in the same category and reframing is again done according to the vision of the leader. As a result, enabling capabilities are realized, defying the prevalent state of technology or even consumer indifference.

- Singapore International Airlines (SIA) crafted the bold aspiration of becoming the world's best airline brand in the aviation industry – a task rendered difficult by the fact that in the '70s, Singapore was not even considered a developed country and did not have the credibility to support such an aspiration.
- Anshu Gupta's vision – to not let anyone die during winter due to inadequate clothing (the founder of the NGO, Goonj) – was because of his experience, having seen deaths on the streets increase during winters. This was testified by the person who disposed of the dead orphan bodies ('Dilli police *ka laash dhonewala*').
- J.F. Kennedy's announcement to the world about the American ambition to 'place a man on the moon' at the peak of the Cold War period, despite the huge risk of loss of face given that preparations were far from complete to warrant such an ambition.
- Kiran Mazumdar Shaw led Biocon from making enzymes to Biosimilar products that are used to mimic a living system and not a chemical process, costing 100 million dollars with a gestation period of over five to six years. Braving adverse opinion on her unusual approach, she stuck by her vision and forayed where professional managers would fear to tread. She was also responsible for making insulin by using Pichia technology, which is different from the E. coli that Eli Lilly and Sanofi use.

The above examples expansively illustrate how seemingly difficult positions can be converted to deliver swashbuckling results. As mentioned before, framing not only requires objectivity to state the position as it is but oodles of creativity and courage to seek solutions that are neither apparent nor easy. Inspired leaders work from a vision, not from their current capability. However, the daily grind of projects is delivered by a team of people who are driven and have relentless energy and purpose. This takes us to the next stage of securing support.

Bolstering

When a great idea is presented, the reaction is predictable. First, there is applause, then follows an exchange of disbelief when the difficulties start to dawn on people. Bolstering is when you put up a scaffold under a new roof to ensure that great ideas don't fall apart under the weight of naysayers and cynics.

Visionaries not only resource the project with the right people, but they also ensure that they are well trained, motivated and rewarded enough to become the eddies of change within the organization. Thus, a cause becomes common and collective energies are deployed to thwart unsurmountable difficulties. And often, those involved aren't the skunkworks in an office who deliver outside the main office system, but very much those within who are known for leading with energy and passion.

For the Nano, a core team of designers, cost accountants and mechanical engineers with a superlative record was constituted and given the power to execute within exacting time limits. For ITC's radical e-Choupal programme, Sivakumar ensured that he had secured full approval. He made sure that he had convinced Yogi Deveshwar well before the critical approval, to the extent that Yogi himself presented to the board to secure their agreement. In Shanta Biotech's case, Varaprasad enrolled the support of doctors to disseminate his Hepatitis B vaccine after their initial rejection. Titan's effort to make the slimmest watch would have come cropper if it wasn't for the wide support that the Titan team elicited from its internal and external stakeholders. From the company supplying the slimmest glass with the highest strength to the coordination between the teams working on design and engineering (marrying functionality with aesthetics), it was literally a clockwork symphony.

If approval is not sought from the right people, not only is the initial movement of the project sabotaged, but even the collective ingenuity of specialists, which is so critical for inventing new ideas, may lead to undesirable results.

Asian Paints demonstrated how innovation can be bolstered with a strong delivery system that can support its popular products. Asian Paints pioneered in IT by buying a mainframe to predict and service at the frequency of every fortnight to most depots, bringing down working capital. Then, it broadened product usage beyond Diwali to year-round purchase by making home painting an expression of one's unique identity, through the campaign: '*Har ghar kuch kahta hai*'. Retail innovation was executed on the ground by working with stores where consumers got an immersive experience – they could choose different colours, finishes and visualize the new look of their homes.

Regrooming

Even with the best of intentions, prototyping and research, mistakes happen and potential successes can be sabotaged. There is no knowing whether the problem was smaller than it was made out to be or whether it could have been fixed mid-course to limit damaging the entire project.

Product corrections can be made on the basis of consumer feedback, but marketing managers either fail to capture this in the wake of the euphoria of the launch or they consider their project to be a one-time hit or miss; it could either rise to a sublime victory or descend to an abysmal fall. This rampant attitude prevents new launches from achieving a conquerable 100 per cent solution to get the product/service into the hands of the consumers. Instead, it ends up at a mere 80 per cent of its potential, fated to die on account of poor consumer experience (which could have been rectified). Another reason why mid-course corrections don't happen is the embarrassment it causes as well as the consequent damage to prospects of future project financing. Needless to say, the damage to the project manager's reputation could be considerable.

Regrooming, therefore, refers to the art of grooming a new project again, through careful isolation and surgical resolution of derailing problems, so the ship doesn't sink due to small leakages, but sails powerfully ahead.

Singapore International Airlines, after the launch of their airline with an ambition of being the best in the aviation industry, set off with the best in-cabin experience and continuously improvised on it, providing one gratifying feature after another. So continuous was the pursuit of excellence that the airlines was, in fact, able to refashion the perception of their country as being world class.

Regrooming depends on constant indefatigable improvements that are not blinded by the notion of an infallible swoop of success. The Formula 1 pit stops, where racing motorists have to stop to change wheels and check pressure in a blazing hurry, managed to reduce the holdover time from over a few minutes to a few seconds through continuous improvements. They turbo-ed through a relentless pursuit of excellence, founded on the belief that no amount of time-crunching is good enough.

Vijay Menon in his book *Innovation stories from India Inc** points out that The Himalaya Drug Company's founder, M. Manal, was inspired to start the drug company based out of Dehradun after seeing a wild elephant calmed by the serpina herb, that later became the world's first antihypertensive drug. But just that initial success would have slowed the company down into oblivion. Years later, it set up a store in the Cayman Islands, offering an opportunity to observe consumers from close quarters – this became the base for a flurry of innovations like Liv 52 for the liver and Cystone for kidney stones. Regrooming the company continued as it launched the unique chewable tablet for menstrual comfort when Manal found a young girl who was hesitant to take a tablet.

After exiting his company, Network 18, Raghav Bahl's Quintillion Media, which owns and runs Quint, a digital news portal, regroomed itself and transitioned from sequential and linear

---

* Menon VIjay, *Innovation stories from India Inc*, Bloomsbury, India, 2017.

TV content to the non-linear and timeless nature of web media consumption with huge success. Regrooming awards those who take change in their stride and make the most of new opportunities.

Expanding

When a project shows early offshoots of growth, it's important to pick them up, attribute them correctly to product approval by consumers and rapidly scale up to gain before competitors gobble it up and come up with a better version, or before the pursuit of regular mundanities blocks the road of new ideas.

Scaling up is the preferred way to take control of a favourable market situation. ITC, with its launch of Bingo chips and snacks, did just that. After the first rash of success, they quickly went on to multiply the display racks of chips in all the stores and also increased the repertoire of flavours, so that newly won consumers would have no reason to lapse back to their old brand. The marketing head of ITC called it a 'stun and awe' approach to corner market share ahead of the target against market leader Lay's and Kurkure.

Tata Motors launched full body buses in collaboration with Marcopolo, even though the norm until then was open bodied buses bringing world-class quality. But they scaled up and worked in every area of innovation, constantly adding scale and might to their offerings. First, they improved the running efficiency of trucks through the first ever Indian innovation of a 'lift axle', where a third axle would lift the tyres off the road on a return trip, after offloading the goods, to reduce tyre wear 'n' tear and consequent costs. Since half of the costs of running a truck goes towards fuel, any reduction in operating costs was embraced in large numbers by their clients. Then followed the introduction of radial tyres for trucks, and then they expanded even further – setting up a service centre every 50 kilometres. The final stroke was to fend off the Japanese competition, and it launched the famous Tata 407 in the light commercial vehicle (LCV) segment.

Expanding causes substantial alignment inside the company, since the risk-reward equation can unfold both ways. And while success breeds many celebrating fathers, failure leads to isolated gallows, therefore requiring that the responsibility be pre-emptively shared.

Also, other support systems need to be built to protect and envelope the fledgling idea with more vested dependencies and interests. For example, Airtel, after spreading its user base, went ahead to share mobile towers with its competitors to increase the average return per user (ARPU) by reducing the total cost to the final user. The move was unprecedented, since it meant giving your critical infrastructure away to your competitors, but the total gain was higher than the loss. The move ensured that newly acquired customers continued to use their services more, thereby making customer acquisition (the initial obsession) worth the initial investment. Efforts to expand into adjacent domains call for fundamental business remodelling, and to that extent, expanding the scope of innovations from being a mere product to a process to an entire ecosystem. The primary objective is not to merely increase the share of the wallet but to increase the size of the wallet, making the business more sustainable.

Once Maruti scored initial successes with its cars, it lost no time in spawning distribution centres to formulate a service experience that made transitioning from the old cars an easy choice. This kind of side bulwarking is not only a competitive advantage, but it is also a source for future inspiration. With a large user and distributor base, they multiplied its range to offer economy to super luxury vehicles, thereby becoming a brand that had aspirational offers (Grand Vitara, Swift, Baleno) and also accessible ones (Maruti 800, Omni).

Branching

Innovation is not just about taking a crack at the top end of the project idea and expecting the rest to follow in a merry trail of successful events. It resembles an image of a tug, where each effort strengthens every ring of the chain. Failures in the industry can be dramatically reduced if every aspect of the value chain is pressed into service through newer ways of servicing a new idea. It must not be a case where a Mercedes is supported by a bullock-cart delivery system.

Sometimes, the radical nature of the innovation causes more innovation to take place along the various steps of making and delivery, but it causes delay and discomfort. Alternatively, project managers could cross-functionalize the entire project to challenge the company members to scrutinize ruthlessly, overcoming existing limitations. This would not only energize even the seemingly lesser creative areas, like logistics and channel management, with fresh ideas, but also surprise consumers with genuine changes, which can only have a positive bearing on the adoption and experience of a new idea.

MakeMyTrip has successfully done just that. By breaking through the drudgery of planning a holiday only to discover that it was a bum deal, it has helped consumers by forging alliances across hotel chains, airlines and tour operators that offer easy and subsidized local sight seeing pleasures. Travel packages, consequently, are not only affordable, but also come without the haggling and negotiation that stresses travellers in an unfamiliar environment. Forging alliances across the entire consumer experience never fails to multiply the delight of the consumer.

A good example of branching is Narayana Health, founded by Dr Devi Shetty to provide affordable healthcare, where they can perform a cardiac surgery for as low as ₹1 lakh. Innovation was done at every level to multiply their chances of success. Buildings were erected with the help of Larsen & Toubro (L&T) at specified costs and within the time limit by keeping all the structures at a single level and keeping it light on assets. Materials like disposable drapes, costing a mere ₹900 per operation, were developed specifically. The cost of post-operation care was reduced by providing digital meters to patients, so they could measure their own vitals, and an easy-to-understand, phone-friendly film was introduced to bring down readmission rates. Finally, to eliminate bedsores and thereby reduce costs, causative reasons were addressed: patients were turned over on their beds, a wrinkled mattress or a damp sheet was replaced regularly, etc. Regular innovation at every level, however small, was undertaken to build on the initial success.

Infosys not only led IT consulting but also went on to branch into many other areas to overcome the image of being a sweatshop with a dodgy governance system, and developed a world-class campus. With impeccable financial reporting, it complied with the Cadbury Report, and provided 35 per cent equity to employees. In essence, it tackled every area of its image to become a world-class company, getting listed on NASDAQ. It took Infosys twenty-four years to reach its first billion, but they clocked the second billion in a mere twenty-three months.

Paytm is about branching into the dynamic e-commerce ecosystem; they ended up encroaching on the terrain of cards to classical banking systems. For the first ten years, they provided recharge services to mobile companies, but as phones got 'smarter', they decided to build their own brand independently, under the leadership of Vijay Shekhar Sharma. Now, Paytm pursues an online-to-offline model, charging merchants a commission for the service rendered and earns interest on the money that consumers have in their e-wallets (through all this, it has amassed nearly ₹2,000 crores in gross merchandise value [GMV]). Its user base exceeds 150 million and through the aggressive campaign, 'Paytm karo', is growing hungrily.

Expanding is fundamentally about constantly innovating on success, however diverse or small its impact. Marico has successfully demonstrated that with not grand, but small steps to innovate, as seen in their packaging of Parachute in cylindrical plastic bottles that are packed easily, don't leak, look trendy and can be differentiated from the foggy metallic pieces (although the trade took over eight years to accept it). The ₹1 sachet in the shape of a bottle is another example of innovation adding value, however small. Finally, acquiring Mediker from P&G and growing it in India, and extending Saffola Oats, the heart-friendly product from, ironically, the unhealthy oil category, by leveraging the inherent heart-healthy platform of Saffola.

Innovation culture thrives in the DNA of Oberoi hotels, who look at properties that promise pure air quality, perhaps a bit like the bars and restaurants in China, where food and beverage is topped with a lungful of fresh air.

In conclusion, innovations are path-setting if they can fundamentally alter the way we think and execute new ideas. Through reframing, we can depart from the old and set up grounds for new ideas to peep through. But around the new idea, path-setting enablers, like reframing, bolstering, regrooming, expanding, branching or R-B-R-E-B pathway, have to be laid so success has a chance to solidify and multiply, not atrophy for want of a facilitating support system.

Innovation: Brainstorming Techniques

Brainstorming is required when something new is to be cast. Yet, very insipid ideas appear at the other end and paucity of time leaves us with no option but to run towards execution with whatever is on hand. Is there a process for innovation here, however paradoxical it may sound? Can creativity be template-ized so companies can routinely wow Indian consumers?

Process of Creativity

Creativity isn't about creating a completely new idea from some never-imagined ingredients. More likely, it is the reordering of the old in new ways. But how is the curtain of obvious thinking parted to let new light pierce through?

Creative processes, as per Henri Poincare and Jacques Hamdard, goes through five seminal steps:

Creative circle

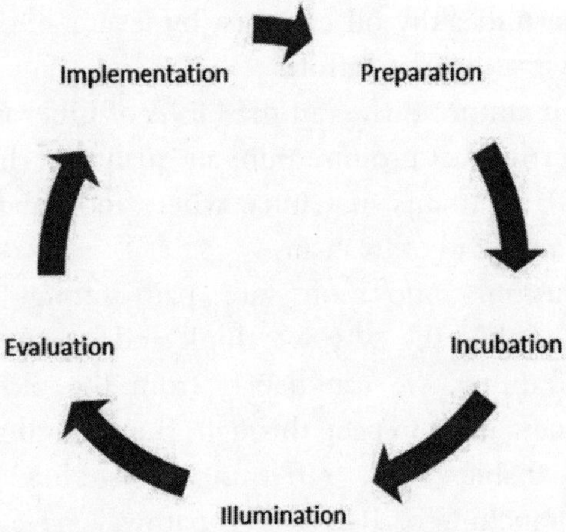

Source: Authors

1. Preparation: When a problem is formulated and a skeletal resolution is mapped. At this point, it is useful to collect information that has a direct bearing on the issue and even information that is distant. Thus, if you find a problem regarding how one can plug a leaky tap, look for adhesives for all kinds, but also evaluate how bridges are made, punctures are fixed or even how rain breaks through the sky. It can be distantly related, but don't let judgment filter through yet, prioritizing what appears to be fun. The brain has a way of connecting unrelated things that are not yet understood.
2. Incubation: When the problem is understood, it is best left to be mulled over in the back of the mind and for it to be made sure it receives no active participation. Put simply, you give up the conscious effort and let the unconscious machinery go ticking.

3. Illumination: This is the Eureka moment, when unexpected ideas appear – much like how solutions appear when thinking about an office problem on the way to work. This is the reality we know but one we don't consciously cultivate and improvise on. Designers admit that the first iterations of creativity are the best, as our subconscious mind makes the best connections much before the thinking mind steps in to dictate logically.
4. Evaluation: When the creators check with other people to assess the idea's worth.
5. Implementation: When the artists chalk out the first impression of their paintings to convert an idea into reality. Above is this process flowchart of this 'creative cycle'. But how does one ensure that the maximum ideas are generated during the Incubation and Illumination stage, so you too are blessed with the luxury of choosing between many greats?

De Bono's six thinking hats offer useful insight and a methodology to generate whimsical ideas through a creative process.

Normally, we suffer from spaghetti thinking, which means that we only think on the basis of our disposition, training or depending on the function we belong to. De Bono's technique allows members in the group to think, for a designated time, by putting on symbolic hats with colours that depict a certain type of thinking. A blue (B) hat helps to manage and state the goal; a white (W) hat is to seek information that is relevant for the subject at hand; red (R) stands for emotions and invites intuition and instinct to be brought into play; black (BL), which is about discernment and judgement, is marked by logic; a yellow (Y) hat forces the members of the group to think of the benefits and the sunny side of a proposition; and finally, a green (G) hat induces creativity with provocative exploration through questioning and alternate paradigm posing. Barring the red that is censorious, enough time is dedicated to each aspect.

The sequence of these hats can vary from subject to subject or depending on the stage of the discussion. For really creative processes, like cracking a communication copy or new innovation, it pays to have the sequence B-W-G-R-Y-BL-G-B at hand. Whereas for something of a strategic nature, just B-Y-BL-W-B-G-B, ending with blue in both cases, works. There is no rigid rule. Only running this a few times gives you a good handle on planning your own sequence.

A simpler one is often followed for product innovation and requires group members to look at every idea from three angles.

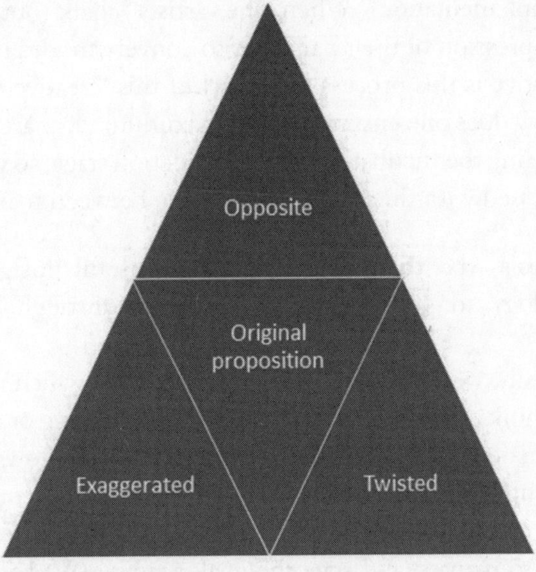

Source: Authors

For instance, if the original idea is a drinking yoghurt, the ideating team could stretch their mind to create a twisted version of it, like a yoghurt with curry flavour or a rubbery texture. Or you could just think of the opposite, which is a running liquid or a vapour-like feel in yoghurt. Or you could exaggerate it, make it like a chunky bar of hard-bites with yoghurt, or into a jelly. As can be seen from merely stretching the idea, we can generate new possibilities that a crack team of specialists can work on, hatching new possibilities that would have been completely evaded in the natural linear innovation process.

What do you retain and where do you take a leap? First, you understand what the essence of the challenge is and where have the borders been cast (refer to reframing in the chapter on innovation). Where has a similar challenge been cracked? Then, you just go ahead and apply it.

Speedo did this very successfully when it identified that they wanted to create the fastest swimsuit. The essence of the challenge or the core obstruction was a swimsuit's resistance to sliding in water. Had other human endeavours or natural forces figured it out? Dolphins and submarines, certainly. What did they have in common? A smooth surface that let water slip through, reducing the natural resistance of the uncovered human body. And Bingo! The new super-fast swimsuit was born.

A new system of hackathon has taken root, for fast, specialized innovation in iconic companies like Google and Apple. A crack team of specialists descend on a topic and they lay down impossible propositions to crack. Then, they isolate themselves in a room for days and nights, till they emerge with a working idea to execute afterwards. Here, the stress of a deadline and the domain knowledge of specialists is manoeuvred to deliver a path-breaking innovation.

However, organizations have more inertia than inherent velocity when it comes to welcoming new ideas. There is no guarantee that creative ideas, even if they take root, will survive the toxic winds of office cynicism. A creative police, as it were, needs to sleuth the office corridors to let freshness flow.

Watch Out!

We outline the do's and don'ts to germinate an idea and let it bloom. Extracted below are things to watch out for, as they fence in creativity – which comes from *The Art of the Idea* by John Hunt (worldwide creative director of TBWA and an award-winning playwright) – is dedicated to making the birth of ideas an organizing principle and not just a Eureka moment.

- You either have **sunrise people** or sunset people, Irrespective of age, gender and race, sunrise people bring ideas and energy into the room, while sunset people dampen and drain out with words like, 'Haven't we done this before?', 'It doesn't work', 'Not practical' or 'Not worth it'. Know them, sift through them and isolate them.
- **Ideas have moods**. A new idea cannot be bossed into existence. Many great ideas take root when you are not trying too hard. But they come half-finished, are fragile and sometimes even silly. But don't ridicule and dismiss them. When ideas surge, let them be knocked about within a group, until everyone participates and the adrenalin flows – refining and fine-tuning as you go along. Very few ideas are born perfect, so being judgemental early on kills truly path-breaking work.
- **Equality before the idea**. Usually, the creative few, if indeed they are creative, are poked to generate new ideas, when actually, ideas can spring up anywhere. But we need to have room for diversity to breathe – calling youngsters into senior meetings, production people to sit in marketing or vice-versa are great ways to break the old and bring in the new. Break the politburo of company borders and usher in the democracy of ideas.
- **Logic is kryptonite**. Logic that is brought on too early during a creative session can turn a brainstorm into a brain-drizzle; hence, it should be only brought in later to finish a filtering process and not as a catalyst.

- **Information is not an idea**. In the age of Google and smart phones, countless datasheets and powerpoints can be brought in to add volume to any discussion, misleading us into the territory of facts – not meaning. The mind needs to be unfettered from the lure of information so it can soar and discover new patterns.
- **Trust your instincts** or they will go away. Prefer years of evolutionary advantage of instinct over uncertainty, defying number-crunching.
- **Incremental change** works only if you are a glacier. Incrementalism doesn't work because it is slower than the vastly changing background, leading up to no change at all. Change is a result of a big leap, not a small hiccup.
- **Expediency is not an idea**. Ideas can't be the middleman, taking the path of least resistance because it suits all. Fresh ideas require courage and tenacity in the hands of people who bounce it amongst themselves to make it revolutionary and not merely adaptive.
- **Embrace diversity** and it'll hug you back. Don't call mini-me's around a table for intellectual incest, but instead, celebrate diversity as multi-source intelligence – not conflicting views. We need others to take our blinkers off for us, otherwise we will perpetuate the game of sameness.
- **Great speakers aren't the greatest idea generators.** Talking about something is not the same as talking through something. Look for discussions that emerge from the fringes of an idea and not from impressive gobbledygook from smart thinkers – words can be deceptively beautiful. Understanding, beyond words, often engenders an idea.
- **Honesty**. Ideas can reach their full potential when the context they are operating in is honest and open. If the

problem is with the product not selling, there is no point in having a brainstorming session with the assumption that the product cannot change. There is no point in calling a group of people and telling them what and where they must think. Conversely, the rewards of an honest discussion are beyond what can be measured.

- **Ideas work in urgency**. Too often, idea generators plead for extended deadlines, pleading for time to make a big difference. In reality, urgency creates a mood and the kinetics to force an idea out, which may otherwise rot in the process – extending deadlines and volumizing meetings.
- **Category lines are blurring**. Ideas needn't sit inside the categories, but as argued in the chapter on segmentation, should be between and outside them. If a bookstore is going out of business, buying better books may be less effective than installing a cappuccino machine; this way, you can go hiking, discover the burrs on your pant and invent velcro.
- **Ideas require small changes**. If it means stepping out of your office to discuss things in a park or even in a different corner of the office where fun and informality prevails. Bring in the necessary stimulus to change and reignite imagination. Small changes make a big difference to the internal wiring.
- **We don't know what we don't know until we do.** Outside of work, indulge in things that break mental conformity, opening up the mind to relay new patterns. From consuming different food to music to art, soak the mind with new stimuli.
- **Revel in ambiguity**. An answer not being known is no reason to not venture; just because you can fail is not a reason to not stand up again. The experience of older folks starts to rust ideas. Being playful, humorous and, occasionally,

> even role-playing as someone else are ways to circumvent yourself. Because ideas require us to be like Don Quixote, and without a bit of lightness, we will never look for new clues that lie hidden, defiant to rules.

Innovation is tough. Without it, you are doomed, and with it, there are frequent disappointments. Pragmarketism advocates that we attempt at various steps to create more fresh and productive plans, with several iterations. We should even create a culture of eradicating dampeners of innovation, as highlighted above. It's a lot of cerebral churning, but in our experience, a few days of extra work of being closed up in the office to seek a solution is a lot less work than months and sometimes years of frustrating failures and crores of money ill-spent.

However difficult the situation, there is always a better way. It can be mined and brought to light if we innovate and persist, pragmatically and flexibly, with tools and examples that we have gleaned above.

13

Selling

'Marketing guys don't do much except making adverts that no one understands,' my sales head once lamented.

'You guys don't place and display what we make and advertise,' I complained.

'I am sending the marketing guys into sales because they don't know what sells, and I am getting the sales guys into marketing because they don't understand what they sell everyday.' Our CEO thus resolved the situation.

Sales and marketing are a mash-up. Often, you can't decide where one's responsibility ends and the other's begins. Magic happens when responsibilities are shared and respected, but it's a disaster when they work at cross-purposes. So, what's the resolution?

Selling to the consumer is at the heart of both.

Selling is as seminal to business as waking is to living out our dreams. It helps convert our dreams to reality. But selling is not just being available at arm's reach, as Coke once expounded, but also about being compellingly enticing. As choices expand and the digital world entices, our brands need to be showstoppers more than ever before.

Selling includes the journey between manufacturing and consumption. It's what gives our products momentum so that consumers don't have to wait for too long. It runs in tandem with marketing, which creates the reason why products need to be consumed. Put it out too soon before marketing and selling is like a stranger in the room. Alternatively, put it too long after marketing and selling it is like a day-old newspaper – everybody knows about it but nobody gets excited to buy it. Selling is, therefore, also about timing. When a huge capital investment is sitting in that simple cookie, it becomes very critical to have a sales structure that makes availability, visibility and timing right, so that every kind of cookie that the consumer wants is available, and such that it bites just right, every time.

Structure of the Sales System: Products

Once products are made, they need to be dispatched far and wide in our country to reach the consumers sitting thousands of kilometres apart, separated by treacherous terrain or just humongous distances. From here, the selling challenge starts.

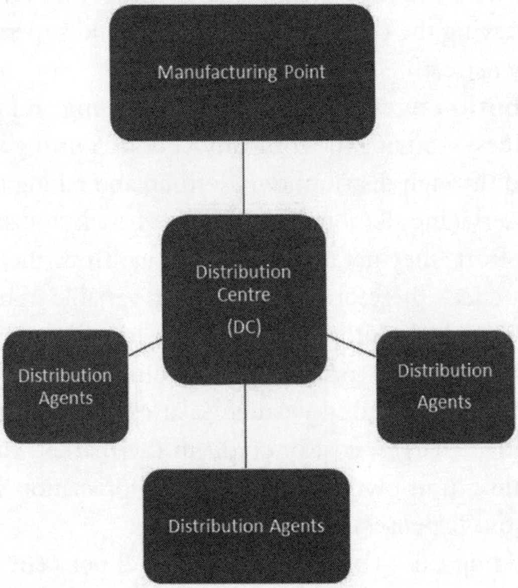

Source: Authors

From a manufacturing location or factory, products move to distribution centres, which are typically owned by the company and facilitate breaking large lots into smaller ones to be passed to distribution agents, who buy these from the companies, leading to primary sale or invoicing, as the title of the goods gets transferred.

Distribution centres are usually located outside leading cities with good transportation facilities and a basic office that handles logistics at the secondary level. They are remunerated by big companies for all the expenses of warehousing rent, administrative expenses and loading costs. Distribution centres never buy the product; hence, they make no margin on the product being transited through them. Instead, they get a commission that is fixed. Clubbed with earnings on logistics that they often own or manage in partnership with a local truck owner, they make a fairly regular income, insulated from the selling fortunes of the products they store. It's a win-win situation since companies value them for just that, leaving the companies free to own and supervise the real selling downstream.

Distribution agents partake in the upswing and downswing of the business – buying the company's goods, putting their feet on the ground through distribution salesmen and taking the physical trouble of servicing all mom and pop stores, tuck shops or '*kiranas*'. For their effort, they get a fixed percentage from the goods they sell. In essence, therefore, they have a variable remuneration. It's usual to calculate their ROI on business by dividing their income (commission percentage x value of sales) by total expense (includes rentals, salesmen salaries, bad goods, bank and administrative charges, cost of credit in the market, running cost of distributing unit owned by them, its depreciation and sundry administrative expenses).

On dividing the two, if you get a 1 to 2 per cent return, the annual return is 12 to 24 per cent. If you compare this with the opportunity cost of his capital (put simply, the money he would have earned by investing in fixed deposit with the bank), this is a good return. However, in reality, smarter distribution agents multiply income in turning the cash around by selling on cash (or credit, not exceeding a week in metros and fifteen days in upcountry) more than twice in a month. So, in effect, their cash investment is halved and their return doubled. But company sales agents know this and prevail on distribution agents to compromise on excess profit and deploy extra manpower or expand distribution through investment in vans.

From distribution agents, products reach retailers, who sell either to **wholesalers** or directly to consumers. Wholesalers are another layer in the distribution circuit; they provide an advantage in reaching smaller retailers whom companies can't reach directly, either because they don't have enough product strength (in terms of both size and range) or because they can't afford it. Wholesalers are disadvantageous because they cost an extra percentage or two for the seller and can be swung with huge discounts, making them somewhat disloyal as channel partners. But many companies that depend on rural penetration, like torches, slippers, confectionery and undergarments (the most ubiquitous product categories in upcountry India) or have low-priced SKUs (stock keeping units), like confectionery, soaps and shampoos, actually find wholesale a boon and have mastered programs for trade (gold, watches, utensils or even a trip to Bangkok) to tie them down through quantity purchase schemes extending into full quarters.

Retailers in India present a unique challenge. They are varied (from a tuck shop that stays half-closed to organized retail like Big Bazaar to e-commerce players like Big Basket), scattered (almost ten million outlets need to be reached for FMCGs at the lowest end), heterogeneous (terms of trade vary from instant cash purchase to credits extending into six months in the hills) and influential (a *kirana* store is the first surrogate brand of India which ensures adulteration-free quality, returns and discounts on frequent purchase and home delivery – all the advantages that modern trade formats are offering now). Hence, designing a route to the market for most companies in India is tedious but rewarding. Large multinationals use the extensive labyrinth to spread their products over a million outlets within a fortnight – a feat that new entrants cannot even imagine.

On the other side, you have organized trade, which is growing in double digits, but still contributes only in single digits to the national sales of most pan-Indian players. Organized trade in India, like other business realities, has unique hybrids that sit between the traditional trade and the modern trade. Unlike the West, which has small, large and hyper formats, the Indian self-service stores are the erstwhile soiled shops with a welcoming bania, who has now receded, allowing direct access to the products in narrow aisles. In some shops, the access is partial, in others it extends into a difficult mezzanine floor on the top, suitable for hunched walking. In Mumbai, Chennai and other metros, these self-service stores also have broadsheets with discounted rates no less attractive than Big Bazaar's front-page splashes in the national dailies. As we move up the scale, we start finding organized local trade, like Margin Free in Kerala, which then goes up all the way to the big ones – ABRL, Big Bazaar, Spencer's, Vishal Mega Mart and so on. All this makes for a great Indian meal, where you can soak your taste buds in a delectable curry of the organized trade, fulfil your appetite with the large chapatti of traditional trade and occasionally relish the thrill of chutneys and 'murabbas' with e-tailers.

The above structure is true of FMCG majors, who have one of the best distribution and sales strategies to maximize their direct contact with consumers. Parts of this chain are reduced or eliminated, depending on the company and the industry. Within the FMCG space, for instance, Procter & Gamble made a strategic choice to concentrate their distribution centres in a few hands, enlarging their scope and calling them super-distributors with a margin structure that allowed these super-distributors to run their own frontline selling force. In durable companies, the long chain of distribution is cut by directly reaching some big retailers from the manufacturing points. In pharma, due to regulation, the movement of stocks from distribution centre to agents and pharmacy shops is tightly controlled. Finally, if you are an original equipment manufacturer (OEM), you directly deliver to the customer from the manufacturing location, or orders are pre-booked alongside manufacturing or even before goods are manufactured.

There are also various adaptations in the retailing space. It can proliferate to unbelievable numbers if you are selling something as small as prepaid mobile recharge cards. Even a paan kiosk is a good enough retailing point, the key determinant being the lingering presence of your consumer – the adult male. Or it can be exclusive and chic as in the apparel industry, where there is backward integration of manufacturing and retailing to lure consumers through snazzy franchisee- or company-owned showrooms.

In such a complex environment, how does one design the best channel strategy? At the start, it's very important to address your **primary objective**, which ought to be aligned with the overall business and marketing priority: is the business focusing on reaching more consumers (penetration) or frequency (more consumption from the same)? Often, this choice is not made, leading to doing a bit of both, which is fine because whichever way the wind blows, you collect some fruits on the ground. But the result of this approach is missing out on maximizing the opportunity through a closer focus.

If the choice is penetration, then the effort and capital should be towards getting more outlets aggressively. With the right portfolio (price, quantity and margins), investments need to be made, targeting a far and wide reach through pilot salesmen who scout for shops, dedicatedly following the data of the outlet universe. This would involve incentivizing or subsidizing distribution reach in far-flung areas (at least in the initial stages) as well as regular monitoring of lapsed outlets and those that are showing returns and having the right visibility devices. By contrast, a frequency objective would mean doing a Pareto analysis (finding where the bulk of the business comes from) of the top-selling outlets and zeroing down on them to increase the availability and visibility of a range of SKUs, improving servicing frequency from once a week to double or more, pushing for ready stock (delivering the products when the order is booked, to avoid a lapse or a revision in the order when the actual delivery happens), dressing up outlets with superlative visibility and designing loyalty programs with key outlets to increase market share and even inter-category market share, with visibility share that is more than a brand's market share (also called forward stock share). By focusing on either, companies can register more revenue for less, but this is often not the case, as managers are not sure where the bulk of the business will come from – a situation which can be redeemed with some research (like doing a source of business study with household panel data) and taking some calculated risks, looking at the pattern of sales with internal data.

After setting a clear business objective that dovetails sales and marketing, the next thing to consider is the **cost of the delivery mechanism.** One may take an aggressive approach and rake up higher costs so as to push for more expansion, but for a limited time, after which they can either increase the scale of the business or, through a deliberate reduction of trade discounts, restore a healthier gross margin to make for a sustainable business expansion plan. Every industry segment has its costs (in the FMCG industry, the cost of distribution ranges from 3-4 per cent of net sales, for instance) and the endeavour should be to lower costs and secure higher reach. Within the cost structure, there could be some working costs and some non-working costs. In marketing, this means separating what is consumer-benefiting directly from the unproductive fat underneath. That typically means that fixed costs are controlled. So, there is no heavy investment in distribution vehicles and administrative costs, but additional outlets are reached through stretching the existing resources. Often, companies cut costs, which results in removing good cholesterol too, when the focus should be on cutting down the *non-working* distribution costs.

The next step would be setting up KPIs on expected deliverables. First, **inventory** – how many stock units are to be held at every point – the distribution centres and with distribution agents. Enough stocks are kept to satisfy consumer demand, allowing for some fluctuation, while keeping working capital costs low – this makes for a demanding challenge. Yet, this contradiction is reconciled by considering the minimum time it takes to physically move stocks to different locations from the manufacturing site and then reducing it, approximating towards a just-in-time replenishment with sophisticated planning through IT systems.

At the retail level, the Inventory in the store is determined by the frequency at which the outlet is visited. For a weekly covered market, as in most big FMCG product beats, a cover of fourteen days suffices. In retail accounts, like Spencer's and Big Bazaar, depending on the velocity of the item and the time of the year, it could range from a week to about a month, but with increasing pressure on retail returns, often calculated per square feet, where low value or low velocity items get knocked out, the emphasis is towards lean inventory norms.

Second, **freshness** – which is linked to the above but is measured from the consumer's perspective. In the category of food, this is especially critical, since freshness has a direct bearing on the consumer delight. However, even for other categories, old stocks run the risk of being outdated in design or by sheer appearance. A tight freshness metric (in terms of days) runs counter to an out of stock metric, measured by a Nielsen report. But, in spite of their contradictory nature, having the two KPIs can achieve a desired resolution and ensure an optimal balance without overdoing either. For a durable industry, a long-standing inventory not only blocks high value capital of trade partners, but may also force them to push stocks of old models to the disadvantage of consumers.

Third, **visibility** – which is lower in preference, since it's difficult to quantify this variable with hard numbers. Visibility has traditionally been with frontline sales in some companies, but with growing complexity, it has been designated to specialists. So, whether it's the merchandisers hired for dressing up the ubiquitous 2x1 feet shelves in *kirana* stores, agencies which merchandise and promote in self-service stores or design specialists who work with Titan and Tanishq showrooms, this cost is well worth bearing as it is known to increase sales by 15 to 25 per cent. The additional benefit of near-purchase visibility is that you catch consumers when they are attitudinally disposed to buying. Wherever companies prefer to place their real estate for display, like visi-coolers for Pepsi or shelf-in-shelf units of shampoos or creams, it's useful to have visibility drives to maintain the purity of your stocks. Otherwise, competitive products feed on your space and increase market share from your real estate. Visibility, therefore, has a direct correlation with share gains, as it prioritizes you over competitors.

In the FMCG industry, visibility has to do with selecting what to push and when to do so. Given the large size of their portfolios and the sheer number of SKUs for the same brand, losing focus is easy. However, selecting what to push at different times of the year, depending on the consumer promotions or seasonality, would give better returns than a blanket approach. For instance, promoting Knorr soups in winters over Kissan Jam makes more sense, but what often seems intuitively correct doesn't get translated into ground action.

In durable companies, the visibility requirement is more sophisticated, as consumers are lured by nothing less than the experience of the product. In Samsung showrooms, experience is given primacy over sales, which can even happen online. This subsequently helps build brand attraction and accelerate conversions. The same is true for automobiles, electronic products, paint and so on. Asian Paints have gone ahead with colour labs and simulated living room examples to convince consumers about their ability to provide a superior experience. In retail channels, brands have to lead the conversation with the trading partner through 'category captaincy' – which means using shopper insight (referred to earlier in the chapter on research) to understand the levers that drive category consideration and purchase. In developed markets, although the lead for the category rests with the market leader, there is still a big opportunity for other players to help understand shelf-utilization better for their trading allies and use it for promoting their interests.

Fourth, **selling control** – it impacts sales as per your strategy. In India's vast retail universe, it's easy to lose control. Sales supervision in sync with strategy (either penetration or frequency from the consumer standpoint, as explained above) delivers in the last mile of business planning. The most intense players in distribution tend to come from FMCG and their deliverables are around call-age (how many outlets are they calling on), productivity (how many outlets place orders, resultantly), range-selling (being able to place the entire range of SKUs and not just the easier ones) and depth of throughput (weighted outlets where category share is high, your brand dominates so as to drive up the market share). Given the vast gamut and complexity of this eco-system, companies prefer to have their own manpower oversee selling or train frontline sales to ensure consistent and comprehensive execution. In industrial sales, selling control is such a strong variable that the frontline sales people are engineers who can converse with ease on technical aspects of their offering, enabling them to convince and close sales.

Along with selling control comes the fifth aspect, **training.** For the most part, sales are conducted by trusting the germane human skill of selling. Organizations like Frito-Lay have perfected this to an art and earned enough trust amongst retailers to virtually own the shop space. They follow the replenishment model, based on consumer offtake, not on what is available with the manufacturer to place. Gradually, through selective placement, they artificially increase the facings of new flavours and bigger packs (party packs instead of the ₹10 or ₹15 packs) in their racks. The planograms, or the display pattern of flavours, is again done on the basis of the offtake of flavours in that region, with an intrinsic understanding of local palate preferences across India. For instance, Mumbai has a higher number of sweet flavours, like tomato and honey chilli; north India prefers masala and cream onion; and east India likes flavours based on mint and coriander, like 'Papdi chaat' (which Uncle Chipps used to dominate till it got acquired and relaunched). Sales management is relatively easier and more fruitful if overlaid with consumer insight, as demonstrated in the case of Lay's.

Training of frontline sales, which was perfected on the streets of Mexico and manualized in their Dallas office, makes a religion out of rack maintenance. This includes the right-sized selection of racks (names like 'Trimurti' and 'Charminar' were used to cue three- or four-tray racks) and baskets, nailing or placing products in vantage locations to drive consumer behaviour, laying high-selling items at an eye level and within easy reach and lower-selling ones below (except when new flavours or larger packs were being pushed strategically) and, finally, servicing so well that shopkeepers were happy to let company salesmen own that piece of real estate of their shop.

In fact, the sales KPIs in Frito-Lay (now part of PepsiCo) are set based on rack placement and planogram, and the marketing KPIs are based on offtake, indicating the appropriate bifurcation of responsibilities. Across levels, the best performers were rewarded, with guys much lower in the selling system going to Dallas for recognition, just as trainers from the US sweated it out in Kanpur in the initial days to convince the entire selling team of the virtues of a regimented system of rack placement and maintenance.

High training cost meant fewer chips for the consumer in the bag, given the costs. But it was more than made up with the quality and ease of product availability that the company ensured. The obsession with the quality of chips is vivid in the training – 'handle like eggs' – amongst staff at various storage and distribution points to ensure that the full chips, in their pristine 'saddle shape', reach the consumers. Training, wherever invested into with strategic backing, yields dividends that widen the competitive gap. However, there is always a while before the returns flow, and those in a hurry will prefer a quick turnaround over cultivating a long-term advantage.

For a good sales channel management system, the benefits across each of these levers, and some smaller ones within, have to be evaluated with respect to costs. It varies from industry to industry. A durable company cannot behave like an FMCG company, and a fertilizer or paint distribution has its own route to market (RTM), but as many are beginning to discover, competitive advantage may lie in taking the best practices from one industry and implanting it onto another. That is how a restaurant company like Haldiram's can launch retail packs based on knowledge of consumer preferences through food doled out from its parlours daily, capturing dazzling success. Though nobody has done the reverse – turning a successful retail brand into a great out-of-home restaurant opportunity – the probability of success is relatively high.

Summing up the above is a cross-evaluation of different sectors of the industry with respect to the four variables of sales management, to understand the critical drivers of success in each industry.

Industry evaluation of sales variables

Industry	Inventory	Freshness	Visibility	Selling control
FMCG	Outlet visit frequency	Product shelf life	Strategic choice of SKU	Call-age, productivity, range
Durables	Season-based	Variety, feature-flexibility	Experiential	Conversion rate
Pharma	A month at DC	Year-round (expiry date critical)	Not important	With doctors, not retailers
Paints, automobiles	Credit policy, Diwali	Technology, model upgrades	Demonstrative – looks/driving comfort	Cost/efficiency/comparative selling
Modern trade	Average one week	Category dependent	Category captaincy	Deals, display
Industrial products	Customer usage	Design	Catalogues, company credentials	Trained manpower, bidding process

While they are varied and unique to their industry circumstances, there is no reason why the cross-pollination of ideas from one segment to the other cannot be done for securing a competitive edge. For instance, detailed product catalogues like the ones used in the pharma industry for a doctor's endorsement can be the inspiration to convince the mom/housewife of a new detergent or durable, or even a nutritious food supplement, to impart gravitas and significance to grocery-purchase decisions. Reversing the approach, a pharma company could take a trick out from the bag of visibility devices of FMCG companies to market an over-the-counter (OTC) product. On the other hand, FMCG companies could open parlours for consumers to sample their brands in a restaurant (if it's a food company) or grooming parlours (for personal care companies), deprioritizing sales over experience. Cross-pollination is rare because industries tend to focus inwards at their competitors who are huffing and puffing, doing the same thing with mere executional differences. A radical approach in availability or experience for consumers beyond the industry's standard way of dispensing products is relatively scarce.

Price promotions and their effectiveness

If advertising has a long reach and impact, promotions have a short reach (limitable by geography, retail channel or SKU size) and more instant impact. Price off, discounts on multiple units or large packs, extra quantity, an added proximal product (conditioner free with shampoo) or distant one (Nivea cream with innerwear brand) are ways to entice consumers to buy more than their usual requirement. The intended impact is to spur more consumption based on higher availability. While that may not always be possible, pantry up-stocking does prevent the purchase of competitive products where market share wars are closely contested.

Price promotions, while providing a shot of relief in a period of distress (which coincidentally is when they are pressed into service most), suffer from the following limitations:

1. Price promotions usually appeal to loyal consumers and those who flit in and out of the category depending on its value. New consumers are not won over due to price promotions – at best, lapsed or infrequent consumers get attracted back.
2. Frequent price-offs blur the reference price. Consumers end up not understanding what the original price was – this dilutes the delight that comes from grabbing a good deal. Worse still, when the price discount is pulled back continuously, consumers may resist it and fall out of the brand since they are too used to the discounted price. In the long term, this can be very damaging as the brand's margin is diluted with no offsetting by commensurate sales up lift.
3. Price promotions work well when the sales, after the promotion period has lapsed, are higher than the average of the previous months. If that happens, then it cues an increase in the repertoire of consumption or in the base of users. If not, it merely prepones the sales that would have happened a week later, indicating that only the usual buyers availed the deal. A good increase is 10 to 15 per cent, equivalent to an extra three to five days of sales in a month. In reality, the increase is around 5 per cent, which barely covers the cost of the promotion or the operational complexity that distracted the whole value chain during the promotion.

So, what is the best way to run a price promotion? **Price elasticity**, which is essentially a way of estimating the impact of price on volumes, is calculated thus: volume increase divided by price cut. It could be one measure to compare one's brand performance over others or across various points of time. Thus, if price is cut by 10 per cent and the sales volume increases by 20 per cent, the elasticity is negative 2 (negative implies inverse correlation). The bigger the value, the higher is the elasticity. So, a more useful question to raise is: how do we ensure that we get higher price elasticity? Some of the best practices in the industry that can be followed for higher elasticity are as follows:

1. Price cut is relative, meaning it should make the consumer sense better value in comparison to competitors. Hence, to encourage the switch, it should be lower than the competition. Going very deep will hurt the company and brand P&L, and a superficial drop without referencing the competition will yield low results and just end up wasting money.
2. Generally speaking, big brands have small price elasticity, but small brands have higher elasticity. A corollary is that big brands suffer more financial loss by dropping the price because of a higher number of sales units involved than smaller brands.
3. In his book, *How Brands Grow*, Byron Sharp argues that price increase involves a bigger drop in volume than volume increase with price drops. This he attributes to the 'loss aversion theory', wherein consumers hate losing money more than the prospect of gaining money.
4. Price elasticity is higher where consumers do pantry stocking, buy frequently and seek value with not much brand differentiation.

We understand that sales and market share can be influenced positively in some cases, but at what level do price promotions become profitable for the company? Byron warns that if the normal contribution margin of a product is 50 per cent, a 10 per cent price cut shaves 20 per cent off the contribution margin. So, brand managers need to be forewarned about the depletion of margins that the sales increase brings.

A win-win situation would be increases in sales and market share without a drop in the gross margin or the contribution margin – in other words, a breakeven for the business. At three levels of gross margin, Byron offers the following break-even scenarios.

Break-even Scenarios	**At 30 % GM**	**At 40% GM**	**At 50% GM**
Price reduction %	Increase in sales required to match GM	Increase in sales required to match GM	Increase in sales required to match GM
5	20	20	11
10	50	33	25
20	200	100	66

Inside the company, people have a good sense of how much volumes can be secured with a price cut, depending on the relative price difference and market shares. As can be seen from above, it's easier to take small price cuts and get offsetting volumes than take large price cuts, which require an impossible increase of volumes if the gross margin (GM) is not good.

To redeem all the above difficulties, some retailers, like Big Baazar, have started loyalty programmes – so, discounts secure heavy purchase from light users and new users to avoid concentrating sales into the hands of heavy users who would have bought anyway. However, there are inherent flaws in this model, as illustrated by the grid below:

	Low brand loyalty	**High brand loyalty**
Light buyers	Unlikely to join due to low interest in brand and category	Likely to join, but don't benefit brand since they are light buyers of the category
Heavy buyers	Likely to join, but not beneficial enough as they value on-spot discounts	Likely to join but would have bought anyway

Thus, only in relatively fewer cases does the loyalty programme provide benefits. However, it has other benefits: it pre-empts consumers from shifting to another brand or retailer, and it creates a database for future communication, insight and even new product or promotional news dissemination. What has worked lately for the big retailers instead is creating thematic promotion days: Wednesday Bazaar or Big Bachat Day; or Big Billion Day and Great Indian Shopping Festival for e-commerce players. These increase footfall and since they are also combined with huge discounts from suppliers, the GM and the price elasticity are presumably enhanced.

With all the considerations above regarding the return on investment on advertising, price promotions and loyalty programmes, do we get some silver bullets to crack the hyper-cluttered and ever-evolving Indian market? Unfortunately, the remedy is more about maximizing some or most of these things to stay competitive in the great Indian market.

1. Brands are beginning to acquire importance, but pricing has also never been as critical as it is now. This is the reality of the Indian market. From being commoditized to being branded to having many branded players who are offering similar products. The result is that consumers are buying brands they value for trust and quality, but will only pay a little extra before switching to the next best alternative, which is usually not far behind in the consumer perceptual map. Hence, building brands, one cannot ignore hawk-like gaze on value and pricing. Consumers like brands, but they like a good deal no less.
2. With increasing clutter and scarce time, consumers are screening out messages more than evaluating them. Therefore, brand messaging has to be sharp, minimalistic and relevant. In Japan, which is at the extreme end of this phenomena, brands are moving to pure symbols, like the Nike swoosh, that has recognizable brand assets (colour,

font, typography, visual imagery, etc.) easily reinforces the memory of the brand in consumer's mind.

3. Brand representation should be minimalist, but expansion of its assets should be complemented with the brand's presence at multiple touchpoints – wherever relevant obviously, or even obscurely. This is a better way to drive brand recall than through the usual multiple long messages of standardized creatives. Better reach is a clear benefit of this approach.
4. High clutter means easy fatigue or poor processing because of fragmentation of creative messaging. To counter these twin problems, brands have to be consistent with their core message, but fresh with their context regarding the occasion and the time. Hence, Haldiram's is better off when talking about 'Indian taste and quality' (which is a consistent message) with varied offers that correspond to different occasions, dishes, times of the day, etc. In this manner, consumers not only distil the brand they need with ease from muddy waters, but also connect to them in various ways without getting bored.
5. Finally, chase penetration, and top that with frequency wherever possible. In a large country that is growing and changing every day, the opportunity to get new consumers is limitless. And with new consumers, different levels of frequency will also follow, extending both the market share and the long tail of brand users, ranging from heavy to light – and we don't need to prioritize them until we are faced with serious stagnation. But then again, it's unlikely to happen in growing India, where even niches become mass segments due to the size of our population – the only condition is that we should know what our consumer needs in each segment.

Offline-Online Interaction

With online attacking, what look will the retail of the future wear? This discussion will have trade pundits in fervent debate, reaching no conclusion, as there are few precedents to go by, even as India carves out its own destination with a unique trade situation. However, some possibilities gleam in these uncertain waters, which can help companies get the best of both worlds.

Buying and exploring are slowly disassociating from each other. Consumers will take a brand experience in one place but buy the product somewhere else. Online marketing can be used by them to purchase or explore, as the category permits. Standardization of products or clear nomenclature becomes important so consumers can spot and order what they like. Complex model names of cell phones, usually seen on large billboards, don't help consumers order them on Amazon, or a great dress on Myntra with no label cannot be recalled when one's fingers linger on the search button with a lack of certainty.

Offline has the advantage of tangibility, which online can only provide virtually. Brands and retail channels playing in this space must enhance the tactile brand and buying experience to draw consumers into their fold. Likewise, online players will have to find avenues to make their offerings more palpable, as we have seen demonstrated in Pepperfry showrooms.

A choice being given to consumers directly translates to making them feel empowered; new innovative products and a range of SKUs greatly influence this feeling. Offline has to learn a thing or two from online here. Rather than being content with selling high selling SKUs, as the ROI logic of floor space dictates, offline has to find ways to thrill visitors who are checking their retail shelves with innovation and wide range, especially as they are used to online scrolling. Otherwise, offline stores are likely to become discounters for bulk purchase, losing consumers who are looking for new ideas and inspiration.

On the other hand, excessive choice for consumers on online portals may become a disadvantage. In his book, *The Paradox of Choice*, Barry Schwartz* convincingly argues that with too many things to choose from, consumers are ironically more dissatisfied than ever before. Because the satisfaction from what they have selected doesn't counter the imagined satisfaction of the many others they have rejected to make such a choice. To avoid deluging consumers with excessive choice, or pushing paid adverts to drive the choice artificially in already crowded screen space, online retailers will have to go with genuine consumers and maybe even a specialist's feedback (which is not possible offline) to guide consumers through the blink 'n' miss virtual aisles.

Deals, discounts and convenience are the reasons why consumers prowl on digital space. Unless efficiencies on traffic drivers (household products, books, grocery) are bought on a large scale and packing/freighting costs are lower, online will struggle to retain loyalty. Consumers then look at benefits like easy returns, cash on delivery options or simply the speed of a delivery to justify choosing Amazon over Flipkart over ShopClues, as e-players lose their distinction in the consumer's eyes. Since switching is as easy as shifting a finger from one app to another, e-commerce will have to find newer ways to grow, as investors start seeking profits over mere customer acquisition, reflected in gross merchandise value (GMV).

Owning content creation (like integrating a publishing house to build content), logistic synergies (economies of scale and sophisticated IT systems) and a range of products with clubbed deals on what consumers want and when (during peak seasons or festivals) will become the next set of determinants for differentiation. On each of these aspects, convenience will drive consumers from offline to online because of the differentiated

---

* Schwartz, Barry, *The Paradox of Choice: Why More Is Less*, USA, HarperCollins, 2004.

offerings provided by e-commerce. This is not currently the case, and it will take some time to evolve into. However, adopting some or many of the steps above would compromise the core competence of e-commerce players, which is essentially in retailing. Therefore, this becomes a classic marketing dilemma – whether to spread wide and thin or go narrow and intense. The war between Flipkart and Amazon is an example of many brands and many horizontal synergies versus one brand seeking consumer loyalty with different offerings. Which is the winning strategy? Where will the competitive edge lie?

The answer lies in the basics, or in knowing one's consumer. Analytics of the consumer buying-pattern will drive who stays relevant to a consumer. Sharper segmentation and more relevant microtargeting for consumers with bundled offers to make their life easier are other opportunities. Further, technology is going to be a driver of differentiation and growth in the long term, as the future of the world will be shaped by artificial intelligence, machine learning and robotics. But again, how far can technology go before it becomes abrasively intrusive? Will consumers like being pried into for better value offerings, or will they prefer being left alone? All these questions cannot be answered today because the road ahead is uncertain, but what would stand each company in good stead is sticking to the vision that it has set up to service its consumers. Today, unfortunately, there is no fundamental distinction among them beyond offering the best deals and getting maximum patrons.

E-commerce

Business circles are abuzz with the meteoric rise of e-commerce in India. Where is it headed, how fast and what impact it is making on retail. Or is this just a blip that has lasted a bit longer than it should have?

A global report from the Ecommerce Foundation shows that India is on an unusual trajectory, and if the global trends are anything to go by, the party may have just begun.

Out of a global population of 7.3 billion people, 1.4 billion have purchased online once a year, which is at a total sum of $2,200 billion in GMV, making it a per capita purchase of $1,382. This shows that once people are online, there is no telling how far they will yield to the lure of a thrill at a single click. Now comes the second interesting statistic: Asia Pacific – and this can hardly be overstated – in spite of the convenience of mom and pop stores, has overtaken the total revenue accruing from America and Europe. That gives it a share of 3.4 per cent of the GDP, with China leading at 7.4 per cent share. China leads the e-commerce sale at $766 billion versus $25 billion of India. The main drivers of e-commerce, apart from local regulation and VAT, are the growth of the adjacent industries, logistics and internet penetration. While India is doing great with the internet, the state of infrastructure means that India will have to bank on its already ubiquitous 'bike boys' to cover the last tortuous mile better than anywhere else in the world.

As per the same report, India has a low $255 per capita expenditure, with clothes leading the categories, followed by information technology (mobile, laptops), media and entertainment, and shoes and personal style. Since the penetration rate of e-commerce is only around 10 per cent, the room to grow is simply astronomical.

E-commerce closes the chasm between need perception and satisfaction, and provides the assurance of cross-brand comparison and unbelievable discounts, making your offline retailer appear horribly uncompetitive. But poor infrastructure, distrust about online payments, ambiguous regulatory policies and the high costs of packaging and returns will check this growth, at least till these issues are sorted out.

As per a Kantar-IMRB report, significant opportunities still remain in FMCG, as consumers show the highest frequency of transactions in this sector, often building the necessary traffic-volume of consumers for e-retailers. As $290 million is spent in this category, it is much bigger than most people realize. Once discounted sales cool off in this category, marketers will be able to spot a big opportunity in the future to drive sales with strong loyalty programmes for their brand. Close to half of the consumers of FMCG are SEC A* and live in metros, which provides scope for both penetrating deeper and for getting consumers with high disposable incomes to spend more. An analysis of eleven million invoices during the festive period shows that, on the basis of the incidence of sale, personal care leads at 65 per cent, followed by food and beverages at 33 per cent and household care at 14 per cent. The expenditure per occasion follows the same sequence, with personal care leading at ₹570 per occasion, followed by food and beverages at ₹320 and household care at ₹190.

How does one maximize this e-commerce opportunity? From 452 million users in 2017, the number is pegged to rise to 829 million by 2021. Considering this number was 40 million in 2014, growth is not just a possibility, but a certainty. Gargantuan numbers apart, what else is the trend foretelling? First, women are estimated to be 45 per cent of the surfers of the web wave. Brands which keep women in mind, not only as consumers but as buyers, will have an edge; they must focus on value, SKU size, pantry stocking patterns, family needs and social aspirations – a fresh and incisive insight will help in building valuable inventories with suppliers and in leading with right pricing and promotions. Second, 75 per cent of users will come from tier II and III towns and rural areas. Again, an understanding of the rural wallet and the extent of urbanization in these areas will improve the offerings. Currently, rural retail looks like an impoverished version of its urban cousin. The time has come to launch SKUs that are designed for rural

* SEC is socio economic-classification of consumers basis attributes like their education, occupation etc. and ranks them between A to E.

folks, incorporating their likes and cultural realities – Bhojpuri or Rajasthani patterned bedsheets, with pictures of their local stars, *langoths*, vests, *gamchas* or even an opportunity for an individual to sell Oriya upcountry products to his Andhra cousin from a similar caste and class.

Third, the user base is expanding fast. So fast that what category users are embracing is foxing everyone. The launch of Amazon Prime Video shows what entertainment can do to draw in new users, ahead of other e-tailers. Fourth, mobile leads penetration, so ease of navigation at the site as well as the quality of e-merchandise and promotions have the potential to swing market shares. Ease of use improves dramatically with app download, but only a few million users have downloaded the Amazon and Flipkart apps. Also, when compared to China, the metric of time spent on the site (averaging five minutes) shows that there is scope to go further, encouraging more searching and more purchasing.

Fifth, how does one get consumers with higher purchasing power? E-tailers will have to offer more offers, products and services to draw and retain their premier clientele. Currently, there is carpet-like bombardment to enlist more customers, but segmenting affluent customers and marketing to them will have to be done by sharpening and fencing them away from the lure of competitors.

Sixth, a search is an important tool (it is the 'I want to' nature of a query), with 60 per cent landing with just a question, and the majority not moving beyond the first page. The quality of answers to queries on categories need to be answered satisfactorily to build loyalty and drive purchase, preferably multiple answers, with algorithms that promote proximal categories (like conditioner with shampoo, leather sofa with leather polish or lifestyle lights), if e-tailers want to be ahead on search engines like Google. Intent-related searches that are specific to products and brands are where e-tailers have a clear advantage over Google, leading to conversions in high multiples.

While the exact course of e-commerce cannot be specifically foretold, the pointers above indicate which areas marketers need to keep foremost in their mind to optimally utilize the emerging opportunities. However, e-commerce is a channel that finally allows faster and more intricate consumer need-satisfaction. By staying focused on consumer need, with a strong understanding of the Indian psyche, Pragmarketers can not only successfully navigate this ambiguous e-commerce space, but also anticipate the developments before the others who look towards the West or towards China (Alibaba) for inspiration.

14

The Future of Marketing

You can never be seasoned enough in marketing. We have found the marketing gurus fail dismally, while novices have come from nowhere and achieved spectacular success. Part of that has to do with the indeterminate nature of consumer demand, which is only grasped by constant listening – however, over time, senior marketers prefer their views to the consumers'. The other part has to do with the inability of managers to change with the volatile, uncertain, complex and ambiguous (VUCA) world, which defeats predictable solutions. The current challenges we face as marketers were neither foreseen nor did they originate within the domain of our work. Sample these.

Plastic wrappers have been the boon of packaging, but are fast becoming its scourge. Companies have to immediately make plans to change to an alternative that preserves the environment without consumers having to pay extra for it. This is a tough ask when one considers that technology is not catching up fast enough.

Plastic straws recently faced public and regulators' ire when a scientists studying sea turtles in Costa Rica discovered and removed a plastic straw from the nostril of an olive ridley sea turtle. The industry faces an imminent ban and the paper substitutes of the same straw, while available, melt while the beverage is being sipped. Even assuming that this is acceptable, the question still remains: who will absorb the higher cost of these straws? This is an even tougher ask.

More uncertainties have started in the environment, impacting marketers more than ever before, as the world gets more interconnected. Sugar tax on sweetened beverages commensurate with the sugar content is around the corner as obesity increases and alternatives like Stevia don't quite taste the same. Unilever faced flak recently because it showed a son deserting his father in the kumbh mela in its new ad for Brooke Bond Red Label, offending Indian sensibilities. Most milk collected at chilling centres recently tested positive on adulterants and contaminants. The industry protested the testing methodology and the accuracy of the instruments, seeking court intervention, but the regulators put a ban on sourcing and farmers subsequently boycotted, disrupting the supply of this critical ingredient for many brands. A social listening of any brand reveals how answerable brands have become to consumers' questions, which span everything from sourcing to trading practices to even social and political views.

Brands can no longer remain limited to just supply and consumption. Instead, there is a need for a shared world view where marketers and consumers have to be on the same page to enjoy a lasting relationship.

Consumer and brand interaction levels

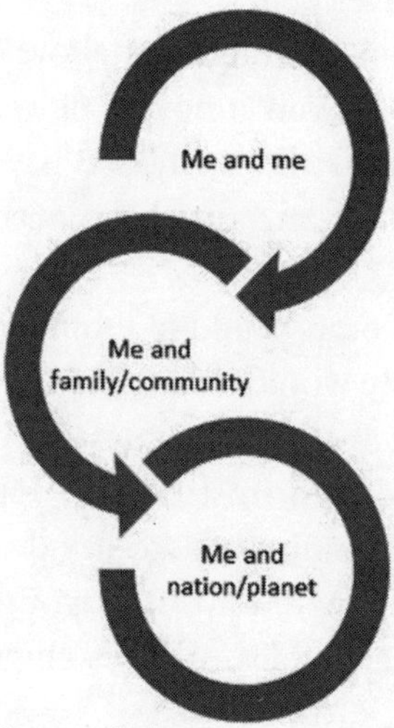

Source: Authors

All this poses the question: what does the future of marketing hold?

While crystal gazing is not our strength, we can certainly hazard the direction that future trends can take, appreciating the evolving brand and consumer interaction. Here is a peek at the three levels of interaction that marketers need to be pragmatically prapare for.

Me and me: Consumers want brands that amplify them. Period. Instagram, Facebook, Twitter and

TikTok are all a global rage because brands are finally helping consumers reflect their personalities. It's worked at various levels, as tabulated below:

My personality	Instagram, Facebook, fitness apps
My views	Twitter
My friends	Facebook
My intimate friends	Tinder
My fun pal	TikTok
My contacts	LinkedIn
My natural beauty	Forest Essential
My distinctive presence/ attraction	Fogg/Axe

These are just a few, and the game hasn't even begun. If we refer to the opening chapter on needs and take a cursory glance through Robert Plutchik's emotion wheel and Buddha's *tanha*, we would see the party has just begun. Brands and marketers can look at these consumer emotions closely and arrive at unique product and service ideas to help them express themselves better.

If we look at what consumers are going through (as above), independent and prior to product ideas, we can innovate newer ways to reflect and help them. However, traditionally, we have always developed the product first and then retrofitted the need that it serves in a post-facto manner.

In the future, Pragmarketism would advocate thinking about the consumer's emotional needs first. Not only would this create new products and services, but it would also create brand interaction opportunities using new technologies. Take, for instance, an app that vents or channelizes anger in a community of like-minded people – Angry Birds; or snacks that surprise with unusual flavours like sweet potato chips or a brand experience idea of Lay's chips wherein people express their ecstatic and unbridled moments in keeping with the brand essence of 'it's irresistible'; or a cosmetic brand that allows you to express yourself in a way that takes you out of mundanities into a spiritual space.

The above emotions of an individual, whether positive or negative, can be a powerful glue to hold consumers and brands together through multiple platforms enabled by technology. Today, the world has just a few of such apps, like Facebook, Twitter, Snapchat and so on, but these will further segment and sub-segment to make new communities that help consumers express their deepest urges like never before. Segmentation based on Indian realities (as detailed in the chapter on the subject) can illustrate several new ways to start interacting with brands in a very relatable and intimate manner.

In the future, only brands that reflect and amplify consumer presence will prevail, while those that stay anchored in basic need-states will perish.

Me and family/community: We talked about the holistic conception of Indian society, wherein individuals draw their identity from the family and community they hail from. In India, where a deep-rooted traditional structure exists, consumers will reward brands that help them connect with their affinity groups, whether they are relatives or friends. The connections may be anchored at various levels.

- Financial help: Banks, NBFCs or even service brands that can enable parents and kids with a comprehensive, end-to-end education/career/family coverage plan will find takers in an increasingly volatile environment of rising expenses and financial vagaries; or micro-finance to help small enterprises, which has already started but needs to go deeper into understanding people's reservations; or the management of the finances of old and uninformed folks in upcountry India through simple, user-friendly and reliable packages.

- Skill reinforcement: Brands that enable one generation to pass their skills to another, as often happens with umpteen self-employed people operating in the small scale cottage industry network of India. This could help families perpetuate their entrepreneurship in their knowledge of food, financial management of giving loans or dealing in small transactions in innumerable *haats* and *mandis*; it may even extend to cultural or musical performances as a means of living – all this will help consumers embrace modernity while retaining the best that their families have to offer in terms of tradition.
- Increasing impact for communities: Indian caste, languages and religious communities regularly congregate and bargain to maximize their gains from the outside worlds. Brands that create technology platforms to bring people with shared aspirations together will add up to a very useful aspect of this political or economic need of the consumers – like focusing on the Marwari samaj or Kayastha sabha. However, care will have to be taken to avoid the negative aspects of such gatherings by identifying it with a larger and nobler cause, without flaring parochialism. Therefore, Kayastha sabha conducting a tree plantation rather than asking for job quotas may be the way to pander to such grouping tendencies in a constructive way.
- Emotional fallback: With rising alienation in urban areas, and as people leave their homes to work in distant lands, brands have a unique opportunity to serve the need of people to connect through new orientations – their workplace, residential neighbourhood, common hobbies, passions and so on. Brands that become the reason for this social glue will last not only this century but also the one after this. In

the West, a furniture brand conducted a campaign wherein it helped migrants settle into a new, unfamiliar city and interact with each other as a community to accelerate their acclimatization to an alien place. In this case, the brand not only increased its visibility and relevance, but also hugely added to its image as being empathetic.

Some of the ideas above may seem distant from a consumer's needs or too small to be pursued. But that would be a grave mistake. Big ideas start small, but if they are resonant with the consumer's need, they tend to multiply when enabled by social media, adding to the brand equity.

Me and planet/nation: While visiting MBA campuses around the country for lectures or recruitment, we are amazed at the increasing concern of young students regarding matters that pertain to the national good, an environmental footprint and the well-being of the planet they reside on.

India, spiritually and philosophically, resonates with the idea of internationalism. This is reflected in our dictum:

> '*Vasudhaiva kutumbakam*' or the entire world is my family, we are related to each other, being descendants of Vasudeva Krishna.

The time has come for brands to reflect on the well-being of the entire planet. If brands, on account of their attitude – from indifference about their sourcing policy to dated manufacturing systems to a hard-nosed and narrow financial approach to insensitive communication or their sheer inability to clean the value creation system – ignore the larger impact on the planet, then they stand risking what their consumers hold very dear.

Conversely, progressive thinking and pro-activity can catapult a brand. This leads us to the new world of **cause marketing** as a way to intimately connect the brand to the consumer in the most expansive and contemporary manner. Cause marketing will be the way through which brands can endear themselves to their consumers by extending their sway from mere consumption to the responsible conservation of our environment. Normally, this aspect of business falls in the domain of CSR. Currently, this word is an afterthought and most corporate boardrooms could be witnesses to a statement like this one: 'When all the slides are done, put a slide on CSR.'

But if consumer need is the foundation of the business, can social needs be far behind? If brands increase their sensitivity towards the community/nation/planet that their consumer live and breathe in, would they not widen the lens of their brand? And would the brand not become progressive and futuristic in doing so? We have created a small model of cause marketing, elevating the idea of CSR.

Cause Marketing

The time has come for the old Indian notion of 'Vasudhaiva Kutumbakam', which means that the whole world is nothing but one big joint family of Sri Krishna. This belief in universal humanity underpins many Indian practices, knowingly or unknowingly. This is evidenced in the way we treat our guests (best expressed in Indian tourism's tagline '*athithi devo bhava*' [the guest is god]), extend monetary and social help towards our communities (Jain Dharmashalas, Marwari trading groups or well-connected Sikh migrant communities, to name a few), give alms to beggars or even feed stray dogs or animals. Most religions practiced in India talk about charity and service towards the community: *zakat* for Muslims, *langar* for Sikhs or *daan* for Hindus. The billion consumers are constantly reminded of the larger community they are obligated to, as a part of their dharma.

Doing business with consumers who have these deep-seated socio-religious beliefs will require this aspect to be integrated into the way business is done. This is not very different from the CSR idea that comes from the West, which is drawn from an increasingly self-evident truth: businesses cannot thrive if the society it draws from is depleted. Essentially, companies need to give back to complete the value creation circle. Apple has the vision to power their business entirely through natural resources with solar, wind and hydropower, and move their supply chain to 100 per cent renewable energy and use 100 per cent recycled and responsibly sourced paper during packaging.

The spirit of CSR is best expressed in the words of J.R.D. Tata: 'The wealth gathered by Tata is held in trust and used exclusively for people's benefit. The cycle is thus complete – what comes from the people, goes back to the people many times over.'

Doing thus, companies cover the journey of profit, people and planet to enter a circular loop of value creation, changing the current linear model of create-utilize-waste. Sustainability, it hardly needs to be said, becomes a natural offshoot.

These are some examples of cause marketing in recent times:

- Dettol's campaign supporting the Indian government's 'Swachh Bharat' campaign, done in conjunction with *hospitals*.
- Unilever's '*Haath muh or bum, bimari hogi kum*' campaign that elevates the commitment to cleanliness while promoting its brand.
- Tata's '*Jaago re*' campaign that triggers conversation around social issues, mirroring the figurative meaning of their product benefit: waking up.

There are many more initiatives by companies that are working in the CSR corridors but haven't been connected at the brand level to draw consumer empathy around their cause.

For instance, ITC has been carbon positive for over thirteen years – it implemented the triple bottomline strategy to positively impact the other two bottomlines: environmental and social capital. Tata Group is one of the leading global companies to pilot Natural Capital Protocol across their four group companies to conserve scarce natural capital. These companies could gain by telling their consumers about the social and environmental causes they promote, turning the user of their products into brand evangelists.

More on this point: our planet is headed towards the ominous sounding 'Earth Overshoot Day' – in a not-so-uncertain future, when resources will outrun demand, India will be the frontrunner. The statistics on this are perilously certain: with 17 per cent of the world population, we have only 2.4 per cent of the world's land, 4 per cent of the world's water and 1 per cent of the global forest resource. Consumers are partially aware and partially perplexed that so little is being done. This represents a great opportunity for brands to champion a larger cause and enlist consumers' support. As the society and consumer is evolving, gender equality and opportunity consciousness has started surfacing, but still remains in a nascent stage. In a growing country like India, there are a lot of issues that are specific to us – exam stress leading to student suicides, female foeticide, lack of cleanliness and hygiene, among various other social and cultural issues. These provide opportunities to brands to stand for the purpose they believe in.

Brands should, however, choose causes that are in keeping with their essence, as explained in the chapter earlier on brand essence. This would not only add authenticity to the cause but also result in positive brand equity if done with consistency, making possible a long-term ownership of the cause.

Consumers can be galvanized to support the brand and the noble cause it promotes by something as inspiring as Apple's corporate philosophy:

'To ask less of the planet, we ask more of ourselves.'

The true multiplier comes when consumers become brand evangelists, speaking up and championing the brands on their own. While its impact on brand loyalty can hardly be overstated, it would further accelerate the adoption of the brand by those who are otherwise cynical or indifferent. This is based on the insight that you can ignore a brand but not a cause, since it has a much larger impact. Cause marketing, therefore, not only expands the base of users, but also deepens the association with a brand.

Imagine a campaign in cities by well-meaning consumers for those brands that support the environment, traffic decongestion, tree plantation and an implied boycott of those that are indifferent to such pressing concerns. The positive rub-off such a campaign would have on brands would far outweigh any self-serving, bought-media or routine advertising.

The last step of cause marketing growth is where brands and their evangelists give back to society through sacrifice. Sacrifice implies a contribution over and above one's selfish motive. That could mean a reduced margin for products and services meant for consumers at the bottom end of the pyramid; a genuine contribution of a percentage of sales or a dedication of their employees' working time towards social services.

Cause marketing not only brings brands really close to consumers from the widest perspective, but also closes the loop of business back to society – from where it originates.

Epilogue

We have ploughed through the pages of *Pragmarketism* as a way to market in India, melding theory and practice, infusing Indian sensibilities into consumer understanding and visualizing the brand and the consumer in a holistic manner.

For those who have patiently navigated through the high seas and are looking at a rich haul on their ship's deck, here is a stock-taking of the entire journey:

- Understand consumers routinely, but also modify and adapt to reflect Indian society and its consumers, unravelling their psyche, which is rooted in history and tradition.
- Establish clearly the vision to inspire people with and clarify the company's objective.
- Understand consumer need, link it to their deep-seated emotions and use the 'want-haunt' pathway to increase brand relevance.
- Research widely and deeply, but also ask towards what end and how best to question, considering the entire gamut of research techniques.
- Segment, target and position like in classical marketing, but also look for gaps between segments. Target and remember to size the market and undertake positioning with clear primary and secondary differentiation.

- Communicate after understanding business, marketing and communication objective, and create Big Ideas that resonate resoundingly with consumers.
- Create brands that build loyalty, but also spawn *sva-bhu* brands that empower consumers in new and unimaginable ways.
- Approach consumers with classical marketing and media, but sharp-shoot with digital marketing, with sharp messaging to build higher relevance and empathy with individual consumers.
- Innovate with products that have the potential for incrementalism, but also disrupt the framework with the R-B-R-E-B model: reframing-bolstering-regrooming-expanding-branching.
- Start nimbly, making the most out of the emerging opportunity and progress with flexibility and suitable opportunism.
- Design a selling strategy that best mirrors the consumer need so that the critical variables of your selling system can deliver maximum consumer satisfaction.
- Stay tuned to the evolving marketing trends for consumers at various levels that pertain to themselves, the family, the community and the planet they live on, which is within the framework of cause marketing in the brand plan – taking the CSR model upfront and promoting the *vasudhaiva kutumbakam* model of the Indian society.

In doing all of this, Pragmarketism will become the DNA of your marketing design, modifying Western theory with Indian context, building Indian frameworks that reflect our society and its ethics and constantly interconnecting different levels of marketing and innovation with the latest trends that build our cult or *sva-bhu* brands.

Indian marketing has come of age. Let's celebrate it with Pragmarketism.

Index

Acknowledgements

A book of this magnitude is not possible without copious contributions from our peers, seniors and associates. We are deeply thankful to all who provided the raw material and inspiration for *Pragmarketism*. Some directly, some indirectly, in shaping our marketing experiences at various levels of our careers.

Organizations and senior leaders we are grateful to:

Arvind: Titan, ITC, J. Walter Thompson, Nestlé India Limited, PepsiCo (Frito Lay).

Leaders – Raveesh Awasthy, Sanjay Katyal, Rohit Ohri, Alok Lall, Nirmal Dayani, Geetu Gidwani Verma, Manu Anand, Deepika Warrier, Jagrut Kotecha, S. Nagarajan, Shivani Hegde, Sullivan o'carroll, Helio Waszyk, Etienne Benet, Suresh Narayanan and Arshad Chaudhry.

Trupti: Reckitt Benckiser, Pfizer (Parke-Davis), Bausch and Lomb, GlaxoSmithKline Consumer Healthcare.

Leaders – Mahesh Samath, Monica Gangwani, Vivek Sharma, Pranab Barua, Pravin Kini, Vivek Nayyar, J P Singh, Sandeep Gupta, Rajat Goel, Zubair Ahmed, Shubhajit Sen, Venu Ambati, Carlton Lawson, Jayant Singh, Manoj Kumar, Sara Bland, Navneet Saluja.

Peers and team members with whom numerous ideas have been bounced off and refined in our formative and leadership years:

Arvind: Amit Arora, Shishir Khirbat, Ashish Arora, Shital Mehta, Neil George, Chetan Gore, Mansi Tripathy, Rishi Ahuja, Suman Dey, Vidur Vyas, Bindu Kulkarni, Umang Vohra, Sriram, Rashi

Gandhi, Awanish N Singh, Rahul Shanker, Alpana Titus, Amitabh Pandey, Payal, Vikas Ahuja, Ashwini Law, Mukesh Kumar, Sanjay Kashyap, Natasha Singh, Michelle Hamm, Mamello Makhoro, Mayur Bhargava, Nikhil Chand, Chandru, Mayur Bhargava, Virat Mehta, Ravi Ramchandran, Ana Sinha, Chandan Mukherji, Rashi Goel, Ritanbra Mundrey, Rashmi Gupta, Priya Beri, Rajat Jain, Alamjeeet Sekhon, Yashashri Vatve, Meenal Raghava, Nobel Dhingra, Mehernosh Malia, Shail Gaurav, Rajneesh Goel, Gopichander J, Mayuri Mukherjee, Mrinalini Mankotia, Pallavi Anand, Ghazal Bajaj.

Trupti: Gaurav Jain, Rajesh Ramakrishnan, Prashant Pandey, Anindya Dasgupta, Charubala Seshadri, T S Dayanand, Soumava Sengupta, Bhavana Mittal, Himanshu Khanna, Alok Agrawal, Kishaloy Basu, Vijay Sharma, Sunil Mehra, Sumeet Saluja, Naveed Ahmed, Rahul Bibhuti, Rahul Sachdeva, Raghav Gupta, Partha Dutt, Sandeep Anand, Vikasdeep Katyal, Gurtashika Gill, Shambhavi Jha, Neha Markanda, Vidhi Singh, Apurv Pandey, Shekhar Saurabh, Karandeep Duggal, Nikita Tamta, Rasneet Kaur, Kanika Juneja, Kishlay Seth, Anjana Alex, Sandhya Rana, Natasha Bahuguna.

Our media and creative agency partners: Group M, Zenith Optimedia, Publicis, Mccann, FCB, Wunderman Thompson, Ogilvy, Havas.

Mona Jain, Nitin Jain, Neelav Bose, Prasanth Kumar, Parthasarathy Mandayam (Maps), Kapil Ohri, Satya, Ambika, Param Saikia, Anupriya Acharya, Atul Sharma, Mishti Bose, Ashutosh Sawhney, Ritu Sarda, Ashish Khazanchi, Ashish Chakravarty, Swati Bhattacharya, John Thangaraj, Debarpita Banerjee, Surjo Dutt, Joy Chauhan, Charu Bhatnagar, Pinaki Bhattacharya, Tista Sen, Sambhit Mohanty, Amarinder Butalia, Shubhrojyoti Roy.

We are indebted to our parents and siblings – B .S. Bhandari, the late Kanchan Bhandari, Suresh Narvekar, Shama Narvekar, Neeta Phatarphekar, Dr Milind Narvekar, Dr Minni Sanganeria, Shonu Jain, Dr Ranu Jain, Dr Tanu Bordia for their constant support and encouragement in shaping our careers.

Finally, our editor Sachin Sharma at HarperCollins India whose effort has been nothing short of monumental to bring this book to its current shape.

About the Authors

Trupti Bhandari is a business leader and marketeer with more than twenty-three years of experience across FMCG, healthcare and lifestyle segments in blue-chip companies like Reckitt Benckiser, Pfizer, Bausch & Lomb and GSK Consumer Healthcare. She has had the opportunity to build and grow iconic brands such as Dettol, Horlicks, Boost, Crocin, Sensodyne, Eno, Listerine, Gelusil etc. catering to a diverse audience in different life stages. Trupti has served in various leadership roles, spearheading strategy, P&L, innovation and communication. She has been recognized through multiple advertising and business awards. Trupti is a regular speaker, writer and jury member on marketing and business forums. Apart from her passion for marketing, Trupti is an executive coach with certification from Consciousness Coaching®, South Africa.

Arvind Bhandari is an Executive Vice President and Director at Nestlé India. He is a corporate veteran with over twenty-three years of work experience. He has served in leading organizations like ITC, JWT, PepsiCo and Nestlé across the South Asia and South Africa region. He has held senior leadership roles, building successful businesses and nurturing classical brands like Maggi, Lay's, Pepsi, Everyday, Milkmaid, to name a few. He has to his credit, some iconic campaigns like Pepsi's '*Mera number kab aayega*' and Lay's '*No one can eat just one*'. Arvind has been awarded the

Asia One India's greatest CMO 2016-17 award for excellence in marketing.

With degrees in management, humanities and law from Institute for Management Development, Lausanne, Switzerland; S. P. Jain Institute of Management and Research, Mumbai; Law Faculty and St. Stephen's College, University of Delhi, Arvind brings together an interesting perspective and understanding of the Indian society and consumer psyche. He is a writer/columnist with several marketing and business publications and lectures at prominent management institutions.

For further conversations on *Pragmarketism*, write in to us at truptiandarvind@gmail.com OR visit the Facebook page https://www.facebook.com/Trupti-and-Arvind/